Schriftenreihe Europäisches Recht, Politik und Wirtschaft

Herausgegeben von

Prof. Dr. Dres. h.c. Jürgen Schwarze,
Direktor des Europa-Instituts Freiburg e.V.,
Universität Freiburg

Prof. Dr. Armin Hatje, Universität Hamburg

Band 402

Alexandra Ellen Hansen

Facts Before the European Court of Human Rights

How does the European Court of Human Rights (ECtHR) contend with facts, and how can principles of scientific method be used to critique the factual analyses by the ECtHR in its case-law?

 Nomos

The prepress was supported by the Swiss National Science Foundation (SNSF).

SCHWEIZERISCHER NATIONALFONDS
ZUR FÖRDERUNG DER WISSENSCHAFTLICHEN FORSCHUNG

The Deutsche Nationalbibliothek lists this publication in the
Deutsche Nationalbibliografie; detailed bibliographic data
are available on the Internet at http://dnb.d-nb.de

a.t.: Zürich, Univ., Rechtswissenschaftliche Fakultät, Diss., 2021

ISBN   978-3-8487-8985-6 (Print)
          978-3-7489-3322-9 (ePDF)

British Library Cataloguing-in-Publication Data
A catalogue record for this book is available from the British Library.

ISBN   978-3-8487-8985-6 (Print)
          978-3-7489-3322-9 (ePDF)

Library of Congress Cataloging-in-Publication Data
Hansen, Alexandra Ellen
Facts Before the European Court of Human Rights
How does the European Court of Human Rights (ECtHR) contend with facts,
and how can principles of scientific method be used to critique the factual analyses
by the ECtHR in its case-law?
Alexandra Ellen Hansen
201 pp.
Includes bibliographic references.

ISBN   978-3-8487-8985-6 (Print)
          978-3-7489-3322-9 (ePDF)

1st Edition 2022

Published by
Nomos Verlagsgesellschaft mbH & Co. KG
Waldseestraße 3–5 | 76530 Baden-Baden
www.nomos.de

Production of the printed version:
Nomos Verlagsgesellschaft mbH & Co. KG
Waldseestraße 3–5 | 76530 Baden-Baden

ISBN   978-3-8487-8985-6 (Print)
ISBN   978-3-7489-3322-9 (ePDF)
DOI   https://doi.org/10.5771/9783748933229

Onlineversion
Nomos eLibrary

To my parents

Acknowledgements

For his expertly supervision, mentoring and encouragement throughout my PhD, I wish to thank Tilmann Altwicker. He managed to keep me on track when my own thoughts led me astray but also allowed me the necessary space and freedom to develop my own mechanism to write this thesis. The many discussions we had during my employment as his research assistant helped me narrow down my research interests. I am extremely grateful for the opportunity to present earlier versions of my work in front of Tilmann Altwicker and the members of the Swiss National Science Foundation research group. I received very helpful feedback in these sessions and am thankful to all members of the research group. I am also grateful to Oliver Diggelmann for having agreed to be the second assessor of my work.

I wish to express my deepest gratitude to Lilian Buchmann, Fabienne Krebs, Aileen Kreyden, Severin Meier, and Sandra Ujpétery for their valuable inputs and support. Their diverse backgrounds provided for invaluable feedback at various stages of my doctoral process.

I am grateful to the Faculty of Law of the University of Zurich for having provided me with funds via the Candoc research credit[*] for my last year of research. Unfortunately, my plans to go to the University of Glasgow as a visiting researcher were thwarted by the Coronavirus pandemic. Nonetheless, I would like to express my gratitude to Lea Raible and James Devaney, who supported my application to the law school in Glasgow.

A very special word of thanks goes to my parents, Margaret and Bjørn, my sister Charlotte, my partner Carim, and my friends. I cannot put into words how much I appreciate the support on all levels imaginable that they have provided to me over the last years. Without them, I would not have been able to complete this project.

This PhD thesis was handed in on 15 July 2021 and accepted by the Faculty of Law of the University of Zurich on 6 October 2021.

Published with the support of the Swiss National Science Foundation.

Basel, 28 May 2022

---

[*] UZH Candoc Grant, grant no. [FK-20-007]

Table of Contents

Abstract

Legal decision-making is not a 'one way street'. Any legal analysis is based on a factual context. Before any legal analysis can commence, the facts of a given case have to be detangled and a decision is reached as to which facts are deemed relevant for the legal analysis that is to follow. The legal norms that are considered applicable to the factual circumstances will, in turn, bring into focus those facts that best fit under the legal norm. There is, thus, a back-and-forth between the factual and the normative; the factual gaze is influenced by the legal gaze and vice versa. It is the factual-side of this back-and-forth, that is of interest in this thesis.

The contribution of this PhD thesis is that it suggests using principles of scientific method as fact-assessment criteria. These scientific principles are employed as a methodology to assess and criticise nine judgments by the ECtHR. In a nutshell, it is shown that reading and analysing the ECtHR's case-law using the principles of scientific method, allows the detection of flaws in the factual analyses. A strong factual analysis, freed of logical flaws and inconsistencies, that is based on principles of scientific method, will provide a strong basis on which the legal analysis can then follow. Any inconsistencies in the factual analyses will impact the legal assessment. This thesis aims at stressing the importance to pay more attention to the factual analysis in legal decision-making, and it outlines how a more appropriate factual analysis can be achieved.

Introduction

The research question that is addressed in this thesis is 'How does the European Court of Human Rights (ECtHR) contend with facts, and how can principles of scientific method be used to critique the factual analyses by the ECtHR in its case-law?'

Facts play an important role in legal decision-making because without the occurrence of a (factual) event, there would be neither a need for legal analysis nor anything to base the legal analysis on. In international adjudication, as opposed to national jurisdictions, there are not many rules on how courts ought to contend with facts. Durward Sandifer famously wrote that 'no rule of evidence [...] finds more frequent statement in the cases than the one that international tribunals are not bound to adhere to strict rules of evidence'.[1] This holds true for the European Court of Human Rights (ECtHR) as well.

Before any legal analysis can commence, the facts of a given case have to be disentangled and decisions have to be made as to which facts are considered relevant for the legal analysis that is to follow. The legal norms that are deemed applicable to the factual context will, in turn, bring into focus those facts that fulfil the legal bill. There is, thus, a back-and-forth between the factual and the normative; the factual gaze influences the legal, and the legal gaze influences the factual.[2] It is the element of fact-analysis, or fact-assessment, within this back-and forth that is of interest in this thesis.

Given that there is no clear framework and few rules are in place with regard to how the ECtHR ought to contend with facts, this thesis aims to shed light on the ECtHR's fact-assessment procedures, and it suggests that principles of scientific method can be applied as a framework to analyse and critique the ECtHR's practice in this regard. Nine judgments by the ECtHR will be analysed in depth using principles of scientific method. It will be shown that the ECtHR's fact-assessment procedure does not follow a clear structure, and that this can result in problematic lines of reasoning in its judgments. A middle-ground pragmatist position, which acknowledges the specificities of the realm of legal decision-making but

---

1 Durward V Sandifer, *Evidence Before International Tribunals* (rev edn, University Press of Virginia 1975) 9.
2 Karl Engisch, *Logische Studien zur Gesetzesanwendung* (3rd edn., Winter 1963) 15.

allows for interdisciplinary approaches, will be outlined and defended as a theoretical framework that allows principles from the realm of science to enter legal thinking.

The contribution of this doctoral thesis is that it provides a framework for detecting flaws in the ECtHR's factual analyses. The added value of reading judgments of the ECtHR through the lens of principles of scientific method is that this provides a new perspective from which the ECtHR's jurisprudence can be analysed and critiqued. The principles provide an analytical and critical framework against which the at times chaotic fact-assessment of the Court can be scrutinised in a structured manner, making it easier for the reader of jurisprudence to detect problems.

This thesis aims at stressing the importance of paying more attention to the factual analysis in legal decision-making, and it outlines a framework for detecting flaws in the ECtHR's fact-assessment.

In Part I, the 'stage is set' by providing an overview of the particularities of the sphere of international adjudication. This will enable the reader to understand why there is no coherent framework regarding rules of evidence, fact-finding, and fact-assessment in international adjudication. The rules of evidence that are in place in different international adjudicative bodies are then discussed, with a focus on the ECtHR.

In Part II, the ways facts and law are intertwined are discussed, and the theoretical and philosophical underpinnings for the interdisciplinary approach to be applied in the case analysis in Part III are outlined.

In Part III, the principles of scientific method are introduced, and three of them are chosen for the case analysis. The principle of simplicity, the – closely related – principles of external validity and explanatory power, and the principle of falsifiability are then used to detect flaws in the fact-assessment by the ECtHR in its case-law. Nine cases decided by the ECtHR are scrutinised using these principles as a framework for analysis, and it will be shown what implications these new categories have for the way we can critique the ECtHR's jurisprudence.

I. Facts and Rules of Evidence in the Sphere of International Adjudication

Part I will provide an overview of the context that is of interest in this thesis: international adjudication, and adjudication by the European Court of Human Rights (ECtHR) in particular. It will be shown that judicial fact-assessment is an important function of international adjudication and that, although there are some rules in place that regulate fact-finding, fact-assessment and the weighing of evidence, these rules are sparse and do not provide a clear framework as to how the international judiciary in general, and the ECtHR in particular, ought to contend with facts. Thus, international adjudicative bodies have quite wide discretion when it comes to the assessment of the information that is brought before them. It is important, thus, to scrutinise these fact-assessment procedures. Part I will provide the background that illustrates why the fact-assessment procedures of international courts matter. This will pave the way for the suggestion of using scientific principles as a methodology to assess and analyse fact-assessment procedures in the ECtHR's case-law.

1. What Are Facts?

To label something a 'fact' usually implies that one wants to insulate this product or statement from debate and give it a certain authority.[3] Depending on the context in which the term 'fact' is used, it may have different meanings. In other words, the answer to the question of what facts are may vary considerably depending on whether one is asking the question in a philosophical discussion, in a legal debate, or in everyday conversation. The Cambridge Dictionary and Merriam-Webster define 'fact' as follows:

> 'something that is known to have happened or to exist, especially something for which proof exists, or about which there is information[4]

---

3 Frédéric Mégret, 'Do Facts Exist, Can They Be "Found," and Does It Matter?' in Philip Alston and Sarah Knuckey (eds), *The Transformation of Human Rights Fact-Finding* (Oxford University Press 2016) 28.

4 See Cambridge Dictionary, available at <https://dictionary.cambridge.org/de/worterbuch/englisch/fact>, last accessed on 12 July 2021.

1: something that has actual existence; an actual occurrence // 2: a piece of information presented as having objective reality // 3: the quality of being actual // […]'[5]

These definitions link facts to certainty, to objectivity, to actuality, and to reality. A person who labels something a fact indicates that she can prove her knowledge in some way or another. This is the traditional Enlightenment notion of what distinguishes facts from opinions: a fact is provable whereas an opinion is not.[6] However, statements cannot easily be categorised as either facts or opinions. Rather, there is a continuum because factual statements often contain some opinion.[7] At one end of the spectrum, I might state that A is holding a cup of tea. I can be quite certain because I can observe the cup in A's hand. At the other end of the spectrum, opinions might diverge on the existence of God. It is not possible to provide the kind of proof that can be provided for the statement about the cup. Between these two extremes, there exist extensive grey areas, or areas 'where statements involve varying degrees of inference and value judgment'.[8] An example that Michaele Sanders provides is the following: a person sees a classmate reading late on a Friday night, and states that that classmate is a diligent student. This statement cannot be placed squarely at one end of the abovementioned spectrum because it is neither purely fact nor purely opinion. It can be said that it is a fact that the classmate was reading, and that fact can be verified in the same manner as the holding of a cup of tea can be verified. The cup of tea might have been a cup of coffee and the classmate might have just been pretending to be reading or just staring at the book, but these 'facts' can be verified through inquiry. However, the inference that the classmate is a diligent student includes an element of opinion. The classmate might have been reading something merely for pleasure, but the observer inferred from the fact 'reading' that the reader was studying.[9] Of course, the judgment of the classmate might also have been made by the observer due to his previous experience of observing the classmate. Thus, even if the book was indeed, at that point in time, merely for pleasure, the previous observations push the statement

---

5 See Merriam-Webster, available at <https://www.merriam-webster.com/dictionary/f act>, last accessed on 12 July 2021.

6 Mégret (n 3) 30.

7 Michaele Sanders, 'The Fact / Opinion Distinction : An Analysis of the Subjectivity of Language and Law' (1987) 70 Marquette Law Review 680.

8 ibid 681.

9 ibid.

slightly closer to the factual end of the spectrum. Not only experience influences the qualification of a statement, but context does so as well. For instance, the place and time of reading may indicate whether the reading is done for pleasure or for studying.

What emerges from the above is that what must be assessed when we are trying to distinguish between facts and opinions is the *reliability* of a statement. The more reliable a statement is, the more likely it can be considered a fact. How do we determine whether a statement is reliable or not? There seems to be something optimistic in the labelling of a product as a fact; it seems to indicate that some things can be called 'true' or 'evident' or 'concrete'.[10] The more true, evident, and concrete a statement is, the more reliable it seems. Designating something a fact also is a form of exercising power. As HLA Hart put it:

> 'To be an authority on some subject matter a man must in fact have some superior knowledge, intelligence, or wisdom which makes it reasonable to believe that what he says on that subject is more likely to be true than the results reached by others through their independent investigations, so that it is reasonable for them to accept the authoritative statement without such independent investigation or evaluation of his reasoning.'[11]

Thus, one might say that a statement is reliable if it is uttered by someone with superior knowledge and whose utterance one is reasonable to believe. However, what should we do about situations in which two people who are both of superior knowledge and whose utterance one has reason to accept make different or even contradicting statements? Norwood Russell Hanson makes an interesting point in his discussion of observation. Two people may see the same thing, i.e. they start from the same visual data, but then they may have different interpretations and construe the evidence differently. 'The task is then to show how these data are moulded by different theories or interpretations or intellectual constructions.'[12]

Thus, when we are asked 'What are facts?', the answer should be: 'it depends.' As the examples above have shown, the context in which we find ourselves will have an impact on what can be considered a fact. And

---

10 Mégret (n 3) 28.
11 HLA Hart, 'Essays on Bentham' [1982] Studies in Jurisprudence and Political Theory 261–262.
12 Norwood Russell Hanson, *Patterns of Discovery* (Cambridge University Press 1958) 5.

as Hanson noted, we need a theory to mould our understanding of facts before we can discuss whether a certain fact-analysis was done well or not. In order to clarify and show on what grounds facts are conceptualised in this thesis, the following sections will first 'set the scene' by elaborating on the context that is of interest here, i.e. international adjudication, the rules of evidence more generally speaking, and the context of the European Court of Human Rights in particular. Then, in a second step, theoretical considerations that serve as a basis for the analysis of the ECtHR's fact-assessment (third step) will follow.

2. Particularities of the International Sphere

This chapter will show that fact-finding is an important function of international adjudication and that there are rules of evidence in place that guide the different courts and tribunals in their adjudicative task. There is no uniform set of rules that applies to all adjudicative bodies equally. Rather, each court or tribunal has its own set of rules and practices with regard to the gathering of evidence. In order to understand the reasons for there not being one coherent evidentiary framework in international law, the peculiarities of the international sphere will be considered before looking more closely at the different rules that are in place.

a. Fragmentation

One first particularity of the international sphere is its fragmentation. The academic field of public international law has its origins in the late nineteenth century. Legal studies were oriented towards the idea of a world that was interdependent, that acted as a community, one with a cosmopolitan future, governed by a global law.[13] After 1989, there was a dynamic increase in new specialised fields and subfields of international law that went hand in hand with a growth in international actors, such as international organisations and non-governmental organisations (NGOs), and the emergence of new types of international legal norms.[14] The num-

---

13 Martti Koskenniemi, 'International Law as "Global Governance"' 199, 199.
14 Anne Peters, 'The Refinement of International Law: From Fragmentation to Regime Interaction and Politicization' (2017) 15 International Journal of Constitutional Law 671, 673.

ber of international tribunals grew dramatically: many ad hoc tribunals were established in the late nineteenth century and existed throughout the twentieth century. After the Second World War, various permanent tribunals were established, including the Permanent International Court of Justice (PICJ), the International Court of Justice (ICJ), the European Court of Justice (ECJ) and the United Nations Administrative Tribunal.[15] The World Trade Organization (WTO) with its dispute settlement body was founded in 1994, followed by the International Tribunal for the Law of the Sea (ITLOS) in 1996. The European Court of Human Rights (ECtHR) became a permanent court that gave individuals direct access in 1998.[16] This development gave rise to fears that rather than heading towards a cosmopolitan future, the international legal system with its specialised courts would become increasingly fragmented and thereby dampen any hope for a coherent international legal system.[17]

The International Law Commission (ILC) tackled the topic in its report on 'Fragmentation of International Law', finalised by Martti Koskenniemi in 2006.[18] Fragmentation entails both risks and opportunities. It can create conflicts between legal obligations and lead to a loss of legal certainty due to potentially overlapping jurisdictions of different international courts, and it can thwart the prospect of a unified and coherent international legal system.[19] At the same time, fragmentation can also make the international legal order more effective due to the division of tasks and the specialised expertise that is available in the specialised institutions. There is less concentration of power and 'the number of decision-makers, their multiplicity, and their competition and rivalry will normally lead to a denser body of law, which also includes more sophistication, and a further elucidation of fundamental principles underpinning the order'.[20]

The laws of evidence in the international sphere are also fragmented in the sense that there is not one coherent system or framework, not one size

---

15 Jonathan I Charney and others, 'The "Horizontal"Growth of International Courts and Tribunals: Challenges Or Opportunities?' (2002) 96 Proceedings of the Annual Meeting (American Society of International Law) 369.
16 Peters (n 14) 673.
17 ibid.
18 Study Group of the International Law Commission, Report on the Fragmentation of International Law: Difficulties Arising from the Diversification and Expansion of International Law, finalized by Martti Koskenniemi, U.N. Doc. A/CN.4/L.682 (13 April 2006).
19 Peters (n 14) 678–680.
20 ibid 861.

that fits all. The different adjudicative bodies all have their own rules on fact-finding and evidence enshrined in their constitutive instruments and their rules of court. However, although the law of evidence seems to be an incoherent framework, similarities do exist between the rules of the different courts and tribunals. One reason for there being some overlap is that the rules of evidence in the international sphere are influenced by the rules and practices of municipal systems. Thus, in the following section, the particularity of international law being coloured by domestic legal systems will be discussed.

b. International Law and Domestic Law

International law was created and developed over centuries by jurists who got their legal education in different legal traditions. Inevitably, these creators brought elements from their own legal systems into the international realm and influenced it with structures and concepts from their municipal traditions.[21] This is reflected in the laws of evidence. Certain principles reflect influences from the common law tradition, whereas others are coloured by civil law. For instance, the power of international adjudicative bodies to order parties to produce evidence is adopted from civil law systems,[22] but the standard of proof 'beyond reasonable doubt' is drawn from common law systems.[23]

Although international courts do draw their rules from municipal laws, a difference between domestic legal systems and the international sphere is that the municipal legal systems have detailed rules on evidence that are applied by the courts in civil and criminal cases.[24] In the international realm, however, the rules that do exist are quite general in nature and are characterised by their flexibility and scarcity.[25]

An important factor that calls for the international realm to adopt a liberal approach to the laws of evidence is the sovereignty of states. This is another difference between the international and domestic sphere: international law's main addressees are states, whereas domestic law addresses

---

21 Colin Picker, 'International Law's Mixed Heritage: A Common/Civil Law Jurisdiction' (2008) 41 Vanderbilt Journal of Transnational Law 1083, 1091–1092.
22 See below, I.5.a.i.
23 See below, I.5.b.iii(3).
24 James Gerard Devaney, *Fact-Finding before the International Court of Justice* (Cambridge University Press 2016) 12.
25 ibid.

individuals. International law is unique in that its subjects are individual states and that those play 'a direct and fundamental role in the creation and maintenance of international law'; due to their sovereignty, states can, for instance, opt out of – or refuse to sign – a given treaty.[26] States can and do surrender their sovereignty to a certain extent when they become members of international institutions such as the WTO.[27] However, tools and procedures have been developed by international courts to accommodate the sovereign nature of the domestic procedures. For instance, the ECtHR provides a margin of appreciation to states when it assesses the conformity of a national measure with the Convention.[28] The margin of appreciation grants Member States the authority, up to a certain point, to determine whether a violation of the Convention has taken place in a case.[29] This doctrine, originally developed by the ECtHR,[30] has also emerged as a doctrine of deference outside Europe.[31] The intricacy of this doctrine is in striking the balance between overreliance on national interpretations and assessments and disregarding the national interpretations completely.[32] When the ECtHR determines whether a margin of appreciation should be granted to a state in a given case, the Court often uses the method of European consensus.[33] The determining feature for establishing a European consensus is whether 'there is consensus or common ground within the member States of the Council of Europe on the approach to the problem at issue'.[34]

---

26 Picker (n 21) 1090.
27 For more on this, see Kent Albert Jones, 'The WTO and National Sovereignty', *Who's Afraid of the WTO?* (Oxford University Press 2004).
28 Peters (n 14) 685.
29 Andreas Føllesdal, 'Exporting the Margin of Appreciation: Lessons for the Inter-American Court of Human Rights' (2017) 15 International Journal of Constitutional Law 359, 359.
30 Eyal Benvenisti, 'Margin of Appreciation, Consensus and Universal Standards' 31 New York Journal of International Law and Policy 850–853; George Letsas, 'Two Concepts of the Margin of Appreciation', *A Theory of Interpretation of the European Convention on Human Rights* (Oxford University Press 2007).
31 Andreas Føllesdal and Nino Tsereteli, 'The Margin of Appreciation in Europe and Beyond' (2016) 20 International Journal of Human Rights 1055, 1055.
32 ibid.
33 For a detailed account on the relationship between the margin of appreciation and the European consensus, see, e.g. Nikos Vogiatzis, 'The Relationship Between European Consensus, the Margin of Appreciation and the Legitimacy of the Strasbourg Court' [2019] European Public Law 445, 445.
34 Luzius Wildhaber, Arnaldur Hjartarson and Stephen Donnelly, 'No Consensus on Consensus?' (2013) 33 Human Rights Law Journal 248.

In a sense, these tools allow for the quality of the national process to be scrutinised at the international level while, at the same time, preserving the sovereignty of the domestic system. This also ties in with the above considerations on fragmentation: given that there are so many different players in the international field, tolerance of another body's assessment is necessary. Without tools such as the margin of appreciation, pluralism could not be preserved and cultural and political differences could not be accommodated.[35] This might, then, lead to states opting out of treaties. For international law to be maintainable, cooperation from the national level is required. And for states to be willing to cooperate, their sovereignty must be preserved to a certain extent. Preserving the parties' autonomy in a dispute is important in order to maintain their confidence in the adjudicative body. Regarding the laws of evidence, the sovereignty of the parties in a case requires international adjudication to accommodate for the parties' understanding of and approach to the presentation and substantiation of their version of events.[36] In the light of the equality of the parties, favouring one party's approach over another would be incompatible with the nature of sovereignty.[37]

Another explanation for the flexible rules in international law is that the obtainment of evidence simply is different and more challenging at the international level as compared to the national one. Managing evidence is more challenging for international bodies because there often is a significant lapse in time between the occurrence of the disputed event and the international legal proceedings. Furthermore, the events usually take place far away from the seat of the adjudicative body, which further complicates the gathering of evidence.[38] If these obstacles were coupled with very restrictive rules of fact-finding and evidence, resolving a case could become very hard.

The international courts might also have an interest in avoiding very technical and rigid rules of evidence because the judges themselves come from different legal traditions and have their own understanding of the laws of evidence. Thus, in sum, although the laws of evidence are influenced by domestic rules and procedures, the laws are flexible because any

---

35 Peters (n 14) 685.
36 Anna Riddell and Brendan Plant, *Evidence before the International Court of Justice* (British Institute of International and Comparative Law 2009) 2.
37 Devaney (n 24) 12, n 60.
38 Anna Riddell, 'Evidence, Fact-Finding, and Experts' in Cesare PR Romano, Karen J Alter and Yuval Shany (eds), *The Oxford Handbook of International Adjudication* (Oxford University Press 2013) 852, with further references 851

too formalistic and technical rules could come into conflict with the parties' own sovereign approach, with the judges' ideas and understandings, and with the fact that in the international realm, the gathering of evidence need not be further complicated by formalistic evidentiary rules.

Multiple perspectives are not only brought into the international system due to the influences from different national legal traditions. Multi-perspectivity also exists due to potential interveners to international disputes. Thus, in the next section, the particularity of these multiple perspectives in the international realm will be discussed, and its influence on agenda-setting will be considered.

c. Multi-Perspectivity and Agenda-Setting

The 'international decision-making system'[39] has changed over the last decade due to the emergence of new participants in the international legal sphere.[40] These actors (e.g. international organisations, NGOs, corporations, private actors, hybrid networks, *amici curiae*) interact in various ways, in different procedures, settings and contexts.[41] These interactions can be controlled, e.g. through agenda-setting. Agenda-setting is the 'process of raising issues to salience among the relevant community of actors'.[42] The decision-making system is inevitably influenced by the multiple perspectives these actors bring with them, and this multi-perspectivity will impact the agenda of the decision-making process. However, an actor can only influence a proceeding if that actor is granted access. Thus, setting the agenda is inextricably linked to exercising power: only actors who are allowed into a proceeding will be able to influence it. A case where experts are involved, where there are third-party interventions or *amicus curiae* briefs, will differ from a case where these stakeholders do not have the right to participate. In a sense, the different courts and tribunals set the agenda of a decision-making process by deciding in their constitutive

---

39   Samantha Besson and José Luis Martí, 'Legitimate Actors of International Law-Making: Towards a Theory of International Democratic Representation' (2018) 9 Jurisprudence 504, 504.

40   For a thorough analysis, see, e.g. Jean D'Aspremont, *Participants in the International Legal System - Multiple Perspectives on Non-State Actors in International Law* (Jean D'Aspremont ed, 2011).

41   Besson and Martí (n 39) 505.

42   Steven G Livingston, 'The Politics of International Agenda-Setting: Reagan and North-South Relations' (1992) 36 International Studies Quarterly 313, 313.

instruments, their rules of proceedings, and their case-law who is allowed to participate and how.

Although many judicial bodies do accept submissions by *amici curiae* and third-party interventions, the manner in which such actors may participate varies between courts.[43] The president of the ECtHR, for instance, can 'invite any High Contracting Party which is not a party to the proceedings or any person concerned who is not the applicant to submit written comments or take part in hearings'.[44] Similarly, the IACtHR, the WTO bodies, and the ICJ allow such participation of interveners who are not parties to the case at hand.[45] With regard to *amicus curiae*, it was held in an ICSID decision that

> 'The traditional role of an *amicus curiae* in an adversary proceeding is to help the decision maker arrive at its decision by providing the decision maker with arguments, perspectives, and expertise that the litigating parties may not provide.'[46]

Thus, ideally, such interventions assist the adjudicative bodies and help them conduct a better hearing. For instance, third-party interveners can supply a court with relevant material for the case. In *S. and Marper v. the United Kingdom*, for instance, the ECtHR agreed with the view held in a report on the forensic use of bioethics that the particular policy on DNA data retention at hand was indiscriminate in nature and amounted to an interference with the applicants' private life.[47]

---

43 See Yen Chiang Chang, 'How Does the Amicus Curiae Submission Affect a Tribunal Decision?' (2017) 30 Leiden Journal of International Law 647, 648.

44 Art. 36(2) ECHR, as modified by Protocol No. 11 in 1998. Rule 44 of the Rules of Court of the ECtHR gives further guidance on third party interventions.

45 For a full analysis, see Philippe J Sands and Ruth Mackenzie, 'International Courts and Tribunals, Amicus Curiae' (January 2008) in Peters A and Wolfrum F (eds), *Max Planck Encyclopaedia of Public International Law* (online ed). Available at <https://opil.ouplaw.com/view/10.1093/law:epil/9780199231690/law-9780199 231690-e8?prd=OPIL>, with the relevant rules and practices, last accessed on 12 July 2021.

46 ICSID, *Suez, Sociedad General de Aguas de Barcelona S.A. and Interagua Servicios Integrales de Agua S.A. v. Argentina* (Order in Response to a Petition for Participation as Amicus Curiae, 2006) ICSID Case No. ARB/03/17, para.13.

47 ECtHR, *S. and Marper v. United Kingdom*, App nos 30562/04 and 30566/04, Judgment of 4 December 2008, para. 124. See also ECtHR, *D.H. and Others v. the Czech Republic*, App no 57325/00, Judgment of 13 November 2007.

However, interventions can also have negative effects such as lengthening a proceeding.[48] For instance, Nicaragua's intervention in the ICJ's decision in *El Salvador/Honduras (Nicaragua Intervening)* did complicate and lengthen the proceedings, in which it took the ICJ five years and nine months to deliver a judgment.[49]

Not only do such interventions influence the length of proceedings, they can influence the decision – as they are intended to – and, in turn, impact and shape international law. Quite far-reaching reactions can ensue when courts decide on politically charged and contentious cases. In the context of the ECtHR, for instance, cases related to the legality of abortion, same-sex marriage, and assisted suicide have attracted considerable attention because the Court's decisions have far-reaching effects.[50] In the ECtHR's famous *Lautsi* case – concerning the compulsory display of a crucifix in a public school, and thus the fundamental question of the relationship between state and church –, third-party interventions were submitted by ten Member States, ten NGOs, and 33 members of the European Parliament.[51] A court ruling will, thus, be influenced by the participants, and it has been recognised that third-party interveners can influence international law.[52] On the one hand, this allows civil society and any stakeholders and other affected entities to participate in the proceedings and to 'positively influence the Court's legitimacy'. On the other hand, states fear that their position and influence may be diluted by the

---

48 For a thorough analysis on lengthy proceedings before the ICJ, see DW Bowett and others, 'Efficiency of Procedures and Working Methods: Report of the Study Group Established by the British Institute of International and Comparative Law as a Contribution to the UN Decade of International Law' (1996) 45 International and Comparative Law Quarterly.

49 ibid 21, n 36. The average case before the ICJ usually takes around four years; some cases have even been decided within a year, see The International Court of Justice: Handbook (2004), p. 50, available at <https://www.icj-cij.org/files/public ations/handbook-of-the-court-en.pdf>, last accessed on 12 July 2021, referencing ICJ, *Appeal Relating to the Jurisdiction of the ICAO Council—Aerial Incident of 10 August 1999 (Pakistan v. India)* (Merits) [1972] ICJ Rep 1972, 46 and ICJ, *Request for Interpretation of the Judgment of 31 March 2004 in the Case concerning Avena and Other Mexican Nationals (Mexico v. United States of America)* (Merits) [2009] ICJ Rep 2009, 3.

50 Nicole Bürli, *Third-Party Interventions before the European Court of Human Rights: Amicus Curiae, Member-State and Third-Party Interventions* (Intersentia 2017) 1.

51 ECtHR, *Lautsi and Others v. Italy*, App no 30814/06, Judgment of 18 March 2011, para. 8.

52 Bürli (n 50) 2.

demand for wider participation.[53] Thus, these different actors may have countervailing interests, making it essential that the interests of the parties, of third parties, and of the relevant court are balanced properly.[54]

In this sense, international courts can be viewed as 'organs of the value-based international community whose values and interests they are supposed to protect and develop': their decisions do affect not only the parties to a case but the international community as a whole.[55] An adjudicative body should keep in mind its adjudicative task and decide on a case-by-case basis whether participation by stakeholders other than the parties to the case is suitable and whether such interventions will have a positive impact on the decision-making process. Another important step in the decision-making process is the finding and assessment of facts. Thus in what follows, the process of fact-assessment in international adjudication will be considered.

3. Defining Fact-Assessment

One important function of international courts is to deliver binding decisions on questions of international law.[56] Thus, art. 38 ICJ Statute holds that the court's 'function is to decide in accordance with international law such disputes as are submitted to it'.[57] An adjudicative body can only reach such a decision if it can ascertain the relevant facts of the case; only then can the principles of law be adequately applied to the given factual situation. Before judicial fact-assessment occurs, usually some sort of fact-finding has already been conducted, for instance by fact-finding commissions or by NGOs.[58] However, these types of fact-finding are not the focus of this study; the discussion will instead pertain mostly to fact-finding or fact-assessment – these terms are used synonymously – by the judiciary. Fact-assessment is understood in this thesis as the judicial process in which

---

53 ibid.
54 Paolo Palchetti, 'Opening the International Court of Justice to Third States: Intervention and Beyond' (2002) 6 Max Planck Yearbook of United Nations Law 139, 175.
55 Armin von Bogdandy and Ingo Venzke, *In Whose Name? A Public Law Theory of International Adjudication* (Oxford University Press 2014) 46.
56 ibid 6–7. For their account on the multifunctionality of international adjudication, see 5pp.
57 Art. 38, Statute of the International Court of Justice.
58 Mégret (n 3) 27–28.

the facts are established and then classified as relevant or irrelevant by an international court for a given case that is being adjudicated.[59]

In the realm of international adjudication, there are many different approaches to fact-assessment. Most international bodies have their own set of rules that regulate their fact-finding and fact-assessment powers.[60] This means that there is no coherent framework as to how fact-assessment is to be conducted. On the one hand, the lack of a consistent approach to fact-assessment in the context of international law has been widely criticised.[61] On the other hand, it seems impossible to create a single coherent framework for how international judges are to conduct fact-assessment, given that the adjudicative bodies differ from each other in terms of their set-up and the area of law they focus on.

The International Court of Justice (ICJ) is the only active body in international adjudication that has general jurisdiction.[62] Other permanent tribunals have been established for specific areas of international law, such as the International Tribunal for the Law of the Sea (ITLOS), the International Criminal Court (ICC), and human rights courts. There are quasi-judicial bodies, *ad-hoc* tribunals, dispute settlement bodies and many other adjudicative bodies, all of which have their own approaches as to how they analyse facts and evidence and what functions the different actors have in the process.[63]

Fact-assessment in the different courts can also take different forms due to the specific characteristics of the area of law that they contend with. Fact-assessment in the realm of human rights will inevitably be different from fact-finding in trade law. Thus Philip Alston and Sarah Knuckey, for example, treat human-rights fact-finding as synonymous with investi-

---

59 This will be the focus in Parts II and III.
60 For instance, Plant refers to the following provisions: 'ICJ—Statute of the International Court of Justice, arts. 43–54, ICJ Rules of Court (1978), arts. 9, 44–72, 101; ITLOS—Statute of the International Tribunal for the Law of the Sea, arts. 16, 26–28, ITLOS Rules of the Tribunal, arts. 15, 44–84 (especially 76–84); WTO—Understanding on Rules and Procedures Governing the Settlement of Disputes, arts. 11–13, apps 3 and 4; Permanent Court of Arbitration—Arbitration Rules 2012, arts. 17, 27–9; Iran–US Claims Tribunal, Rules of Procedure, arts. 15, 25, 27.', in Brendan Plant, 'Expert Evidence and the Challenge of Procedural Reform in International Dispute Settlement' (2018) 28 Journal of International Dispute Settlement 464, 466.
61 Anna Riddell, 'Evidence, Fact-Finding, and Experts' (n38) 852, with further references.
62 ibid 850.
63 Riddell, 'Evidence, Fact-Finding, and Experts' (n 38).

gation, documentation, and research.[64] In the WTO context, Michelle T. Grando equates the process of fact-finding with the process of proof.[65] She defines the process of fact-finding as

> '[t]he process through which a panel formulates its conclusions with respect to the facts of a case, that is, it is the process through which the facts of a case are established. In this regard, it is important to note that panels consider and establish facts against the background of a legal provision – ie a provision in the WTO agreements. [...]'[66]

The Max Planck Encyclopaedia of Public International Law (MPEPIL) defines fact-finding as follows:

> 'Fact-finding' or 'inquiry' is a recognized form of international dispute settlement through the process of elucidating facts, given that it is the varied perceptions of these facts that often give rise to the dispute in the first place. [...] Fact-finding is a process distinct from other forms of dispute settlement in the sense that it is aimed primarily at clarifying the disputed facts through impartial investigation, which would then facilitate the parties' objective of identifying the final solution to the dispute.'[67]

This definition treats fact-finding synonymously with 'inquiry' and 'the process of elucidating facts'. The practice of different international courts as to how they use their fact-finding or fact-assessment powers and how they approach this task is different, as will be shown in detail below. Despite these differences and nuances, what all these definitions have in common is that the elucidation of facts is seen as a process. For the purpose of this work, fact-assessment is also seen as a process. However, it will be viewed as a necessary step for a court to rule on a case, rather than a process that 'stands by itself'.[68] It is seen as a strategic practice that is embedded in the judicial procedure and aimed at producing truth claims that

---

64 Philip Alston and Sarah Knuckey, 'The Transformation of Human Rights Fact-Finding: Challenges and Oppotunities' in Philip Alston and Sarah Knuckey (eds), *The Transformation of Human Rights Fact-Finding* (Oxford University Press 2016) 7.

65 Michelle T Grando, *Evidence, Proof, and Fact-Finding in WTO Dispute Settlement* (Oxford University Press 2009) 9.

66 Grando (n 65)., p. 5.

67 Agnieszka Jachec-Neale, 'Fact-Finding' (March 2011) in Peters A and Wolfrum R *Max Planck Encyclopaedia of Public International Law* (online edn).

68 Mégret (n 3) 28.

add to the clarification of the dispute at hand.[69] Does this entail that the goal of fact-assessment by the international judiciary is the ascertainment of truth? One would be inclined to answer in the affirmative. However, as will be shown in the next section, a clear answer as to what the goal of international fact-assessment is, is not easily provided.

4. Goals of International Fact-Assessment

a. Ascertaining 'the Truth'?

The topic of truth has been one of the most central topics in philosophy.[70] Some of the most widely held views on this subject in modern philosophy are correspondence theories of truth, which require truth to reflect how reality actually is; coherence theories of truth, where truth is seen to cohere with a set of beliefs; pragmatist views that focus on what is practicable; constructivist theories that analyse how the world is interpreted and how these interpretations shape traditions and choices; and deflationist theories that do not give much significance to the concept of truth and rather raise the question of what it means to say that something is true.[71]

In a paper titled 'Rethinking Bias and Truth in Evidence-Based Health Care', Wieringa et al. apply philosophical concepts of truth to decisions in the health care sector. They discuss a theory of truth called the ideal limit theory, 'which assumes an ultimate and absolute truth towards which scientific inquiry progresses'.[72] The authors criticise this dominant way of conceptualising truth in the discourse and practice of evidence-based health care as being conceptually insufficient. They argue that this conception of truth does not ask the fundamental question of 'how truths differ from untruths (and what is the nature of the grey zone in the middle)' and that it wrongly assumes truth to be unproblematic and that the right decision will be made once biases have been removed. Such a conception puts constraints on any analysis of what 'good decision-making' in the clinical context entails.[73] The questions that are raised in the paper are

---

69 This definition is inspired by ibid 29.
70 See <https://plato.stanford.edu/entries/truth/>, last accessed on 12 July 2021.
71 Sietse Wieringa and others, 'Rethinking Bias and Truth in Evidence-Based Health Care' (2018) 24 Journal of Evaluation in Clinical Practice 930, 931.
72 ibid 930.
73 ibid 931.

highly relevant to international adjudication: how do truths differ from untruths in the context of international decision-making? How should we approach grey areas (which are extensive in legal decision-making)? And what is 'good decision-making' in this context?

The approach to ascertaining truth differs between common law systems and civil law systems. In common law countries, the truth is seen to lie somewhere in between the parties' submissions, with the national courts taking a more passive role, similar to that of a referee.[74] In these traditions, the procedures are adversarial: the lawyers have the most active role in questioning witnesses and presenting the evidence. The judges or juries analyse the versions of events presented by the prosecutor on the one hand and the defence on the other hand; by applying the relevant standard of proof, they then decide which version of the facts convinces them most.[75] In civil law countries, judges take a more active role in establishing the facts. Here, the procedures are inquisitorial: the judges question witnesses and are responsible for the discovery of the facts.[76] Albeit these approaches differ, Cesare Romano holds that at the national level, the purpose of a trial is to ascertain the truth, or at least to reach 'factually correct verdicts'. He contrasts this with the international realm, where 'the ultimate purpose of international adjudication is not establishing facts, or truths, or even "the truth", but rather to settle the dispute'.[77]

These points seem to indicate that, although at the national level the ascertainment of truth may be the primary goal of fact-assessment, at the international level, this is not the case. Several points support this position. First, the decisions of international courts and tribunals are usually final and without appeal.[78] It would, thus, seem too commanding to give them

---

74 Riddell, 'Evidence, Fact-Finding, and Experts' (n 38) 849.

75 See the Research Project on 'Standards of Proof in International Humanitarian and Human Rights Fact-Finding and Inquiry Missions' by Stephen Wilkinson, under the auspices of the Geneva Academy of International Humanitarian Law and Human Rights in close cooperation with Geneva Call, p. 17, available at <https://www.geneva-academy.ch/joomlatools-files/docman-files/Standards%20of%20Proof%20in%20Fact-Finding.pdf>, last accessed on 12 July 2021.

76 Riddell, 'Evidence, Fact-Finding, and Experts' (n 38) 849.

77 Cesare PR Romano, 'The Role of Experts in International Adjudication' [2009] Legal Studies Paper No . 2011-04, Société française pour le droit international.

78 For instance, in the context of the ICJ: 'The ICJ is a court of first and last instance […]'. See Karin Oellers-Frahm, 'Article 92 UN Charter' in Andreas Zimmermann and others (eds), *The Statute of the International Court of Justice: A Commentary* (2nd edn, Oxford University Press 2012) 178. See also the wording of art. 60 ICJ Statute: 'The judgment is final and without appeal.'

the monopoly on the last version of the truth. This ties in with the idea that international courts may be reluctant to enforce their version of the truth due to considerations of respect for the sovereignty of the litigating states and their version of the events.[79] Second, it may be more difficult or even impossible for international courts to ascertain 'the truth' given that by the time they do decide a dispute, often several years have passed since the events took place.[80]

Third, the absence of rigid rules on evidence in international adjudication may also reflect that the ascertainment of truth is not the prime goal of international fact-assessment.[81]

A fourth point is the level of complexity that cases have reached in modern times;[82] ascertaining 'the truth' may simply not be possible. Fifth, there is no rule in the international law of evidence that states that a court must ascertain 'the truth'. Given the increase in complexity of the cases and the fact that expert disagreement does exist, such a rule would seem unpracticable and undesirable. Thus, the ideal limit theory Wieringa et al.[83] deem insufficient in the context of evidence-based health care also seems unhelpful in the context of international legal decision-making. As truth does not seem to be the (only) goal of fact-finding, in what follows, other goals of fact-assessment will be discussed.

b. Other (Potentially Competing) Goals

Although fact-finding missions are not the focus of this study, looking at what goals they pursue is worthwhile because they illuminate one point that holds true for judicial fact-finding as well: fact-finding can have multiple goals, and these goals potentially compete with each other. In the 1991 UNGA Declaration on Fact-finding by the UN in the Field of the Maintenance of International Peace and Security, the stated goals were to maintain international peace and security and to 'obtain detailed

---

79 Riddell, 'Evidence, Fact-Finding, and Experts' (n 38) 851.
80 ibid.
81 Sandifer (n 1) 9. The quote from Sandifer was already reproduced above in the Introduction: 'no rule of evidence [...] finds more frequent statement in the cases than the one that international tribunals are not bound to adhere to strict rules of evidence'.
82 Devaney (n 24) 6.
83 Wieringa and others (n 71) 930.

knowledge of the relevant facts'.[84] In other fact-finding missions as well, the ascertainment of facts alone was not the main goal. Rather, the tasks included 'determining state and individual responsibility for violations of international law, making recommendations regarding reform and reparations, and promoting accountability'.[85] These goals cannot all be attained at the same time, and again, certain goals will never be attainable due to limitations to human knowledge. Conflict resolution may be at odds with reconciliation, and the goal of 'finding the truth' can conflict with the aim to hold someone accountable as soon as possible. These examples show that considerations of efficiency might call for a 'quick fix' rather than lengthy procedures in certain cases – 'Who after all can wait for a trial to determine that genocide occurred?', as Frédéric Mégret asks.[86] Thus, there is a tension between the appeal to certainty and the 'need for actionable, real-time information'.[87]

In the context of the WTO dispute settlement system, potential goals are 'accuracy, participation impartiality, equality, good faith cooperation, the efficient use of resources (time and money), and the protection of confidential information'.[88] Again, these ideals cannot all be achieved simultaneously. Striving for a certain determination of the facts will inevitably conflict with the desire for an actionable and efficient solution to a case, and focusing on the protection of confidential information and privacy will inevitably prolong the process of adjudication. Thus if we acknowledge that goals and values can conflict, that there are limits to human knowledge, and that the existence of a dispute in itself reflects a non-ideal situation, the question becomes: what is an achievable goal under non-ideal circumstances?

c. Truth Founded on Evidence

Under the title 'the goals of legal adjudication', Michelle Grando writes that '[a]ccuracy, or the search for the truth is considered a – if not the – major objective of adjudication'.[89] However, can 'accuracy' and 'the search

---

84 UN GA Res. A/RES/46/59.
85 Shiri Krebs and others, 'The Legalization of Truth in International Fact-Finding' (2017) 211 Chicago Journal of Internadional Law 95–96.
86 Mégret (n 3) 27–28.
87 ibid.
88 Grando (n 65) 4.
89 ibid 10.

for the truth' really be used synonymously? I would argue that 'accuracy' is about 'conforming exactly to truth', as Merriam-Webster[90] defines it. And, as I have argued above, the exact truth will hardly ever be ascertainable. René Descartes wrote the following:

> 'It is very certain that, when it is not in our power to determine what is true, we ought to act according to what is most probable; and even although we should not remark a greater probability in one opinion than in another, we ought notwithstanding to choose one or the other, and afterwards consider it, in so far as it relates to practice, as no longer dubious, but manifestly true and certain, since the reason by which our choice has been determined is itself possessed of these qualities.'[91]

In a sense, this can be read as meaning that something can be considered true if the probabilities point in that direction. However, a certain qualifying element is required, one cannot simply arrive at qualifying something as 'true', rather, this decision-process must have certain qualities. What one ought to believe, according to the dominant view among philosophers, is what one can base on evidence. In other words, one only has good reason to believe something if this belief is based on evidence.[92] And as David Hume wrote in *An Enquiry Concerning Human Understanding*, '[a] wise man [...] proportions his belief to the evidence'.[93] Thus, depending on the quality of the evidence, and on the requirements that are emphasised in the rules of evidence, a belief can have more weight or less; a belief may qualify as true or not; a decision reached may qualify as 'good' or not. What could these qualities be in international adjudication?

What truth is in international adjudication in the context of this thesis can be equated with what can meet the requirements under the laws of

---

90 See <https://www.merriam-webster.com/dictionary/accurate>, last accessed on 12 July 2021.

91 René Descartes, *Discourse on the Method of Rightly Conducting the Reason, and Seeking Truth in the Sciences* (John Veitch trans., Cosimo Books 1st ed. 2008) (1924), 25; quoted in Makane Moïse Mbengue, 'International Courts and Tribunals as Fact-Finders: The Case of Scientific Fact-Finding in International Adjudication' (2011) 34 Loyola of Los Angeles International and Comparative Law Review 53, 61.

92 For a discussion of evidentialism and pragmatism, see Miriam Schleifer McCormick, *Believing Against the Evidence: Agency and the Ethics of Belief* (Routledge 2015).

93 David Hume, *An Enquiry Concerning Human Understanding* (Oxford University Press 1902), L. A. Selby-Bigge (ed.), 110.

evidence, i.e. what can meet the standard of proof that is required in a given case. Acquiring evidence is not an exact science, and the results of any fact-finding process can vary and produce different results; sometimes the information obtained will be satisfactory, other times the information may be insufficient. Thus, the belief will have to be proportioned depending on the amount and quality of the information. In the context of reaching a conclusion in international adjudication, this can be translated as meaning the conclusion reached by an international court should reflect the specifics of the case and the quality of the evidence; the standard of proof and the attainment thereof being a qualifying element. There is not 'the truth', then, but rather a qualified truth that is considered true because there is evidence to support it, and that evidence is in turn considered evidence because the rules of evidence and fact-finding that are in place have been followed. If more evidence is produced or comes to light at a later point, the truth may change. Harking back to Descartes' quote above,[94] what is required is a qualification: not any fact will amount to truth; the process of fact-assessment and the rules of evidence must be followed, and if a statement is then deemed sufficient by the deciding court or tribunal, it can be qualified as true.

Truth can have different colours in international adjudication due to the fact that there are different standards of proof, as will be shown next.[95] The standard of 'proof beyond reasonable doubt' and that of 'preponderance of evidence' require different levels of certainty or different qualities of the information. In other words, not any submitted piece of information will qualify as proving something beyond reasonable doubt.

However, as will be shown in what follows, the rules of evidence and the rules as to how a court should conduct its fact-assessment procedures are quite scarce and leave the decision-makers with a lot of discretion. It, thus, is important to scrutinise the quality of fact-assessment procedures. It will be suggested in Part II that principles of scientific method can operate as 'qualifying elements' which will allow us to analyse and critique the fact-assessment procedure by the ECtHR in its jurisprudence. However, first, an overview will be provided of the rules of evidence that are in place, and a more detailed account will be given of the rules that guide the ECtHR.

---

94 Above at p. 19.
95 The standards will be discussed in detail below under I.5.b.iii.

5. Rules of Evidence in International Adjudication

The Max Planck Encyclopedia of Public International Law (MPEPIL) defines evidence as follows:

> 'Evidence in international adjudication embraces information submitted to an international court or tribunal by parties to a case or from other sources with the view of establishing or disproving alleged facts.'[96]

In his work on evidence-based jurisprudence, Hanjo Hammann equates the German term 'Evidenz' with knowledge of factual relationships, but only to the extent that such evidence is obtained through a systematic procedure of illustration or demonstration, not solely through introspection.[97] Thus, he emphasises the procedure of the obtainment of evidence and requires a certain level of objectivity in order for the factual basis to qualify as evidence. As Chester Brown rightly notes, evidence 'in itself is not a type of procedure; "evidence", properly understood, refers only to facts and opinions put before the court'.[98] This shows that, unlike fact-finding, evidence is not a process. Rather, evidence is (ideally) the outcome of the process or procedure of fact-finding. A proper administration of evidence requires rules on forms, standards, and burdens of proof, and on powers with regard to the gathering of facts.[99] Thus, in international adjudication, the emphasis is on the procedure of the gathering of information. If this procedure follows certain rules, the information may qualify as evidence.

As will be shown below, in international adjudication, the procedural aspects of who collects evidence and how it is assessed can vary between international courts or tribunals. The rules of the different courts, especially their rules of procedure, usually contain some provisions on evidence.

---

96 See Rüdiger Wolfrum and Mirka Möldner, 'International Courts and Tribunals, Evidence' (August 2013) in Peters A and Wolfrum R (eds), *Max Planck Encyclopedia of Public International Law* (online edn), available at <https://opil.ouplaw.com /view/10.1093/law:epil/9780199231690/law-9780199231690-e26>, last accessed on 12 July 2021.

97 Hanjo Hamann, *Evidenzbasierte Jurisprudenz* (Mohr Siebeck 2014) 3. In the original: 'Wissen über tatsächliche Zusammenhänge, und auch nur soweit es durch systematische Verfahren zur «Veranschaulichung» oder zum «Nachweis», und nicht allein durch Introspektion, gewonnen wird.'

98 Chester Brown, *A Common Law of International Adjudication* (Oxford University Press 2009) 84.

99 ibid 85.

a. The Powers of International Courts and Tribunals Regarding Evidence

Although there is no coherent framework with regard to evidence in the procedural laws of international tribunals, some rules can be found in the statutes and the rules of the courts and tribunals. In what follows, three roles or powers of international adjudicative bodies will be discussed: the power to require the parties to produce evidence; the power to conduct own investigations; and the power to consult experts.

i. Power to Order Parties to Produce Evidence

International adjudicative bodies can request the production of evidence.[100] This is a power that is closer to civil law procedure than to common law traditions. In common law countries, the production of evidence is mainly upon the parties. Although judges could request the production of further evidence, they seldom make use of this power. In the civil law systems, these powers tend to be used more extensively. A civil law judge will more often call for a further witness, take initiative on the examination of a witness, request an expert inquiry or inspection, or request that more documentary evidence be produced.[101]

The power of international adjudicative bodies to order the production of further information is conferred upon them in their constitutive instruments or rules of procedure.[102] This power to request is uncontroversial even in cases where an international court does not have an explicit power conferred to it in the relevant legal texts. The argument is that in order to fulfil their functions in the adjudicative process, international courts need to have some powers to obtain the evidence necessary to reach a conclusion.[103] However, it is somewhat controversial how far this power extends, i.e. whether international courts have the power to (coercively)

---

100 Sandifer (n 1) 154–163.

101 ibid 154–155.

102 For instance, for the ICJ, see arts. 34(2), 49 ICJ Statute and art. 62(1) ICJ Rules; for ITLOS, see art. 77 ITLOS Rules; for ICSID, see art. 43(a) ICSID Convention and Rules 34(2)-(3) and 37 ICSID Rules; in the WTO-Context, see art. 13(1) DSU; for the ECtHR, see art. 38(1)(a) ECHR and art. 42(1) of its Rules of Court; for the IACtHR, see art. 48 ACHR and art. 44(2) of its Rules of Procedure.

103 Mojtaba Kazazi, *Burden of Proof and Related Issues: A Study on Evidence Before International Tribunals* (Kluwer Law International 1996) 166.

demand the production of evidence and what the consequences are of a party's non-compliance if a court requests further evidence.[104]

There is wide consensus that a general obligation exists for parties in international litigation to produce evidence in their possession that is not available to the opposing party, even if the evidence might be adverse to that party's own interest.[105] As will be discussed in more detail below, it ordinarily is upon the party alleging a fact to introduce the relevant evidence to establish it.[106] However, as was held by the Mexico/U.S.A. General Claims Commission in *Parker v. Mexico*, even though this general rule does exist, it 'does not relieve the respondent from its obligation to lay before the Commission all evidence within its possession to establish the truth, whatever it may be'.[107] Other international tribunals have followed this rule,[108] and this 'duty of collaboration'[109] can be found in the constitutive instruments of some international courts and tribunals.[110] In the context of the WTO, a broad power to request information from the parties is given to the Panels in art. 13 of the DSU.[111] It provides Panels with the right 'to seek information and technical advice from any individual or body which it deems appropriate'[112] and to 'seek information from any relevant source'.[113] This investigative power is, thus, not limited to seeking scientific or technical advice or expert evidence.[114] Whether this right to seek information amounts to a binding power to compel the production of information is contested. Arguably, such a binding power has been established through judicial interpretation by the WTO's adjudicative bodies.[115] In *Argentina – Textiles and Apparel*, the Panel stated

---

104 Brown (n 98) 104.
105 Sandifer (n 1) 153.
106 See below, I.5.b.ii.
107 Reports of International Arbitral Awards, General Claims Commission, *Parker v. Mexico*, 4 RIAA 35, 39, para. 6 (US—Mexico GCC, 1926).
108 See, e.g. Reports of International Arbitral Awards, General Claims Commission, *Lillie S. Kling (USA) v. United Mexican States*, 4 RIAA 581–584 (US—Mexico CC, 1930); Reports of International Arbitral Awards, General Claims Commission, *Pinson v. Mexico*, 5 RIAA 411–414.
109 Devaney (n 24) 180.
110 See, e.g. arts. 86–87 Rome Statute and art. 24(3) Rules of Procedure of Iran-US Claims Tribunal.
111 Art. 13 DSU.
112 Art. 13(1) DSU.
113 Art. 13(2) DSU.
114 Joost Pauwelyn, 'The Use of Experts in WTO Dispute Settlement' (2002) 51 International & Comparative Law Quarterly 325, 329.
115 Devaney (n 24) 181.

that 'the most important result of the rule of collaboration appears to be that the adversary is obligated to provide the tribunal with relevant documents which are in its sole possession'.[116] However, the extent of this obligation and the consequences of non-compliance are uncertain.[117] A literal reading of art. 13 DSU does not seem to impose a binding legal obligation upon parties to a dispute to comply with a Panel's request for information.[118] However, the Appellate Body's interpretation suggests otherwise: in its report on *Canada – Civilian Aircraft*, it held that a Panel is 'vested with ample and extensive discretionary authority to determine *when* it needs information to resolve a dispute and *what* information it needs'.[119] Furthermore, the Appellate Body interpreted art. 13 DSU as evoking a duty to comply with a Panel's request and held that if the right to seek information were not an enforceable one, this would 'reduce to an illusion' the Members' right to have disputes resolved.[120] Not everyone agrees with the AB's interpretation of art. 13(1) DSU.[121] Still, the AB's assertion of a power to compel did not provoke an outcry from the WTO Member States, and it has been suggested that the ICJ could achieve the same result through its case-law.[122]

The starting point for this discussion is art. 49 of the ICJ Statute, which reads as follows: 'The Court may, even before the hearing begins, call upon the agents to produce any document or to supply any explanations. Formal note shall be taken of any refusal.'[123] This article does not express a mandate to comply, as the ICJ can only 'call upon' the parties rather than 'demand' or 'compel' the production of evidence. The stated consequence of non-compliance is that the ICJ would take 'formal note', suggesting that the repercussions would not be that serious. Similar wording can be found in art. 77(1) of the ITLOS Rules and art. 43(a) ICSID Convention,

---

116 WTO, *Argentina: Measures Affecting Imports of Footwear, Textiles, Apparel and Other Items–Report of the Panel* (25 November 1997) WT/DS56/R, p. 90, para. 6.40.
117 Brown (n 98) 105.
118 For an in-depth discussion on this issue, see Devaney (n 24) 184–187. See also Brown (n 98) 104–110.
119 WTO, *Canada: Measures Affecting the Export of Civilian Aircraft–Report of the Appellate Body* (2 August 1999) WT/DS70, para. 192 (emphasis in the original).
120 ibid, para. 189.
121 See Rambod Behboodi, '"Should" Means "Shall": A Critical Analysis of the Obligation to Submit Information Under Article 13.1 of the DSU in the Canada - Aircraft Case' (2000) 3 Journal of International Economic Law.
122 Devaney (n 24) 187.
123 Art. 49 ICJ Statute.

according to which parties can also be 'called upon' to produce evidence. These rules do not seem to imply that there is an obligation to cooperate; however, it is up to the relevant courts to interpret the rules in their case-law. It is possible for them to push in a similar direction as the adjudicative bodies have been doing in the WTO context. This was done by the ICSID Tribunal in *Biwater Gauff (Tanzania) Ltd v. Tanzania* where the Tribunal stated that the respondent state was under 'an international legal obligation' to produce the requested documents.[124] Compared to the WTO's adjudicative bodies, the ICJ has taken a more reactive approach to requesting information and has been criticised for under-utilising its power to request information under art. 49 ICJ Statute.[125] Judge Owada, in a dissenting opinion in the *Oil Platforms* case, criticised the Court for being too concerned about respecting the parties' sovereignty and being impartial, and argued for the Court to adopt a more active approach regarding issues of evidence and fact-finding.[126] It has been claimed that the ICJ's deferential and passive approach is 'a hindrance to the proper administration of justice'.[127]

The European Court of Human Rights has a basic adversarial set-up that is coined with strong investigative powers.[128] These powers are provided in art. 38 ECHR, which holds that '[t]he Court shall examine the case together with the representatives of the parties and, if need be, undertake an investigation, for the effective conduct of which the High Contracting Parties concerned shall furnish all necessary facilities'.[129] Rules 44A – 44C of the Rules of Court and the Annex to the Rules of Court include further details on the duties to cooperate.[130] Rule A1 of the Annex to the Rules of Court states that the Chamber may 'invite the parties to produce documentary evidence'.[131] In the case of *Shamayev v. Georgia and Russia*, the

---

124 ICSID, *Biwater Gauff (Tanzania) Ltd v. Tanzania*, (Procedural Order No. 2 of 24 May 2006) ICSID Case No. ARB/05/22, paras. 8–9.

125 Devaney (n 24) 188.

126 ICJ, *Oil Platforms (Islamic Republic of Iran v. US)* (Merits) [2003] ICJ Rep 2003, 161, Dissenting Opinion of Judge Owada at 321.

127 Devaney (n 24) 188.

128 Astrid Wiik, *Amicus Curiae Before International Courts and Tribunals* (Nomos/Hart 2018) 449, n 55.

129 Art. 38 ECHR.

130 Rules 44A–44C of the Rules of Court. See also Alix Schlüter, 'Beweisfragen in der Rechtsprechung des Europäischen Gerichtshofs für Menschenrechte' in Armin von Bogdandy and Anne Peters (eds), *Beiträge zum ausländischen öffentlichen Recht und Völkerrecht*, vol Band 288 (Springer 2019) 69ss.

131 Rule A1, Annex to the Rules of Court.

Court held that there was a 'duty to cooperate with [the Court] in arriving at the truth'.[132] The refusal of the Russian Government to cooperate in this case amounted to 'accepting that those refusals obstruct the functioning of the system of collective enforcement established by the Convention'.[133] Furthermore, the Court held that '[i]n order to be effective, this system requires [...] cooperation with the Court by each of the Contracting States'.[134] In the case of non-cooperation, and if the Contracting State cannot provide any 'convincing explanation for its delays and omissions in response to the Court's requests for relevant documents, information and witnesses'[135], the Court may draw inferences that can be to the detriment of the uncooperative government.[136] Adverse inferences may also be drawn in the context of the ICJ and the WTO if a party to a dispute does not submit the requested information.[137]

ii. Power to Conduct Own Investigations

International courts have powers to conduct investigations *proprio motu*, i.e. to gather information on their own initiative. The ICJ, for instance, has the power to 'make all arrangements connected with the taking of evidence' according to art. 48 of its Statute.[138] From their power to make own investigations, international tribunals can, for instance, arrange visits to the sites that are linked to the dispute.[139] Art. 44(2) of the ICJ Statute allows the Court to 'procure evidence on the spot'[140], meaning that the ICJ has the power to conduct on-site visits. ICSID tribunals also have an express power under art. 43(b) ICSID Convention to 'visit any place con-

---

132 ECtHR, *Shamayev and Others v. Georgia and Russia*, App no 36378/02, Judgment of 12 April 2005, para. 502. With further reference to ECtHR, *Artico v. Italy*, App no 6694/74, Judgment of 13 May 1980, para. 30.

133 ECtHR, *Shamayev and Others v. Georgia and Russia*, App no 36378/02, Judgment of 12 April 2005, para. 502.

134 ibid.

135 ECtHR, *Tepe v. Turkey*, App no 27244/95, Judgment of 9 May 2003, para. 135.

136 ECtHR, *Shamayev and Others v. Georgia and Russia*, App no 36378/02, Judgment of 12 April 2005, para. 503.

137 Pauwelyn (n 114) 329. E.g. Panels may, with reference to art. 13 DSU, draw adverse inferences.

138 Riddell, 'Evidence, Fact-Finding, and Experts' (n 38) 855.

139 ibid. See, e.g. art. 81 ITLOS Rules of the Tribunal.

140 Art. 44(2) ICJ Statute.

nected with the dispute or conduct enquiries there'.[141] The ECtHR has the power to conduct investigations *proprio motu* under its Rules of Court.[142] The Annex to these Rules specifies in Rule A1(3) that the Chamber has the power to take evidence by delegating to one or more judges of the Court the task and responsibility of conducting an inquiry, which includes carrying out on-site investigations.[143] It has made use of these powers in a number of cases. In *Ilascu and Others v. Moldova and Russia*, for instance, a delegation of the ECtHR conducted an on-site investigation in March 2003.[144] The ITLOS, too, has the mandate to make site visits to gather information and evidence.[145] International tribunals that do not explicitly have this right in their constitutive instruments still have an inherent power to do so.[146] However, it is a power that is not used frequently.

The first time an international judge made a 'descente sur les lieux' was in 1896, when an arbitrator in the case of *Ben Tillett* visited a prison for several days in order to gather evidence.[147] The PCIJ conducted its first on-site investigation in the dispute between the Netherlands and Belgium before the PCIJ in 1937.[148] An occasion where the ICJ made a 'descente sur les lieux' was in the *Gabčíkovo-Nagymaros* case where Slovakia asked the Court to 'visit the locality to which the case relates' and 'to exercise its functions with regard to the obtaining of evidence'.[149] The judges visited various sites along the Danube and spoke to representatives (designated by the parties) who gave them explanations on the technicalities of the case.[150] In *El Salvador/Honduras*, the ICJ refused El Salvador's request to conduct an on-site visit.[151] Riddell suggests that this reluctance could be 'related to the rather antiquated view that the ICJ primarily decides disputes on the law,

---

141 Art. 43(b) ICSID Convention.

142 Rule 42(2) ECtHR Rules.

143 Rule A1(3) Annex to the ECtHR Rules of Court.

144 Press release issued by the Registrar, ECtHR, *Ilascu and Others v. Moldova and Russia*, App no 48787/99, available at <https://hudoc.echr.coe.int/eng-press#{"ite mid":["003-1047258-3021881"]}>, last accessed on 12 July 2021.

145 Art. 81 ITLOS Rules.

146 Brown (n 98) 111.

147 ibid 111 with further reference in n 204.

148 JH Leurdijk, 'Fact-Finding: Its Place in International Law and International Politics' (1967) 14 Netherlands International Law Review 141, 143.

149 ICJ, *Gabčikovo-Nagymaros Project, (Hungary v. Slovakia)* (Order, Site Visit) [1997] ICJ Rep 1997, 3, para. 10.

150 ibid.

151 *Land, Island and Maritime Frontier Dispute (El Salvador v. Honduras: Nicaragua intervening)* [1992] ICJ Rep 361–2, para. 22.

not disputes based on complex facts'; it may also stem from potentially high costs and safety considerations.[152] Site visits were also proposed but then refused in the *South West Africa* case. Here, the ICJ acted under art. 48 of its Statute and deemed it unnecessary to comply with the request.[153]

What is the use of such on-site visits? Judge Schwebel held with regard to the *Gabčíkovo-Nagymaros* case that insights into the complexity of the case were gained that could not have been attained if the judges had remained in The Hague.[154] Thus, such visits can have an illustrative function that helps the Court understand the localities better, and this background information could be helpful to the understanding of complex facts.[155] Given that the complexity of the cases in the international realm is on the increase, conducting more on-site visits to improve the understanding of cases could make sense. However, as Devaney rightly notes, establishing a commission of experts might well prove more useful than having a bench of judges travel to a site.[156] This was done by the ICJ in the *Corfu Channel* case. Here, the Court sent experts to the site to gather additional evidence.[157] In the following section, this power to engage experts will be discussed in more detail.

iii. Power to Engage Experts

International adjudicative bodies often have the power to engage experts.[158] Since adjudicative bodies have expertise in their field of law but usually not in other (scientific) fields that may play a role in a case at hand, they are often given the right to seek information and ask for technical advice from experts to help them deal with complex factual questions.[159] They can request expert reports in cases where the parties submit large

---

152 Riddell, 'Evidence, Fact-Finding, and Experts' (n 38) 855.
153 ICJ, *South West Africa (Ethiopia v. South Africa)* (Order of 29 November 1965) [1965] ICJ Rep 1965, 9.
154 Stephen Schwebel, 'A Site Visit of the World Court', *Justice in International Law: Further Selected Writings of Stephen M. Schwebel* (Cambridge University Press 2011) 96.
155 Devaney (n 24) 18.
156 ibid.
157 ICJ, *Corfu Channel Case (United Kingdom v. Albania)* (Merits) [1949] ICJ Rep 1949, 4, p. 21.
158 Riddell, 'Evidence, Fact-Finding, and Experts' (n 38) 856.
159 See, e.g. <https://www.wto.org/english/tratop_e/dispu_e/disp_settlement_cbt_e/c3s6p1_e.htm>, last accessed on 12 July 2021.

amounts of complex technical and scientific material and appoint their own experts when needed.[160] Due to the rising number of highly complex cases, it has become more common for parties to submit expert evidence to international courts. Such party-submitted evidence can put the court into a difficult position if the expert reports conflict.[161] Notably, experts may disagree even though they base their findings on the same factual data.[162] In the WTO's *US – Shrimp* case, there was expert disagreement on issues regarding sea turtle biology because there was only 'limited to anecdotal information', which lead to confusion 'or even disagreements in some of the documents'.[163] The expert evidence submitted by the parties can also be criticised as being biased because it is difficult not to see such party-experts as 'hired guns'.[164] International courts themselves will often not be in a position to assess the submitted expert material; thus, the power of courts and tribunals to appoint their own experts who help them assess this evidence but do not have a right to vote becomes all the more important.[165]

The power to appoint experts is often explicitly provided for in the constitutive instruments of international courts and tribunals. For instance, UNCLOS provides this right in art. 289 for disputes 'involving scientific or technical matters',[166] and the UNCITRAL Arbitration Rules provide that 'after consultation with the parties, the arbitral tribunal may appoint one or more independent experts to report to it, in writing, on specific issues to be determined by the arbitral tribunal'.[167] Art. 13(1) DSU provides a Panel with the power 'to seek information and technical advice from any individual or body which it deems appropriate', and under art. 13(2) Panels may 'seek information from any relevant source and consult experts to obtain their opinion on certain aspects of the matter'.[168] Similarly,

---

160 Brown (n 98) 112–113.
161 ibid 113. See, e.g. ICJ, *Temple of Preah Vihear (Cambodia v. Thailand)* (Merits) [1962] ICJ Rep 1962, 6, Dissenting Opinion of Judge Wellington Koo, para. 51, p. 99, who refers to the 'conflicting character of the two expert recommendations' as presenting a 'perplexing problem'.
162 ibid.
163 Dr. Eckert in WTO, *United States: Import Prohibition of Certain Shrimp and Shrimp Products–Report of the Panel* (6 November 1998) WT/DS58/23, para. 9 at p. 361.
164 Pauwelyn (n 114) 334.
165 See, e.g. art. 289 UNCLOS and art. 30(2) ICJ Rules.
166 Art. 289 UNCLOS.
167 Art. 29(1) UNCITRAL.
168 Art. 13(1) DSU.

the ICJ may 'entrust any individual, body, bureau, commission, or other organisation that it may select, with the task of carrying out an enquiry or giving an expert opinion'.[169] These provisions show that the powers of international adjudicators range from appointing their own independent experts to give evidence, to inviting them to sit on the tribunal through-out the proceedings (without having a vote), to commissioning expert investigations.[170] In the EU, too, there is a tendency to involve experts in decision-making.[171] The ECJ has an explicit power to commission an expert report under art. 22 ECJ Statute,[172] and for instance in the European Food Authority, scientists also play an important role.[173]

How frequently these powers are used varies from court to court. The ICJ, for instance, only rarely makes use of it. In *Gulf of Maine*, the Court appointed an expert to help determine the maritime boundary after Cana-da and the US specifically requested it to do so.[174] In *Corfu Channel*, the ICJ appointed experts to conduct on-site visits and to collect and evaluate the evidence[175] and employed experts 'on account of the technical nature of the questions involved in the assessment of compensation' due to the UK.[176] Very recently, in the *Armed Activities on the Territory of the Congo (DRC v. Uganda)* case, the ICJ arranged for an expert opinion on the question of reparations.[177] In other instances, however, the ICJ refused to appoint experts. In *Nicaragua*, the Court considered that an enquiry according to art. 50 of its Statute would be neither practicable nor desirable.[178] In the *Case Concerning the Frontier Dispute (Burkina Faso v. Mali)* the Court did appoint experts; however, it did so under the Special

---

169 Art. 50 ICJ Statute.

170 Riddell, 'Evidence, Fact-Finding, and Experts' (n 38) 857.

171 Pauwelyn (n 114) 327.

172 Art. 22 ECJ Statute; see also art. 22 EFTA Statute, art. 23 Euratom Statute, and art. 25 ECSC Statute.

173 See <http://www.efsa.europa.eu/en/science/scientific-committee-and-panels>, last accessed on 12 July 2021.

174 The technical expert was nominated jointly by the parties, see art. II(3) of the Special Agreement of 25 November 1981, ICJ, *Case Concerning Delimitation of the Maritime Boundary in the Gulf of Maine Area (Canada v. US)*.

175 ICJ, *Corfu Channel (United Kingdom v. Albania)* (Special Agreement concluded on 25 March 1948) at pp. 142–162.

176 ICJ, *Corfu Channel (United Kingdom v. Albania)* (Assessment of Compensation) [1949] ICJ Rep 1949, 244, at pp. 258–260.

177 Justine N Stefanelli, 'ICJ Arranges for Expert Opinion on Reparations in DRC v. Uganda' (*American Society of International Law, International Law in Brief*).

178 ICJ, *Military and Paramilitary Activities in and against Nicaragua (Nicaragua v. United States of America)* (Merits) [1986] ICJ Rep 1986, 14, para. 61.

Agreement between the parties and its right to make orders under art. 48 of the ICJ Statute rather than under art. 50. It has been criticised for this reluctance. For instance, in *Temple of Preah Vihear (Cambodia v. Thailand)* Judge Wellington Koo, in his dissenting opinion, stated that due to the technical character of the case, the Court would have been 'well advised under Articles 44 and 50 of the Statute, to send its own expert or experts to investigate on the spot and make a report of their observations and recommendations, as was done in the *Corfu Channel* case'.[179] Why the Court shows such a reluctance in its use of its powers under art. 50 ICJ Statute is unclear.[180] In *Pulp Mills on the River Uruguay*, an ad hoc judge suggested that this reluctance may be due to the Court's fear of additional investigations delaying proceedings.[181] Riddell suggests that another possible explanation could be that international courts do not want to delegate because such delegation of a judicial function may be perceived as undermining the legitimacy of the decision. Furthermore, using independent experts causes additional costs that the tribunal has to cover if it appoints experts *proprio motu* rather than leaving the appointment to the parties.[182]

In comparison to the ICJ's practice, WTO Panels have made use of their power to appoint experts more frequently. Their power under art. 13 DSU is reinforced in art. 11(2) SPS Agreement and art. 14(2), 14(3) and Annex 2 of the TBT Agreement.[183] Where experts have been consulted, their opinion has had a clear impact on the Panels' decisions.[184] The Panels have used their consultation powers in cases that involved complex scientific and technical evidence,[185] but also when expert translating skills were

---

179 ICJ, *Temple of Preah Vihear (Cambodia v. Thailand)* (Merits) [1962] ICJ Rep 1962, 6, Dissenting Opinion of Judge Wellington Koo, para. 55. Similarly, ICJ, *Case Concerning Kasikili/Sedudu Island (Botswana v. Namibia)* (Merits) [1999] ICJ Rep 1999, 1045, Separate Opinion of Judge Oda at para. 6; ICJ, *Military and Paramilitary Activities in and against Nicaragua (Nicaragua v. United States of America)* (Merits) [1986] ICJ Rep 1986, 14, Dissenting Opinion of Judge Schwebel at para. 134.

180 Devaney (n 24) 22.

181 ICJ, *Case concerning Pulp Mills on the River Uruguay (Argentina v. Uruguay)* (Merits), [2010] ICJ Rep 2010, 14, Dissenting Opinion of Judge *ad hoc* Vinuesa, p. 281, at para. 95.

182 Riddell, 'Evidence, Fact-Finding, and Experts' (n 38) 857.

183 See also arts. 19(3), 19(4) and Annex 2 of the Agreement on Implementation of Article VII of GATT 1994 and arts. 4(5) and 24(3) of the SCM Agreement.

184 Grando (n 65) 340.

185 See, e.g., WTO, *Japan: Measures Affecting the Importation of Apples–Report of the Panel* (10 December 2003) WT/DS245/R, paras. 6.1–6.194 and WTO, *Australia:*

required.[186] The opinion of the experts is not binding on the Panel.[187] Still, in many cases, Panels have decided to give much weight to the expert analysis.[188]

The European Court of Human Rights also has the power to hear experts if their statements seem likely to assist in clarifying the facts of a case according to Rule A1(1) Rules of Court, Annex to the Rules. Paragraph 2 of the same provision allows the Chamber to 'ask any person or institution of its choice to express an opinion or make a written report on any matter considered by it to be relevant to the case'.[189] The practicalities and technicalities of expert participation are detailed in Rules A5–A8 of the Annex to the Rules of Court.[190] Although the ECHR does not include any provisions regarding the format in which, e.g., forensic-science findings should be reported, procedures regarding the appointment of experts must conform with art. 6(1) ECHR: the Court must assess whether the right to a fair trial was respected.[191] In the ECtHR's case-law, it has been recognised that a lack of neutrality on the part of an expert may give rise to a breach of the principle of equality of arms under art. 6 ECHR.[192] An expert's procedural position and his or her role in the proceedings must be taken into account.[193] In cases where an expert reports on highly technical issues that are outside the judges' knowledge, the judges' assessment of the facts will be highly influenced by the expert.[194] In such a case, an expert report

---

Measures Affecting the Importation of Salmon–Recourse to Art. 21.5 by Canada–Report of the Panel (18 February 2000) WT/DS18/RW; Brown (n 98) 115 n 230.

186 WTO, *Japan: Measures Affecting Consumer Photographic Film and Paper–Report of the Panel* (23 April 1998), paras. 1.8–1.11.

187 Grando (n 65) 340. Grando also mentions the exception to this rule on p. 340, n 488: thus, in certain cases, a panel may be obliged to accept expert conclusions.

188 ibid.

189 Rule A1 ECtHR Rules of Court, Annex to the Rules (concerning investigations).

190 See also Caroline E Foster, 'Court-Appointed Experts' (February 2019) in Ruiz-Fabri H (ed), *Max Planck Encyclopaedia of Public International Law* (online edn).

191 Joëlle Vuille, Luca Lupària and Franco Taroni, 'Scientific Evidence and the Right to a Fair Trial under Article 6 ECHR' (2017) 16 Law, Probability and Risk 55, 55.

192 ECtHR, *Placì v. Italy*, App no 48754/11, Judgment of 21 January 2014, para. 74.

193 See, e.g., ECtHR, *Sara Lind Eggertsdóttir v. Iceland*, App no 31930/04, Judgment of 5 July 2007, para. 47.

194 For an in depth analysis of the role of experts in judicial procedures, see Déirdre Dwyer, *The Judicial Assessment of Expert Evidence* (Cambridge University Press 2008).

constitutes 'an essential piece of evidence and the parties must be able to comment effectively'.[195]

In sum, there seems to be a general consensus in the literature that the power to appoint experts is an inherent one and that international adjudicatory bodies have the right to consult with experts even if they are not expressly permitted to do so in their rules.[196]

Now that the basic powers of the international adjudicative bodies with regard to evidence have been established, the next step is to ask what basic concepts apply in this context. Before a court can analyse the evidence, it must first assess whether the evidence is admissible. Then, the court will decide who bears the burden of proof and whether the bearer of this burden meets the applicable standard of proof. Thus, in the following, these basic concepts will be discussed.

b. Basic Concepts

i. Admissibility of Evidence

International courts' approach to the admissibility of evidence is quite similar to that of civil law systems. Whilst common law systems are restrictive with regard to the admission of evidence but less strict in their rules regarding the weight and probative value they attribute to the different forms of evidence (e.g. oral and documentary), civil law systems have less exclusionary rules for the admission stage, but are stricter about the weight they attach to different forms of evidence. In civil law systems,

---

195 Guide on Article 6 European Convention on Human Rights, Right to a fair trial (civil limb), updated on 30 April 2019, p. 68/97 available at <https://www.echr.coe.int/Documents/Guide_Art_6_ENG.pdf>, with reference to ECtHR, *Mantovanelli v. France*, App no 21497/93, Judgment of 18 March 1997, para. 36; and ECtHR, *Storck v. Germany*, App no 61603/00, Judgment of 16 June 2005, para. 135.

196 See Christian J Tams, 'Art. 50' in Andreas Zimmermann and others (eds), *The Statute of the International Court of Justice: A Commentary* (2nd edn, Oxford University Press 2012) 1289. Agreeing with this position, see Gillian M White, *The Use of Experts by International Tribunals* (Syracuse University Press 1965) 73. However, Sandifer considered that 'it is to be doubted whether an international tribunal has the power to appoint a commission of inquiry in the absence of a specific grant of authority in the arbitral agreement', see Sandifer (n 1) 329.

documentary evidence is preferred over the oral testimony of witnesses, which is deemed 'untrustworthy'.[197]

Along the civil legal systems' lines, international courts are restrictive with regard to the types of evidence they deem admissible: 'evidence in written form is the rule and direct oral evidence the exception'.[198] But with regard to the admission of evidence, the rules are generally not restrictive.[199] The idea behind a more flexible approach to the admissibility of evidence is that an international tribunal should have free discretion in estimating the value of the parties' submissions, and to this end, it must be able to consider 'all the evidence and all the assertions made on either side'.[200] The principle of free assessment of evidence is also reflected in the ICJ's statement in the *Nicaragua* case where it held that 'within the limits of its Statute and Rules, it has freedom in estimating the value of the various elements of evidence'.[201] The ECtHR also adopts a flexible approach and has stated that it is 'entitled to rely on evidence of every kind [...] in so far as it deems them relevant [...]'.[202] As was held in *Nachova and Others v. Belgium*,

> '[i]n the proceedings before the Court, there are no procedural barriers to the admissibility of evidence or pre-determined formulae for its assessment. It adopts the conclusions that are, in its view, supported by the free evaluation of all evidence, including such inferences as may flow from the facts and the parties' submissions.'[203]

If the general principle is that international courts enjoy wide discretion in their assessment of the evidence, the next question is: when can a fact that is brought before a court be regarded as proven?

---

197 Brown (n 98) 89–91.

198 Sandifer (n 1) 3.

199 Brown (n 98) 91.

200 PCA, Reports of International Arbitral Awards, *Island of Palmas* 2 RIAA 829, 840–841 (US-Netherlands, PCA, 1928). See also ibid 91, n 50.

201 ICJ, *Military and Paramilitary Activities in and against Nicaragua (Nicaragua v. United States of America)* (Merits) [1986] ICJ Rep 1986, 14, para. 60.

202 ECtHR, *Ireland v. the United Kingdom*, App no 5310/71, Judgment of 13 December 1978, para. 209.

203 ECtHR, *Nachova and Others v. Bulgaria*, App no 43577/98, Judgment of 6 July 2005, para. 147.

ii. The Burden of Proof

In order to answer the question as to when a fact can be regarded as proven, one must first identify the party who bears the burden of proof, i.e. who carries 'the onus of proving an assertion made in judicial proceedings'.[204] International procedure is, again, closer to civil law proceedings. Unlike in common law systems, the concept of the burden of proof is not subdivided into the burden of persuasion and the burden of going forward, nor is there a procedural motion to challenge the sufficiency of evidence.[205] Furthermore, a clear claimant/respondent distinction is not always possible in the international sphere.[206]

As a general principle in international procedures, the party who asserts a fact bears the burden of providing the proof for the assertion (*actori incumbit probatio*).[207] If the asserting party fails to provide sufficient evidence and thus fails to persuade the court, the decision will be unfavourable to the party bearing the burden of proof.[208] A second general principle that applies in international adjudication is that the party who invokes an exception to a general rule bears the burden of proof.[209]

Although nuances may exist in the way and the degree to which the rule of *actori incumbit probatio* is applied, most adjudicative bodies have applied it consistently. This holds true for tribunals such as the ICSID and the WTO Panels and Appellate Body, the PCIJ, the ICJ, and also for human rights bodies.[210] The ICJ famously held in its *Nicaragua* case that

---

204 Brown (n 98) 92.

205 Grando (n 65) 80. For more on the differences between common law and civil law systems, see ibid, 74ss and Kazazi (n 103) 23ss.

206 James Crawford, *Brownlie's Principles of Public International Law* (9th edn, Oxford University Press 2019) 546.

207 Kazazi (n 103) 85.

208 Grando (n 65) 81.

209 Devaney (n 24) 144.

210 See Anna Riddell, 'Evidence, Fact-Finding, and Experts' (n 38) 858–856, n 51–54. For the ICSID, see e.g. ICSID, *Plama Consortium Ltd v. Bulgaria* (Decision on Jurisdiction of 8 February 2005) ICSID Case No. ARB/03/24, paras. 118–20, 167; UNCITRAL, *Canfor Corporation v. US* (Order of the Consolidation Tribunal of 7 September 2005), para. 93. For the WTO, see e.g. *European Communities: Tariff Preferences–Report of the Appellate Body* (20 April 2004) WT/DS246/AB/R., paras. 87–8. For the PCIJ, see, e.g. PCIJ, *Legal Status of Eastern Greenland*, PCIJ Series A/B No. 53, 1933, at 49, paras. 100–1; PCIJ, *SS Lotus*, PCIJ Series A No. 9, 1927, at 18; PCIJ, *Mavrommatis Jerusalem Concessions*, PCIJ Series A No. 5, 1925, at 6. For the human rights context, see, e.g. HRC, *Bordes and Temeharo* (1996)

ultimately, 'it is the litigant seeking to establish a fact who bears the burden of proving it; and in cases where evidence may not be forthcoming, a submission may in the judgment be rejected as unproved, but is not to be ruled out as inadmissible in limine on the basis of an anticipated lack of proof'.[211] This rule has even found its way into a legal code; the Rules of the Iran–US Claims Tribunal hold in art. 24(1) that '[e]ach party shall have the burden of proving the facts relied on to support his claim or his defence'.[212]

The burden of proof has a slightly different role in international human rights tribunals. Here, there usually is no onus of proof on any particular complainant.[213] The ECtHR, for instance, applies quite a flexible approach as regards questions of proof; it held in *Ireland v. the United Kingdom* that 'the Court examines all material before it, whether originating from the Commission, the Parties or other sources, and, if necessary, obtains material *proprio motu*'.[214] Whilst an applicant does bear an initial burden of proof in the sense that they have to make a *prima facie* case that is accepted by the court, once the court has accepted a case, the burden of proof falls onto the respondent government. It is then up to the state concerned to prove that it did not commit the alleged human rights infringement or that the actions in question were justified.[215]

Given that a clear applicant/respondent distinction is not always possible in international cases, where the parties present competing claims, the burden is on both of them to prove their claim accordingly.[216] According to Chittharanjan Felix Amerasinghe, the ability to determine who bears the onus 'is an inherent power which is essential for the proper function-

---

HRC Decision No. 645/1995, para. 5.5 and the IACtHR, *Velásquez Rodriguez* (Reparations and Costs) [1989] 28 ILM 291, at 315.

211 *ICJ, Military and Paramilitary Activities in and against Nicaragua (Nicaragua v. United States of America)* (Judgment on Jurisdiction and Admissibility) [1984] ICJ Rep 1984, 392, para. 101.

212 Art. 24(1) Iran-US Claims Tribunal Rules.

213 Bertrand G Ramcharan, *International Law and Fact-Finding in the Field of Human Rights* (Bertrand G Ramcharan ed, 2nd edn, Brill Nijhoff 2014) 61.

214 ECtHR, *Ireland v. the United Kingdom*, App no 5310/71, Judgment of 13 December 1978, paras. 160–161.

215 Riddell, 'Evidence, Fact-Finding, and Experts' (n 38) 859.

216 This was the case, e.g. in the ICJ's case *Temple of Preah Vihear (Cambodia v. Thailand)* (Merits) [1962] ICJ Rep 1962, 6, Dissenting Opinion of Judge Wellington Koo, at 15.

ing of international tribunals'.[217] Chester Brown notes that courts will be reluctant to decide who bears the burden in cases where the evidence is competing.[218] Still, courts will have to determine pragmatically – in some way or another – who bears the burden of proof.[219] This requires the courts to ascertain which party is relying on which facts and whether the evidence produced meets the required standard of proof.

iii. Standard of Proof

Closely linked to the burden of proof is the standard of proof. It determines whether the burden of proof was met.[220] It is 'the measure against which the value of each piece of evidence as well as the overall value of the evidence in a given case should be weighed and determined'.[221] In international law, there are no rigid rules on the standard of proof.[222] This flexible approach is reflected in a statement made by the IACtHR in the famous *Velásquez Rodríguez* case: 'international jurisprudence has recognised the power of the courts to weigh the evidence freely, although it has always avoided a rigid rule regarding the amount of proof necessary to support the judgment'.[223] In *US – Shirts and Blouses*, the Appellate Body of the WTO held that:

> 'in the context of the GATT 1994 and the WTO Agreement, precisely how much and precisely what kind of evidence will be required to establish such a presumption will necessarily vary from measure to measure, provision to provision, and case to case.'[224]

Thus, there are no clear rules and no uniform standard of proof that applies to all cases. The difficulty in pinning down the concept of the

---

217 Chittharanjan Felix Amerasinghe, *Evidence in International Litigation* (Martinus Nijhoff 2005) 75.

218 Brown (n 98) 97.

219 Riddell, 'Evidence, Fact-Finding, and Experts' (n 38) 859.

220 Kazazi (n 103) 323.

221 ibid.

222 Brown (n 98) 98.

223 IACtHR, *Velásquez Rodríguez* (Merits) [1988] 95 ILR 259, referring to the ICJ's *Corfu Channel* case and *Nicaragua*. See ibid 98, n 109.

224 WTO, *United States: Measures Affecting Imports of Woven Wool Shirts and Blouses from India–Report of the Appellate Body* (23 May 1997) WT/DS33/AB/R and Corr. 1, at 335.

standard of proof stems from the different approaches that are adopted in common versus civil law systems.[225] In common law traditions, usually two standards of proof are applied: in civil law cases, there is the standard of 'preponderance of evidence' (or 'balance of probabilities'), whereas in criminal law cases, the standard of proof 'beyond reasonable doubt' is required.[226] The approach is different in civil law countries. In this legal tradition, the key question is whether the judge is convinced or persuaded by the presented evidence or not; it is about the 'inner, deep-seated, personal conviction of the Judge'.[227] However, although the common law approach may appear to be more objective and clear, there still exists a degree of subjective weighing on the judge's part if the evidence from one party has to be weighed against the evidence presented by the other party.[228]

What, then, is an acceptable standard of proof before international tribunals? The issue is that the judgment as to what is acceptable or sufficient will vary from one person to another, it is 'discretionary and subject to human judgment'.[229] Chester Brown identifies five different standards that have been applied in international proceedings: the 'requirement to show prima facie evidence', the proof of facts 'beyond reasonable doubt', 'proof in a convincing manner', the 'preponderance of evidence' (or 'balance of probabilities'), and the judiciary's own evaluation of whether the presented evidence meets the standard of 'sufficient evidence'.[230] Whether these are all distinct standards that can be clearly distinguished from each other is debatable. Mojtabar Kazazi, for instance, only lists three benchmarks: prima facie evidence, proof beyond reasonable doubt, and preponderance of evidence.[231] These are also the three standards that Joost Pauwelyn distinguishes in a more recent analysis of questions of proof in international law.[232] Thus, in line with Kazazi and Pauwelyn, in the following, the focus will also be on these three standards. What can be said is that the highest

---

225 Riddell, 'Evidence, Fact-Finding, and Experts' (n 38) 860.
226 ibid.
227 Kevin M Clermont and Emily Sherwin, 'A Comparative View of Standards of Proof' (2002) 50 American Journal of Comparative Law 243, 243.
228 Riddell, 'Evidence, Fact-Finding, and Experts' (n 38) 860–861.
229 Kazazi (n 103) 325.
230 Brown (n 98) 100–101.
231 Kazazi (n 103) 344.
232 Joost Pauwelyn, 'Defenses and the Burden of Proof in International Law' in Lorand Bartels and Federica Paddeu (eds), *Exceptions and Defences in International Law* (Oxford University Press) 4.

standard is the requirement of proof 'beyond reasonable doubt' while the standard of 'prima facie evidence is the lowest.

(1) Prima Facie Evidence

The lowest degree of proof is, arguably, the standard of 'prima facie evidence'. It is questionable whether it even constitutes a standard of proof in its own right, or whether it is a concept that is just very much entangled with other concepts such as the questions pertaining to the admissibility of a case, the use of presumptions, the shifting of the burden of proof, and the overarching question of what constitutes sufficient evidence. For instance, Kazazi writes that '[i]n international procedure the question of whether prima facie evidence is acceptable as a standard of proof sometimes appears in the guise of the question whether the probative value of the evidence adduced in a given case is sufficient for it to be considered prima facie evidence.'[233] Looking at this sentence, one might ask what the difference is between the standard of 'prima facie evidence' and the question of what constitutes 'sufficient evidence'. According to Kazazi, the question is 'whether the evidence in question is sufficient for it to be accepted *prima facie*'.[234] However, would that not be a question concerning admissibility rather than a question pertaining to the relevant standard of proof? This also seems to follow from, e.g., statements made by the ILO and the European Commission of Human Rights: if no *prima facie* case was made, or if the applicants failed to provide *prima facie* evidence, an application may not be further pursued by the ILO or may be rejected by the Commission.[235] Grando, in her analysis of the WTO, mentions the idea of *prima facie* evidence as an 'initial standard of proof'.[236] However, what the distinction is – if there is any – between an 'initial standard of proof' and questions of admissibility seems questionable.

Yuval Shany points out that '[i]nstances of prima facie incompatibility with the governing legal text or lack of factual substantiation represent one set of situations in which international courts may sometimes invoke

---

233 Kazazi (n 103) 336.
234 ibid.
235 ibid 328.: Kazazi refers to ILO and Commission in n 13 and 14.
236 Grando (n 65) 118.

questions of merit in the jurisdictional phase of the proceedings'.[237] Thus, arguably, questions pertaining to 'prima facie' can be situated between the admissibility and the merits phase of a ruling. For instance, the ECtHR can decide that a case is inadmissible under art. 35 ECHR if it deems a claim 'manifestly ill-founded'. This is a conclusion on a matter of substance.[238] Thus, one might argue that 'prima facie' analyses may serve as a tool to discuss substantive rights before the merits stage.

In the literature, *prima facie* evidence is also mentioned in connection to presumptions and the shifting of the burden of proof.[239] Chester Brown discusses the *prima facie* case rule under the title of the burden of proof and the shifting thereof. He quotes the Appellate Body stating in *Japan – Apples* that:

> 'It is important to distinguish, on the one hand, the principle that the complainant must establish a *prima facie* case of inconsistency with a provision of a covered agreement from, on the other hand, the principle that the party that asserts a fact is responsible for providing proof thereof.'[240]

Thus, in his view, having to establish a fact on a *prima facie* basis is not the same thing as having the obligation to establish a fact upon which one wants to base a claim. However, what happens once a *prima facie* case has been made? Does the burden then automatically shift onto the other party to the dispute? The case-law of the WTO seems to indicate that such a shift does take place and that the respondent party has to rebut the claim that was established *prima facie*.[241] However, whether a 'real' shift of the burden of proof really does take place in these cases is highly debated.[242] Even if one argued that the burden does shift onto the other party, the question

---

237 Yuval Shany, *Questions of Jurisdiction and Admissibility before International Courts* (Cambridge University Press 2016) 91–92. With references to the Behrami and Bankovic cases.

238 ibid 93.

239 This is the case, for instance, in the context of the WTO: see, e.g. the analysis by John J Barceló III, 'Burden of Proof, Prima Facie Case and Presumption in WTO Dispute Settlement' (2009) Paper 119 Cornell Law Faculty Publications.

240 Brown (n 98) 97; (references omitted).

241 See, e.g. WTO, *United States: Measures Affecting Imports of Woven Wool Shirts and Blouses from India–Report of the Appellate Body* (23 May 1997) WT/DS33/AB/R and Corr. 1, at 14 and WTO, *European Communities: Measures Concerning Meat and Meat Products (Hormones)–Report of the Complaint by Canada* (13 February 1998) WT/DS48/R/CAN, para. 9.264.

242 Grando (n 65) 120ss.

becomes whether such a shift also relieves the asserting party from the burden of proof. In the context of the WTO, Joost Pauwelyn argues that such a relief does not take place. He states that despite the French translation of 'prima facie' in official WTO reports being *'un commencement de preuves'*, in his opinion, 'it is hard to imagine that a mere scintilla of evidence or mere *prima facie* evidence would be enough not just to shift the burden of production (that may well be the case) but also to formally discharge the real burden of proof or persuasion'.[243]

Much confusion thus persists around the concept of *prima facie* evidence. The Oxford Handbook[244] does not mention a 'prima facie' standard in its discussion of evidence and the standards of proof. And in Brown's analysis,[245] *prima facie* evidence is discussed before 'standard of proof'; in fact, he discusses prima facie under the title of 'burden of proof'. One could argue that *prima facie* is a threshold requirement; something that has to be discussed even before the burden or standard of proof can apply. Only if there is a *prima facie* case of a violation or infringement of a right does the burden of proof have to be determined more precisely. If no *prima facie* case is established, the case will be dismissed. What seems uncontroversial still is that the party asserting a fact must establish it. Thus, on a *prima facie* basis, the party who wants to bring a case must 'make the first move'.

(2) Preponderance of Evidence

The 'preponderance of evidence' standard is a mid-range standard of proof adopted from the common law tradition.[246] This standard has been interpreted as 'meaning that the party having the burden of persuasion on a proposition must prove that the proposition is "more probably true than false." It is also said that the "weight" or "convincing force" of the evidence in favour of the proposition must be "greater than" the weight of evidence tending to establish the assertion's falsehood.'[247] In other words, preponderance of evidence means that one party succeeded in presenting

---

243 Pauwelyn (n 232) 24.
244 Riddell, 'Evidence, Fact-Finding, and Experts' (n 38).
245 Brown (n 98).
246 Riddell, 'Evidence, Fact-Finding, and Experts' (n 38) 861.
247 Vern R Walker, 'Preponderance, Probability and Warranted Factfinding' (1996) 62 Brooklyn Law Review 1075, 1076, references ommitted.

evidence outweighing that presented by the other party.[248] The rationale behind such a mid-range standard is that in certain cases, an exact standard of proof could never be met; the level of absolute certainty will often be impossible to reach, and without a mid-range standard, the party bearing the burden of proof would always be disadvantaged as any doubt would lead to a decision in favour of the opponent.[249] More broadly speaking, it would seem unfair to require a high standard in cases where such a standard is impossible to attain.

But where is this threshold for an assertion to be more probably true than not? Some argue that this should be a statistical calculation, based on a cardinal scale between 0 and 1, in which the threshold of preponderance of evidence would be at 0.5.[250] But there is much discussion as to how high the required probability should be and whether this should vary from one case to another, for instance taking into account what is at stake. Thus, 'a higher degree of probability within the more probable than not range' would be required for claims of greater gravity.[251] Do these considerations and possible calculations really lead to more clarity or a clearer standard of proof? Grando argues that the standard of 'preponderance of evidence' provides less room for the judiciary to exercise discretion. However, a certain margin of discretion does remain. 'When applying this standard the adjudicator determines whether a certain proposition is more probable than not on the basis of her assessment of the evidence, that is to say, the adjudicator does not apply a mathematical formula which yields an exact probability of the occurrence of the fact at issue.'[252] Whatever formula one wants to apply, the standard of 'preponderance of evidence' seems closest to what Descartes required. Let me quote him again here:

> 'It is very certain that, when it is not in our power to determine what is true, we ought to act according to what is most probable; and even although we should not remark a greater probability in one opinion than in another, we ought notwithstanding to choose one or the other, and afterwards consider it, in so far as it relates to practice, as no longer dubious, but manifestly true and certain, since the reason

---

248 Kazazi (n 103) 349.
249 Grando (n 65) 138–139.
250 Walker (n 247) 1076.
251 Grando (n 65) 140.
252 ibid 138.

by which our choice has been determined is itself possessed of these qualities.'[253]

Thus, harking back to the above discussion of truth, this standard seems to most reflect that 'the truth' is hardly ever attainable and that, therefore, we need a standard that allows a situation of imperfect information to be resolved. It also allows a case to be resolved if a party fails to cooperate. For instance, in *Trepashkin v. Russia (No. 2)*, there was much disagreement between the parties 'as to many aspects of the physical conditions of the applicant's detention' and with regard to the manner and condition in which the transport of the applicant to and from prison had taken place.[254] The Court decided that it was not necessary to ascertain whether each statement and allegation was true, and primarily based its factual conclusions on the standard of preponderance of evidence because the specific context of the case, i.e. a complaint with regard to prison conditions, allowed to Court to deviate from its 'go-to' standard of 'beyond reasonable doubt'. It held that

> 'In such cases the Court may draw adverse inferences from the Government's failure to produce sufficient evidence or explanations, and decide on the basis of preponderance of evidence.'[255]

(3) Beyond Reasonable Doubt

This standard places a high burden onto the parties and has not often been invoked in international contexts.[256] It is applied by criminal courts in common law jurisdictions.[257] At least in some cases, international

---

253 René Descartes, *Discourse on the Method of Rightly Conducting the Reason, and Seeking Truth in the Sciences* (John Veitch trans., Cosimo Books 1st ed. 2008) (1924), 25.

254 ECtHR, *Trepashkin v. Russia (No. 2)*, App no 14248/05, Judgment of 16 December 2010, para. 107.

255 ibid. With further references to ECtHR, *Kokoshkina v. Russia*, App no 2052/08, Judgment of 28 May 2009, para. 59; and ECtHR, *Ahmet Özkan and Others v. Turkey*, App no 21689/93, Judgment of 6 April 2004, para. 426; see also ECtHR, *Gultyayeva v. Russia*, App no 67413/01, Judgment of 1 April 2010, para. 151.

256 Riddell, 'Evidence, Fact-Finding, and Experts' (n 38) 861.

257 Kazazi (n 103) 344. International criminal tribunals are not the focus of this study, but see, e.g., the Rome Statute of the ICC that requires proof beyond reasonable doubt in art. 66 of its Rules of Procedure and Evidence.

tribunals do adopt this high standard of proof.[258] This was implicitly confirmed by the ICJ in the *Corfu Channel* case, where a 'high degree of certainty' was required due to the gravity of the charge put forward by the UK against the Albanian Government.[259] Along the same lines, in *Velásquez Rodríguez* the IACtHR took account of 'the special serious-ness' of the case at hand and required the truth to be established 'in a convincing manner'.[260] The WTO Panel in *Canada – Dairy (Article 21.5 – New Zealand and US II)* rejected applying the 'beyond reasonable doubt' standard because such a standard would have required information the Canadian government would hardly have had access to; such an approach was considered to be unworkable and too costly.[261]

The ECtHR usually uses the standard of 'beyond reasonable doubt' as its standard of proof.[262] In the *Greek case*, the Commission held that

'A reasonable doubt means not a doubt based on a merely theoretical possibility or raised in order to avoid a disagreeable conclusion, but a doubt for which reasons can be drawn from the facts presented.'[263]

In *Ireland v. the United Kingdom*, the ECtHR followed the Commission in adopting the standard of 'beyond reasonable doubt',[264] and it has continued to use this standard as its 'go-to' standard.[265] It considers as

---

258 ibid 346.

259 ICJ, *Corfu Channel Case (United Kingdom v. Albania)* (Merits) [1949] ICJ Rep 1949, 4, pp. 16–17.

260 IACtHR, *Velásquez Rodríguez* (Merits) [1988] 95 ILR 259, para. 129. Here, Chester Brown disagrees and states that this standard should be considered a separate one, one that sits in between 'proof beyond reasonable doubt' and 'preponderance of evidence'. See Brown (n 98) 99.

261 WTO, *Canada: Measures Affecting the Importation of Milk and the Exportation of Dairy Products– Report of the Panel Second Recourse to Article 21.5 of the DSU by New Zealand and the United States* (26 July 2002) WT/DS103/RW2, WT/DS113/RW2, at V.323.

262 Schlüter (n 130) 26.

263 See *Yearbook of the European Convention on Human Rights* (Brill Nijhoff 1969) 196, para. 30.

264 ECtHR, *Ireland v. the United Kingdom*, App no 5310/71, Judgment of 13 Decem-ber 1977, para. 161.

265 ECtHR, *Denmark, Norway, Sweden and the Netherlands v. Greece*, ECHR, Com-mission Report, 1969, para. 30; ECtHR, *Ireland v. the United Kingdom*, App no 5310/71, Judgment of 18 January 1978, para. 61; ECtHR, *Aydin v. Turkey*, App no 57/1996/676/866, Judgment of 25 September 1997, para. 72; ECtHR, *Mentes and Others v. Turkey*, App no 58/1996/677/867, Judgment of 28 November 1997, para. 66; ECtHR, *Kaya v. Turkey*, App no 158/1996/777/978, Judgment of 19

'reasonable' not 'a doubt based merely on a theoretical possibility or raised in order to avoid a disagreeable conclusion, but a doubt for which reasons can be drawn from the facts presented'.[266] For instance, in *Tanrikulu v. Turkey*, the seriousness of the allegation that Turkish security forces had been involved in the killing of Zeki Tanrikulu had led the Commission to adopt the standard of proof beyond reasonable doubt. The ECtHR reiterated[267] that this evidentiary standard 'may follow from the co-existence of sufficiently strong, clear and concordant inferences or unrebutted presumptions', and that their 'evidential value must be assessed in the light of the circumstances of the individual case and the seriousness and nature of the charge to which they give rise against the respondent State'.[268] The Court agreed with the Commission that this threshold had not been reached in the case at hand.[269]

The Court can thus be seen as usually employing the 'beyond reasonable doubt' standard; however, as seen above in the case of *Trepashkin v. Russia (No. 2)*, due to the flexible approach the Court has opted for regarding questions of evidence and proof, it may adapt the standard of proof depending on the Convention right that is in question.[270]

These cases show that international tribunals may adopt the standard of proof beyond reasonable doubt in cases where the charges are serious and the nature of the allegation or the right at stake calls for a high degree of certainty. However, under certain circumstances, requiring such a high standard of proof would be illusionary and unattainable. This can be linked back to the discussion above on different concepts of truth. Applying the standard 'beyond reasonable doubt' in a rigid manner may suggest that there is a truth that can be ascertained.[271]

February 1998, para. 38; ECtHR, *Veznedaroğlu v. Turkey*, App no 32357/96, Judgment of 11 April 2000, para. 30; ECtHR, *Çakıcı v. Turkey*, App no 23657/94, Judgment of 8 July 1999, para. 92; ECtHR, *Kılıç v. Turkey*, App no 22492/93, Judgment of 28 March 2000, para. 64.

266 *Denmark, Norway, Sweden and the Netherlands v. Greece*, ECHR, Commission Report, 1969, para. 30.

267 Originally used in ECtHR, *Ireland v. the United Kingdom*, App no 5310/71, Judgment of 13 December 1977, para. 161.

268 ECtHR, *Tanrikulu v. Turkey*, App no 23763/94, Judgment of 8 July 1999, para. 97.

269 ibid, para. 99.

270 Schlüter (n 130) 25.

271 For an in-depth analysis of the ECtHR's rules and practice with regard to questions of proof, see Schlüter (n 130).

6. The ECtHR's Institutional Variations

a. Applications Before the ECtHR

As of 31 May 2020, 59'650 applications were pending before the ECtHR.[272] Many such applications are rejected before the merits stage because the criteria for admissibility are not satisfied.[273] Due to the massive workload of the Court, Protocol No. 14 to the Convention was brought into force on 1 July 2010, the purpose of which was to ensure the effectiveness of the ECtHR.[274] It empowered the Court to deal with applications within a reasonable time and provided a filtering mechanism.[275]

The ECtHR's supervision is, mainly, triggered by individual applications.[276] Art. 34 ECHR guarantees the right of individual application. It states that '[t]he Court may receive applications from any person, non-governmental organisation or group of individuals claiming to be the victim of a violation by one of the High Contracting Parties of the rights set forth in the Convention or the Protocols thereto.'[277] Thus, this provision guarantees the right to legal action at the international level. It is also 'one of the fundamental guarantees of the effectiveness of the Convention system of human rights protection'.[278] In its well-established case-law, the Court refers to the Convention as 'a living instrument', meaning that interpretations must take into account present-day conditions.[279] The Court itself has clarified that this applies not only to the substantive provisions of the Convention, but also to the procedural ones.[280] For instance, Rule

---

272 See <https://www.echr.coe.int/Documents/Stats_pending_month_2020_BIL.PDF>, last accessed on 12 July 2021.

273 For an in-depth analysis of the statistics of inadmissibility or strike out decisions in 2019, see p. 4 of ECHR – Analysis of Statistics 2019, available at <https://www.echr.coe.int/Documents/Stats_analysis_2019_ENG.pdf>, last accessed on 12 July 2021.

274 Protocol No. 14 to the ECHR.

275 Anne Peters and Tilmann Altwicker, 'Die Verfahren Beim EGMR' [2018] MPIL Research Paper Series n 1.

276 ECtHR, 'Practical Guide on Admissibility Criteria' (2019) 7.

277 Art. 34 ECHR.

278 ECtHR, *Mamatkulov and Askarov v. Turkey*, App nos 46827/99 and 46951/99, Judgment of 4 February 2005, para. 100.

279 See, e.g. ECtHR, *Tyrer v. the United Kingdom*, App no 5856/72, Judgment of 25 April 1978, para. 31.

280 ECtHR, *Loizidou v. Turkey*, App no 15218/89, Preliminary Objections of 23 March 1995, para. 71.

47(1)(e) of the Rules of Court requires 'a concise and legible statements of the facts'.[281]

The proceedings before the ECtHR are adversarial. The parties to a case must substantiate their claims and provide the factual evidence and make the legal arguments to show that the Convention rights were violated (applicant's perspective) or not violated (Government's perspective). The requirements with regard to the contents of an individual application can be found in Rule 47 of the Rules of Court.[282] The application must contain, among other things, a concise description of the facts of the case, allowing the Court to assess the nature and extent of the complaint without having to consult additional documents.[283] Complaints that do not fulfil the requirements are sorted out 'administratively' by a Judge Rapporteur or, following Rule 49(1) of the Rules of Court, are rejected by a single-judge formation.[284]

The Court can request further documents at any time in the proceedings.[285] As mentioned above, non-cooperation may have detrimental effects on the parties who fail to comply with their duty to cooperate.[286] If parties fail to provide sufficient evidence to substantiate their claims, and do not comply with the request to provide further information, they run the risk of the Court itself not conducting further investigations of its own, which may lead to the complaint being deemed inadmissible or unfounded due to a lack of factual evidence. Moreover, the Court often draws negative conclusions from the failure to comply with the duties to cooperate under art. 38 ECHR with regard to the credibility of the submission of the respective party.[287] In general, the Court largely follows the submissions of the parties and merely can be seen as switching back-and-forth between the factual submissions of the parties in its own assessment of the facts. The ECtHR also emphasises that, as a rule, it does not want to deviate from the findings of fact of the national courts and authorities, given that they are closer to the events and can be considered in principle to be in a better position to make the relevant findings of fact.[288] This idea of the national

---

281 Rule 47(1)(e) of the Rules of Court.
282 Rule 47 Rules of Court.
283 Schlüter (n 130) 17.
284 Rule 49(1) of the Rules of Court.
285 Rule 54(2)(C) of the Rules of Court.
286 See above, I.5.a.i.
287 Schlüter (n 130) 18.
288 ibid.

authorities being 'better placed' will be discussed in more detail below in the context of the principle of subsidiarity.

b. Final Assessment of the Facts

A decision has *res iudicata* force when it is final and the parties to a case are bound by the judgment.[289] This is a shared feature of common and civil law systems.[290] The rationale of this doctrine is two-fold: on the one hand, there must be an end to litigation, and on the other hand, the rule of *ne bis in idem* states that one should not be proceeded against twice for the same cause of action.[291]

The doctrine of *res iudicata* is widely accepted and is applied by the ECtHR. This rule is reflected in art. 46(1) ECHR, according to which States Parties to the ECHR 'undertake to abide by the final judgment of the Court in any case to which they are parties'. In the Grand Chamber case *Scozzari and Giunta v. Italy*, the Court clarified the implications of art. 46 in stating that

> 'a judgment in which the Court finds a breach imposes on the re-
> spondent State a legal obligation not just to pay those concerned the
> sums awarded by way of just satisfaction, but also to choose, subject
> to supervision by the Committee of Ministers, the general and/or, if
> appropriate, individual measures to be adopted in their domestic legal
> order to put an end to the violation found by the Court and to redress
> so far as possible the effects [...].'[292]

Thus, the *res iudicata* force of a judgment has implications on the domestic level. Depending on how the national legal system in question is set up, a

---

289 Brown (n 98) 153. Brown discusses post-adjudication roles of international courts and tribunals, for the rare cases where there is a possibility of recourse, see pp. 153ss. This is also reflected in the Statute of the International Court of Justice, arts. 59–60, International Court of Justice Rules of Court, art. 94. In the ECHR, arts. 44 and 46 are relevant.

290 Niccolò Ridi, 'Precarious Finality? Reflections on Res Judicata and the Question of the Delimitation of the Continental Shelf Case' (2018) 31 Leiden Journal of International Law 383, 384.

291 William S Dodge, 'Res Judicata' (January 2006) in Peters A and Wolfrum R (eds), *Max Planck Encyclopedia of Public International Law* (online edn) para 2.

292 ECtHR, *Scozzari and Giunta v. Italy*, App nos 39221/98 and 41963/98, Judgment of 13 July 2000, para. 249.

reaction upon a decision by the ECtHR could come from the legislative, executive, or judicial branch.[293] The European Convention on Human Rights does not include any obligation or requirement for Member States to follow a specific action or legal process in order to be in compliance with an ECtHR decision.[294] It is established case-law that the Court does not have jurisdiction to order a government to reopen proceedings.[295] On the national level, most State Parties allow for a reopening of proceedings in criminal cases, and some others also allow for a reopening in civil cases.[296]

The effect of *res iudicata* would seem to imply that the ECtHR's finding of a violation only affects the State Parties to the case concerned. However, it has been argued that judgments of the Court may also have *erga omnes* effect due to the principle of *res interpretata*.[297] The aim of *res interpretata* is to go beyond art. 46(1) ECHR, under which ECtHR judgments are only binding *inter partes*.[298] Thus, although there is no legal obligation in the ECHR for Member States to adhere to a judgment made by the ECtHR, once the Court in Strasbourg has decided an issue, for reasons of 'legal certainty, foreseeability and equality before the law', the ECtHR has itself stated that it 'should not depart, without good reason, from precedents laid down in previous cases'.[299] Thus, it is expected that the Court's interpretation will be applied in the same manner if a similar claim is brought to the Court against a different state.[300]

---

293 Marten Breuer, '"Principled Resistance" to ECtHR Judgments: An Appraisal' in Marten Breuer (ed), *Principled Resistance to ECtHR Judgments - A New Paradigm?* (Springer 2019) 327.

294 ibid.

295 See, e.g., ECtHR, *Saïdi v. France*, App no 14647/89, Judgment of 20 September 1993, para. 47; ECtHR, *Pelladoh v. The Netherlands*, App no 16737/90, Judgment of 22 September 1994, para. 44; ECtHR, *Kudeshkina v. Russia (No. 2)*, App no 28727/11, Judgment of 17 February 2015, para. 57.

296 For an overview of different States Parties approaches with regard to the reopening of cases, see Breuer (n 293) 327–328.

297 Oddný Mjöll Arnardóttir, 'Res Interpretata, Erga Omnes Effect and the Role of the Margin of Appreciation in Giving Domestic Effect to the Judgments of the European Court of Human Rights' (2017) 28 European Journal of International Law 819.

298 Breuer (n 293) 334.

299 See ECtHR, *Christine Goodwin v. United Kingdom*, App no 28957/95, Judgment of 11 July 2002, para. 74.

300 Arnardóttir (n 297) 823–824.

c. Rules on Fact-Assessment and Evidence Before the ECtHR

The Court has elaborated in its case-law that art. 35(2)(b) ECHR, which refers to the exhaustion of domestic remedies, ties the Court to base its decision on the factual complaint as presented by the applicant.[301] In other words, while the Court may 'view the facts in a different manner',[302] 'it is nevertheless limited by the facts presented by the applicants in the light of national law'.[303] The enforcement of Convention rights largely takes place before the national administrative authorities and courts rather than before the ECtHR, and the determination of the facts in the national proceedings follows the evidentiary rules of the national legal system.[304] Although it is the responsibility of the parties to a case to substantiate their claims, it is up to the Court to assess and establish the facts. This can be derived from art. 38 ECHR, which states that '[t]he Court shall examine the case together with the representatives of the parties and, if need be, undertake an investigation, for the effective conduct of which the High Contracting Parties concerned shall furnish all necessary facilities'.[305] Thus, this provision allocates the task of fact-finding to the ECtHR and provides it with the necessary competences. However, it also clarifies that investigations should only be carried out when necessary, e.g. because the facts were insufficiently established in the preceding national procedures. Other than in art. 38 ECHR, the Convention does not provide any further information regarding the fact-finding proceedings conducted by the Court.[306] Some further rules can be found in the Rules of Court.[307]

The Court's competence to provide itself with its own rules of procedure regarding fact-assessment and evidence is derived from art. 25(d) ECHR. Since there are hardly any rules on evidence and fact-finding to be

---

301 ECtHR, *Radomilja and Others v. Croatia*, App nos 37685/10 and 22768/12, Judgment of 20 March 2018, para. 123.

302 See ECtHR, *Foti and Others v. Italy*, App nos 7604/76; 7719/76; 7781/77; 7913/77, Judgment of 10 December 1982, para. 44.

303 ECtHR, *Radomilja and Others v. Croatia*, App nos 37685/10 and 22768/12, Judgment of 20 March 2018, para. 121.

304 Arthur Brunner, 'Subsidiaritätsgrundsatz und Tatsachenfeststellung unter der Europäischen Menschenrechtskonvention', *Max-Planck-Institut für ausländisches öffentliches Recht und Völkerrecht, Beiträge zum ausländischen öffentlichen Recht und Völkerrecht 283* (Springer 2019) 28.

305 ibid, 29.

306 ibid.

307 See <https://www.echr.coe.int/documents/rules_court_eng.pdf>, last accessed on 12 July 2021.

found in the Convention itself, the Court enjoys a great deal of freedom in designing the laws of evidence within its own proceedings.[308]

Art. 25(d) ECHR allows the Court to adopt the Rules of Court. In those rules, more information on the establishment of facts can be found. Because the ECHR itself contains no other rules on facts and evidence, it is to a great extent up to the discretion of the ECtHR to formulate these rules, which concern the procedure before the Court itself.[309] But even in the Rules of Court, there are not that many provisions. The ones that are relevant with regard to facts and evidence are art. 38 (procedural rules on the written pleadings); arts. 44A–44E (rights and duties of the parties to cooperate and participate), arts. 46–47 (contents of inter-State and individual applications), and arts. 63–70 (rules on the hearings).[310]

Neither the Convention nor the Rules of Court provide any clear rules regarding the burden or standard of proof or the exact process and procedure of how the Court conducts its fact-assessment. Many of these questions have been addressed, and procedures and standards have been developed in the Court's case-law.[311] An important role is played by the principle of subsidiarity that will be discussed below.

d. Subsidiarity and Fact-Assessment

The embeddedness of an international court within a framework matters with regard to how it engages in fact-finding and fact-assessment.[312] For the ECtHR, this means that its institutional embeddedness within the wider institutional framework of its Member States has an influence on the Court's decision-making process and on how proactive it can, or wants to, be. The ECtHR only decides a case subsidiary to the Member State in question.[313] The principle of subsidiarity is reflected in art. 13 ECHR

---

308 See Jens Meyer-Ladewig, 'Art. 25', *Europäische Menschenrechtskonvention Hand-kommentar* (4th edn, Nomos 2017) n 6.

309 See ibid.

310 Brunner (n 304) 30.

311 ibid.

312 José E Alvarez, 'Are International Judges Afraid of Science?: A Comment on Mbengue' (2011) 34 Loyola of Los Angeles International and Comparative Law Review 81, 92.

313 ECtHR, *Kudła v. Poland*, App no 30210/96, Judgment of 26 October 2000, para. 152.

and art. 35(1) ECHR.[314] Art. 13 ECHR provides everyone with the right to an effective remedy before a national authority in case of a violation of a Convention right.[315] It ensures that Convention rights are already effectively implemented at the national level.[316]

Conceptions of subsidiarity are often used by academics, judges, and politicians 'as a normative framework for assessing how to allocate and exercise authority within a multilevel political and legal order'.[317] This principle espouses a rebuttable presumption that authority is situated at the local level.[318] The presumption is that decision-making should take place at the local level and that centralisation of powers – in this case the allocation of decision-making powers to the ECtHR – should only be allowed for particular reasons.[319] In the context of human rights, the principle of subsidiarity leaves States with the primary responsibility to ensure that human rights standards are adhered to, and only provides international human rights institutions with a subsidiary, supervisory function.[320] Thus far, the principle of subsidiarity has been a jurisprudential one. For instance, in *S.A.S. v. France*, the Court held:

'It is also important to emphasise the fundamentally subsidiary role of the Convention mechanism. The national authorities have direct democratic legitimation and are, as the Court has held on many occasions, in principle better placed than an international court to evaluate local needs and conditions. In matters of general policy, on which opinions within a democratic society may reasonably differ widely, the role of the domestic policy-maker should be given special weight.'[321]

---

314 Brunner (n 304) 87.

315 Art. 13 ECHR.

316 Anne Peters and Tilmann Altwicker, *Europäische Menschenrechtskonvention* (2nd edn, Beck 2012) 173.

317 Andreas Føllesdal, 'Subsidiarity and International Human-Rights Courts: Respecting Self-Governance and Protecting Human Rights - Or Neither?' (2016) 79 Law and Contemporary Problems 147, 147.

318 ibid 148.

319 Markus Jachtenfuchs and Nico Krisch, 'Subsidiarity in Global Governance' (2016) 79 Law and Contemporary Problems 1, 1.

320 Samantha Besson, 'Subsidiarity in International Human Rights Law-What Is Subsidiary About Human Rights?' (2016) 61 American Journal of Jurisprudence 69, 69.

321 ECtHR, *S.A.S. v. France*, App no 43835/11, Judgment of 1 July 2014, para. 129. See also famously: ECtHR, *Case 'Relating to Certain Aspects of the Laws on the Use of Languages in Education in Belgium' v. Belgium* (Belgian Linguistic case), App nos 1474/62, 1677/62, 1691/62, 1769/63, 1994/63, 2126/64, Judgment of 9

However, Protocol No. 15 to the ECHR was adopted on 16 May 2013 by the Committee of Ministers and as soon it is in force, the principle will also be added at the end of the Preamble to the Convention.[322]

Part I has shown that the international sphere is influenced by different legal traditions.[323] Different constitutional values and historical developments at national levels have led to divergences in the fundamental rights standards at the European level. Thus, the European Court of Human Rights is faced with the challenge of balancing 'the need for uniform and effective human rights protection with respect for diversity'.[324] The margin of appreciation doctrine, which is one aspect of the principle of subsidiarity,[325] is seen by some as the main tool for striking this balance; however, it has been criticised by others as having become an 'empty rhetorical device'.[326] From the perspective of fact-assessment, the principle of subsidiarity has an influence on the ECtHR's practice.

As was shown above, unlike in national legal systems, there are not many rules of evidence, fact-finding, and fact-assessment in the ECHR or in the Rules of Court. Unlike in national legal systems, where courts are usually tied to the factual analyses by the previous national authority, there is no rule that ties the Court to the factual analyses of another institution.[327] It can, thus, be seen as having free cognition.[328] However, due to the principle of subsidiarity, the Court is reluctant to make use of this broad factual cognition.[329] In this regard, the margin of appreciation

---

February 1967 and ECtHR, *Handyside v. the United Kingdom*, App no 5493/72, Judgment of 7 December 1976.

322 'Affirming that the High Contracting Parties, in accordance with the principle of subsidiarity, have the primary responsibility to secure the rights and freedoms defined in this Convention and the Protocols thereto, and that in doing so they enjoy a margin of appreciation, subject to the supervisory jurisdiction of the European Court of Human Rights established by this Convention.' (art. 1 Protocol No. 15 ECHR), <https://www.echr.coe.int/Documents/Protocol_15_E NG.pdf>, last accessed on 12 July 2021.

323 See above, I.2.b.

324 Janneke Gerards, 'Margin of Appreciation and Incrementalism in the Case Law of the European Court of Human Rights' (2018) 18 Human Rights Law Review 495, 495.

325 Besson (n 320) 69.

326 Gerards (n 324) 495.

327 Brunner (n 304) 74.

328 However, see ECtHR, *Annenkov and Others v. Russia*, App no 31475/10, Judgment of 25 July 2017, para. 80.

329 Brunner (n 304) 74.

doctrine can be considered 'a self-imposed restraint'.[330] For instance, in *Klaas v. Germany* the Court refrained from conducting its own fact-assessment due to the principle of subsidiarity;[331] it has done so in more recent cases as well.[332] The Court held in *Klaas v. Germany*:

> 'It is further recalled that it is not normally within the province of the European Court to substitute its own assessment of the facts for that of the domestic courts and, as a general rule, it is for these courts to assess the evidence before them [...].'[333]

In this case, the applicant and the Government put forward different accounts as to the facts of the case. The question pertained to whether or not the treatment of the first applicant (mother) by the police officers during her arrest amounted to inhuman and degrading treatment under art. 3 ECHR. The first applicant argued that the police officers had assaulted her. The police officers denied this.[334] The first applicant's neighbour and the second applicant (daughter) gave evidence in the proceedings before the national authorities, in favour of the first applicant.[335] The police officers, however, argued that the mother had been extremely violent and that it had thus been necessary for them to use force in order to ensure that the mother would not escape.[336] After hearing the diverging accounts given by the two witnesses, by the applicant, and by the police officers, the Detmold Regional Court concluded that the police officers had provided convincing arguments, and dismissed the first applicant's complaint.[337] The Hamm Court of Appeal dismissed the first applicant's appeal and

---

330 Sabino Cassese, 'Ruling Indirectly Judicial Subsidiarity in the ECtHR' Paper for the Seminar on "Subsidiarity: a double sided coin?" held to coincide with the ceremony marking the official opening of the judicial year of the European Court of Human Rights, 30 January 2015 1, 6. available at <https://www.echr.c oe.int/Documents/Speech_20150130_Seminar_Cassese_ENG.pdf>, last accessed on 12 July 2021.

331 ECtHR, *Klaas v. Germany*, App no 15473/89, Judgment of 22 September 1993, para. 29. See also ECtHR, *Vidal v. Belgium*, App no 12351/86, Judgment of 22 April 1992, para. 33; and ECtHR, *Edwards v. the United Kingdom*, App no 13071/87, Judgment of 16 December 1992, para. 34.

332 ECtHR, *R.D. v. France*, App no 34648/14, Judgment of 16 June 2016, para. 37.

333 ECtHR, *Klaas v. Germany*, App no 15473/89, Judgment of 22 September 1993, para. 29.

334 ibid, paras. 6–7.

335 ibid, para. 16.

336 ibid, paras. 9ss.

337 ibid, para. 17.

upheld the Detmold Regional Court's decision that Mrs. Klaas had not been treated with excessive force by the police officers.[338] Subsequently, a panel of three judges of the Federal Constitutional Court upheld the Court of Appeal's assessment, as this assessment was not considered to appear arbitrary in any manner that would constitute a violation of constitutional law.[339] Thus, the ECtHR was confronted with two different accounts of the facts. With six votes to three, the Court held that there had been no violation of art. 3 ECHR with respect to the first applicant.[340] Given that the injuries that the applicant had suffered could have originated from the version of events described by the applicant as well as from the version of events that the police officers had provided, and given that the national authorities had heard the witness statements and assessed the evidence, the majority did not see it fit to depart from the findings of fact reached by the national courts.[341] In the majority's opinion, there was no material 'which could call into question the findings of the national courts and add weight to the applicant's allegations'.[342] There were three dissenting opinions in this case arguing that the burden of proof to provide more evidence for her allegations of having been arrested and treated with undue force should not have been pushed onto the applicant, and that rather the Government should have carried the onus to provide sufficient evidence to show that the force had been proportionate. Given that this burden of proof had not been met by the Government, the Court should have ruled in favour of the applicant.[343]

This case exemplifies how important the role of fact-assessment is for the substantive outcome of the proceedings before the ECtHR.[344] The majority gave more weight to the ECtHR's institutional variation, i.e. the principle of subsidiarity, than the dissenters. And as the disagreement between the majority and the dissenters with regard to the allocation of the burden of proof showed, this allocation is of pivotal importance for the outcome of a case.

This sensitivity to the principle of subsidiarity with regard to the Court's role as a fact-assessor was further developed and clarified in *Tanli v. Turkey*:

---

338 ibid, para. 18.
339 ibid, para. 19.
340 ibid, para. 36.
341 ibid, para. 30.
342 ibid.
343 ibid, Dissenting Opinions of Judges Pettiti, Walsh and Spielmann.
344 Brunner (n 304) 76.

'The Court is sensitive to the subsidiary nature of its role and must be cautious in taking on the role of a first instance tribunal of fact, where this is not rendered unavoidable by the circumstances of a particular case [...]. Where domestic proceedings have taken place, it is not the Court's task to substitute its own assessment of the facts for that of the domestic courts and, as a general rule, it is for those courts to assess the evidence before them [...]. Though the Court is not bound by the findings of domestic courts, in normal circumstances it requires cogent elements to lead it to depart from the findings of fact reached by those courts [...].'[345]

The Court remains reluctant to depart from the fact-assessment conducted by the national authorities. It takes into account 'the quality of the domestic proceedings and any possible flaws in the decision-making process', but 'sound evidence' must be provided rather than 'mere hypothetical speculation' to call the domestic courts' assessment into question.[346] This reluctance has been reiterated by the Court in *Sadkov v. Ukraine* where it held that it would only depart from the fact-assessment reached by the national authorities if this were 'unavoidable by the circumstances of a particular case'.[347]

Of course, this leaves room for interpretation and speculation, as it is not clear where the threshold is for national proceedings to be deemed so flawed as to trigger the Court to re-evaluate the domestic fact-assessment; and what exactly 'unavoidable by the circumstances' is supposed to mean.

There are several reasons for the Court's reluctance to depart from the national fact-assessments. The Court considers the national authorities 'better placed' to assess the evidence and to establish the facts due to multiple factors, including the time lapse between the events in question and the Court being presented with the case, the geographical distance, and the Court's immense workload.[348] Reasons such as these mean that the Court is unable to fully determine all the facts of a given case, let alone fully grasp the general situation in the respondent Member State.[349] The

---

345 ECtHR, *Tanli v. Turkey*, App no 26129/95, Judgment of 10 April 2001, para. 110.

346 ECtHR, *Khlaifia and Othes v. Italy*, App no 16483/12, Judgment of 15 December 2016, para. 208.

347 ECtHR, *Sadkov v. Ukraine*, App no 21987/05, Judgment of 6 July 2017, para. 90.

348 Brunner (n 304) 77–81.

349 Jonas Christoffersen, *Fair Balance: Proportionality, Subsidiarity and Primarity in the European Convention on Human Rights* (Nijhoff 2009) 276. For a critical

Court's fact-assessment abilities are, thus, limited due to it being unable to obtain all facts and re-evaluate them.

The 'better placed' argument was first used in the *Handyside* case where the Court held:

> 'By reason of their direct and continuous contact with the vital forces of their countries, State authorities are in principle in a better position than the international judge to give an opinion on the exact content of [the requirements of morals] as well as on the 'necessity' of a 'restriction' or 'penalty' intended to meet them.'[350]

However, as Judge Pinto de Albuquerque, joined by Judge Sajó, wrote in their dissenting opinion in the case of *Correia de Matos v. Portugal*, the 'better placed' rule 'should not be mistaken for a carte blanche to rubber-stamp any policy adopted or decision taken by national authorities'; the Court must – and usually does – provide an explanation for why it considers the domestic authorities better placed to make a certain assessment.[351] Thus, the Court's own assessment of the facts – or its decision not to make its own assessment of the facts – can and must still be scrutinised. Since there are no clear rules as to how factual arguments should be evaluated, I propose in Part II that one way of assessing the Court's factual analyses is to employ principles of scientific method to detect potential flaws in the factual conclusions.

7. Conclusion

What follows from the above is that although rules of fact-finding and evidence exist in international adjudication, there is no one coherent framework. Unlike national jurisdictions, the international realm approaches questions of evidence and proof in a flexible manner. This is necessary

---

analysis, see Stefan Schürer, 'Der Europäische Gerichtshof für Menschenrechte als Tatsacheninstanz – Zur Bedeutung divergierender Sachverhaltsfeststellungen durch den EGMR am Beispiel einiger Schweizer Fälle' (2014) Europäische Grundrechte Zeitschrift 512, 513ss.

350 ECtHR, *Handyside v. the United Kingdom*, App no 5493/72, Judgment of 7 December 1976, para. 48. See also, e.g. ECtHR *Chapman v. the United Kingdom*, App no 27238/95, Judgment of 18 January 2001, para. 91.

351 ECtHR, *Correia de Matos v. Portugal*, App no 54602/12, Judgment of 4 May 2018, Dissenting Opinion of Judge Pinto de Albuquerque, joined by Judge Sajó, para. 7.

due to the fact that the cases tend to be highly complex and thus an ascertainment of 'the truth' cannot be the sole aim. In the international realm, an added layer of complexity exists due to the fragmentation of the international legal sphere, the influences from different national legal traditions, and the fact that multiple actors and potential interveners must be taken into account.

Pinning down the concepts of the burden of proof and the standards of evidence turned out to be quite a difficult task. As Kazazi notes, it is not possible to specify strict standards because it is equally impossible to 'specify the different degrees of belief which may strike human minds'.[352] International tribunals and courts have rather, 'whenever necessary', 'combined them or adopted other standards justifiable under the circumstances of a given case'.[353] The rules and standards in the international sphere are less formal than those that exist in municipal systems. It is much up to the discretion of the tribunals to assess the facts. Because international courts enjoy wide discretion with regard to their fact-assessment, it is important to pay attention to how they contend with facts and to critically analyse the fact-assessment procedures.

In the context of the ECtHR, neither the Convention nor the Rules of Court provide many clear rules as to how the Court ought to contend with facts. The institutional embeddedness of the Court, and its subsidiary position to the Member States must be taken into account when one wants to analyse the manner in which the Court conducts its fact-assessment. For instance, in certain circumstances, the national authorities may be 'better placed' to assess the facts of a given case. However, when and how the ECtHR decides to conduct its own fact-assessment must still be scrutinised.

In what follows, it will be suggested that scientific principles can be used as a methodological framework to analyse the quality of the ECtHR's fact-assessment procedures.

---

352 Kazazi (n 103) 350.
353 ibid 351.

II. Facts, Law and Interdisciplinarity

This section provides the theoretical ground that will allow for principles of scientific method to be used to analyse the fact-assessment conducted by the European Court of Human Rights in its case-law. In a first step, it will be shown why an interdisciplinary approach is permissible in the (international) legal realm. For this purpose, two contrary positions will be discussed. Pragmatism will be presented as a school of thought with an optimistic stand towards interdisciplinarity. As a counter position, positivism will be presented, which is sceptical about interdisciplinary approaches in law. A middle-ground pragmatist position will be defended here that allows for the application of principles of scientific method as modes for critiquing the fact-assessment conducted by the ECtHR in its case-law. This section will also demonstrate that the line between facts and law, or factual and legal analysis, is sometimes blurred.

1. Interdisciplinarity and International Legal Theory

Any new approach or methodology that is applied to the legal domain will present a challenge to prevailing formalist traditions.[354] Although 'traditional' legal scholarship does embrace a variety of approaches such as legal philosophy and legal history, the predominant methodology is doctrinal.[355] This traditional, or 'black-letter' approach to law 'aims to understand the law from no more than a thorough examination of a finite and relatively fixed universe of authoritative texts', such as case-law and legal statutes, and it gains its importance from within the legal tradition itself.[356] There is no room for interdisciplinarity in such traditional approaches to law.

Oliver Wendell Holmes once famously stated that 'for the rational study of law the black-letter man may be the man of the present, but the man

---

354 Andrea Bianchi, *International Law Theories* (Oxford University Press 2016) 9.
355 Douglas W Vick, 'Interdisciplinarity and the Discipline of Law' (2004) 31 Journal of Law and Society 163, 177.
356 ibid 178.

of the future is the man of statistics and the master of economics'.[357] The twentieth century saw this expectation come true: the realist movement grew as a reaction to the dominant formalist conception of law and drew on insights from psychology, economics, and other branches of the social sciences to address normative questions in law.[358] Although realists did not form a cohesive group, they collectively condemned the rigidity and inadaptability of the formalist interpretation of legal rules and criticised classical analysis for its failure to account for the indeterminacy of legal rules and legal reasoning being manipulable.[359] The realist movement paid attention to the role of values in legal decision-making, an aspect absent from classical legal theory. Traditional approaches viewed law as being autonomous from other disciplines; such autonomy was considered necessary for the law to be neutral and objective. This prerequisite of neutrality implies denying any relevance of substantive values to law-processes such as legal adjudication.[360]

Through American legal realism, pragmatism, and various 'International Law & [...] Movements',[361] interdisciplinary approaches have entered legal education, while political upheavals have eroded the (dominant) position of legal positivism, resulting in legal thinking becoming more and more policy-oriented.[362] The idea of progress entered the international legal discourse.[363] However, intellectual tensions persist between 'black-letter' academic lawyers and interdisciplinary scholars. Traditional approaches are criticised as being inflexible and 'intellectually rigid', whereas interdisciplinary approaches are deemed amateurish by their critics because their practitioners are seen as 'dabbling with theories and methods' they do not fully master.[364] This thesis aims at applying principles of scientific method to the fact-analysis in legal adjudication. Thus, this thesis is interdisciplinary in that it aims at incorporating principles from another

---

357 Oliver Wendell Holmes, 'The Path of the Law' (1897) 10 Harvard Law Review 469.

358 Nancy Levit, 'Listening To Tribal Legends: An Essay on Law and the Scientific Method' (1989) 58 Fordham Law Review 263, 277.

359 ibid.

360 Bianchi (n 354) 27.

361 ibid 11.

362 Hans W Baade, 'Social Science Evidence and the Federal Constitutional Court of West Germany' (1961) 23 The Journal of Politics 421, 422.

363 Tilmann Altwicker and Oliver Diggelmann, 'How is Progress Constructed in International Legal Scholarship?' (2014) 25 European Journal of International Law 425.

364 Vick (n 355) 164.

discipline for the purpose of gaining insights in the legal domain. The integration of these principles can be seen as a partial integration of discrete elements from another discipline.[365]

Whether or not interdisciplinary approaches should or even can be used to gain insights in the legal realm can be discussed by presenting two contrary positions: pragmatism, which argues in favour of interdisciplinarity, and positivism, which points to the limitations of such approaches.[366] Thus, in what follows, these two extremes will be presented and a decision will be made as to which school of thought is used here to embed the idea of using insights from the principles of scientific method to scrutinise the fact-analysis in legal decision-making.

2. Pragmatist Optimism towards Interdisciplinarity

a. Pragmatism

Pragmatism has been criticised for being an empty theory that has nothing of substance to contribute to legal theory.[367] The consequentialist and problem-oriented approach adopted in pragmatist accounts may be inappropriate for the context of the legal discipline. It has been argued that legal pragmatism reduces law to being an instrument for achieving political goals and that it is useless in the realm of law.[368] However, as will be shown in the following, there are strands of pragmatism that take into account a broad range of consequences without narrowing them down to any 'ultimate goal'. Pragmatism thus differs from the utilitarian version of consequentialism that specifies the 'ultimate goal' as the maximisation of the satisfaction of the preferences of the largest group. Whereas utilitar-

---

365 Moti Nissani, 'Fruits , Salads , and Smoothies: A Working Definition of Interdisciplinarity' (1995) 29 The Journal of Educational Thought 121, 124.

366 There are of course many alternative points of discussion, e.g. Jürgen Habermas, *Faktizität und Geltung* (Suhrkamp 1998); Martti Koskenniemi, *From Apology to Utopia* (Cambridge University Press 2009).

367 See, e.g. Richard Posner, *Law, Pragmatism, and Democracy* (Harvard University Press 2003) 41; Ronald Dworkin, 'Pragmatism, Right Answers and True Banality' in Michael Brint and William Weaver (eds), *Pragmatism in Law and Society* (Westview Press 1991) 370; Brian Z Tamanaha, *Realistic Socio-Legal Theory: Pragmatisam and a Social Theory of Law* (Claredon Press 1997) 34.

368 Sanne Taekema, 'Beyond Common Sense: Philosophical Pragmatism's Relevance to Law' [2006] The Tilburg Working Paper Series on Jurisprudence and Legal History. Working Paper 06-02 2.

ian conceptions focus on a single criterion, more differentiated forms of pragmatism take into account a plethora of influences and actors and pay great attention to the legal context.[369] Sanne Taekema has opted for such a differentiated pragmatist approach that sees law as 'both a means and end in itself', serving 'a plurality of ends, which cannot easily be measured on a single scale', and having 'value in itself through the way it upholds ideals of justice and certainty in its application'.[370]

As Taekema puts it, '[p]ragmatist philosophy aims at developing a theory of meaning and truth that does not define truth in terms of correspondence to reality but rather looks at the practical effects.'[371] Louis Menand describes pragmatism as being 'an account of the way people think – the way they come up with ideas, form beliefs, and reach decisions. What makes us decide to do one thing when we might do another thing instead?'[372]

Pragmatist accounts of truth often have their basis in the Peircean account where 'truth is the end of inquiry'; or 'truth is satisfactory to believe'.[373] Charles Sanders Peirce is considered the founder of pragmatism.[374] William James, another influential figure in pragmatism, used a clock-metaphor in his explanation of pragmatism's conception of truth. He asks readers to close their eyes and imagine a clock on a wall. The picture in our heads will be of a clock. However, the closer we look, the more detailed our imagination of the clock needs to be, the more difficult it will get. Unless we are clockmakers, it will be quite difficult for us to imagine and reproduce the inner workings and mechanics of a clock. Thus, James asks: '[w]here our ideas cannot copy definitely their object, what does agreement with that object mean?'[375] Or, translated to the sphere of international adjudication: what does it mean for us to agree with a decision reached by an international court where we cannot definitely understand and replicate all the relevant aspects of a case by ourselves? What does agreement between judges mean if they are deciding

---

369 ibid 10.
370 ibid 15–16.
371 ibid 4.
372 Robert Danisch, *Pragmatism, Democracy, and the Necessity of Rhetoric* (University of South Carolina Press 2007) 13.
373 Michael Glanzberg, 'Truth' (*Stanford Encyclopedia of Philosophy*, 2018) <https://plato.stanford.edu/entries/truth/> accessed 1 September 2020.
374 Cheryl Misak, *Truth and the End of Inquiry* (Oxford University Press 2004) 3.
375 Williams James, 'Pragmatism's Conception of Truth' in Simon Blackburn and Keith Simmons (eds), *Truth* (Oxford Readings in Philosophy 2010) 54.

a factually highly complex case where they themselves will not be able to explain in great detail every scientific aspect that plays a pivotal role in the decision-process?

Where some theories require truth to be a static property in the sense that once you have your 'true idea', you have fulfilled your epistemic duties, pragmatism asks: '[g]rant an idea or belief to be true, [...] what concrete difference will its being true make in any one's actual life? How will the truth be realized? What experiences will be different from those which would obtain if the belief were false? What, in short, is the truth's cash-value in experiential terms?' William James defined true ideas as follows: 'True ideas are those that we can assimilate, validate corroborate and verify. False ideas are those we can not.'[376]

Pragmatism does not require us to verify everything. The overwhelming majority of our beliefs can pass for true without us ever attempting to verify them. We believe something to be a clock without taking it apart and analysing its inner workings. We assume a country to exist even though we have never visited it. William James explained that indirect verification can pass muster, that '[w]here circumstantial evidence is sufficient, we can go without eyewitnessing. [...] Verif*iability* of wheels and weights and pendulum is as good as verification.'[377] Our thoughts and beliefs 'pass' as long as they have not been challenged; we rely on each other's accounts and accept others' verifications without ourselves verifying. 'But beliefs verified concretely by somebody are the posts of the whole superstructure.'[378]

In the context of international adjudication, granting a decision to be true is important from the perspective of reaching a justified belief.[379] Of course it is important to analyse and scrutinise judgments after they have been made. But if we start from the premise that a judgment must reflect 'the truth', then any criticism raised against a decision, or any diverging or dissenting opinion by a judge, will chip away at 'the superstructure' of international adjudication and may cause it to collapse. However, if we take a pragmatist stance, changes in law due to, e.g., societal changes, are accommodated, as is the acknowledgement that mistakes are part of any human decision-making process. It also allows the judges to consult experts who help them reach conclusions in areas where the judges themselves will not be epistemically capable of fully comprehending the 'inner

---

376 ibid.
377 ibid 56–57. Emphasis in the original.
378 ibid 57.
379 For a thorough discussion of justified legal belief, see, e.g. Dwyer (n 194) 40ss.

workings' of the issue at hand. It also allows different opinions to be uttered without this implying that the entire superstructure must be called into question. Such diverging opinions may, rather, suggest a different approach to a similar problem that may arise in the future.

Pragmatist approaches acknowledge that inquiry 'is not standing upon the bedrock of fact. It is walking upon a bog, and one can only say, this ground seems to hold for the present. Here I will stay till it begins to give way'.[380] Cheryil Misak explains this Peircean quote and clarifies that when the 'bedrock of fact' does shift, it only gives way rather than collapsing. What she means by this is that this shift only pertains to a certain belief; an instability in one area will not lead our entire belief system to collapse. As Misak puts it: '[s]ome things have to be held constant.'[381] John Dewey makes a similar point in his piece on *Context and Thought*. In the process of inquiry, there need to be some things that can be considered constant. 'If everything were literally unsettled at once, there would be nothing to which to tie those factors that, being unsettled, are in process of discovery and determination.'[382] We all make considerations and reflections based upon some background conditions. What might be right today may be proven to be wrong tomorrow. If it is proven to be wrong tomorrow, we will inevitably have to adapt our beliefs and reflections to the new situation we find ourselves in.

b. The First Step to Interdisciplinarity: Pragmatist Wariness of Dichotomies

Pragmatist thinkers are generally wary of dichotomies; distinctions should only be drawn, and entities only held apart, if doing so is useful. According to John Dewey, distinguishing 'thinking' from 'doing' does make sense, however, turning every category into a separate entity is not something we should aim for because in reality, categories are interconnected in complex manners. A separation of categories (e.g. of facts vs. values, or

---

380 Charles Sanders Peirce, *Collected Papers of Charles Sanders Peirce, Vol. V: Pragmatism and Practicism* (Charles Hartshorne and Paul Weiss eds, Harvard University Press 1934) n 5.589. See also Cheryl Misak, *Cambridge Pragmatism: From Peirce and James to Ramsey and Wittgenstein* (Oxford University Press 2016) 18.

381 Misak, *Cambridge Pragmatism: From Peirce and James to Ramsey and Wittgenstein* (n 380) 18.

382 John Dewey, 'Context and Thought' (1931) 12 University of California Publications in Philosophy 203, 213.

of different scientific disciplines) is, thus, only useful from a pragmatist perspective if this separation improves or clarifies our reasoning.[383]

One dichotomy that pragmatists are especially wary of is the distinction between facts and values. In his work on the collapse of the fact/value dichotomy, Hilary Putnam understands law as a profoundly value-oriented practice.[384] Facts in the law must thus be interpreted in an interdisciplinary manner that allows the connections between law and moral philosophy to come to the fore. Any interpretation of facts in the legal sphere is connected to social and moral values.[385] This pragmatist account can be traced back to William James and John Dewey, who also rejected the clear categorisations of fact/value and fact/theory that positivism is based on because human experience cannot be categorised into such dichotomies. Rather than as 'outside observers', they viewed human beings as parts of the world who cannot take a detached point of view.[386] This pragmatist perspective influenced legal realists. Pragmatism inspired 'the view of law as a social practice in a social and historical context'.[387] Putnam's general claim is that any knowledge of facts presumes knowledge of values, and vice versa.[388] He argued that, e.g., the classification of behaviour into categories such as 'good' or 'bad' cannot be clearly separated from factual judgments. This distinction is mistaken because the factual judgment that 'your behaviour was rude' and the (value) assessment that 'being rude is bad' are entangled.[389] This can be illustrated by the way criticism of the judgment works: if someone denies that a certain behaviour was rude, the denial involves appealing to facts that allow for challenging the judgment of the circumstances at hand: '[m]y behaviour may have seemed rude, but

---

383 Bart Van Klink and Sanne Taekema, 'A Dynamic Model of Interdisciplinarity. Limits and Possibilities of Interdisciplinary Research into Law' (2008) 8 Tilburg Working Paper Series on Jurisprudence and Legal History 3.

384 Hilary Putnam, *The Collapse of the Fact/Value Dichotomy and Other Essays* (2nd edn, Harvard University Press 2003).

385 Jaap Hage, 'Facts, Values and Norms' in Sanne Taekema, Bart van Klink and Wouter de Been (eds), *Facts and Norms in Law: Interdisciplinary Reflections on Legal Method* (2016) 14.

386 Wouter de Been, Sanne Taekema and Bart van Klink, 'Introduction: Facts, Norms and Interdisciplinary Research' in Wouter de Been, Sanne Taekema and Bart van Klink (eds), *Facts and Norms in Law - Interdisciplinary Reflections on Legal Method* (Edward Elgar 2016) 13.

387 ibid 14.

388 Hilary Putnam, *Pragmatism: An Open Question* (Blackwell 1995) 14.

389 Putnam (n 384) 36.

I could not stop and talk to you because I was late for a meeting.'[390] It is possible to distinguish between factual and value judgments in principle, but they are entwined in complex manners.[391] In the context of legal judgments, if a defendant wants to deny that a violation of a legal rule has occurred, the argument will be based on the facts and it will be argued that the facts do not fulfil the legal bill. In other words, criticising the argument of the accuser, who seeks to demonstrate that a violation has occurred, will involve an appeal to the facts that will allow the defendant to challenge the accuser's assessment of the situation.

Regarding the separation of disciplines, in Dewey's opinion, scientific method should be applied more generally, not only to physical science but also to the normative realm, and even to farming and mathematics. His argument is that the scientific method of inquiry is much more advanced and has progressed enormously, whereas more normatively coloured forms of inquiry (e.g. morals and religion) are still determined by fixed rules; thus, other (more static) fields of inquiry can benefit from the knowledge that has been gained in the realm of scientific method and inquiry.[392]

With regard to law, the question is whether the legal discipline allows for testing like in the sciences. John Dewey's pragmatism calls for values and rules to be both treated as provisional hypotheses that must be tested like scientific hypotheses.[393] Both legal realism and pragmatism share a belief in scientific method and the view that law ought to be changeable. Formalism is criticised because it is incompatible with the pragmatist requirement that concepts be linked to experience and practice. Pragmatist explanations reflect the natural, they consider real examples and aim for philosophy to remain connected to real-life expertise.[394] However, applying scientific method to the legal domain does not amount to 'genuine experimenting' as known in scientific contexts. What it means instead is that 'the consequences of adopting a particular solution must be thought through'.[395]

---

390 Klink and Taekema (n 383) 4.
391 ibid.
392 John Dewey, 'The Quest for Certainty' in Jo Ann Boydston (ed), *The Later Works, 1925-1953, Volume 4* (Southern Illinois University Press 1984) 200.
393 Taekema (n 368) 3.
394 Cheryl Misak, 'The Pragmatist Theory of Truth' in Michael Glanzberg (ed), *The Oxford Handbook of Truth* (Oxford University Press 2018) 283.
395 Taekema (n 368) 5.

Despite pragmatist approaches advocating the application of scientific methods of inquiry across all disciplines, pragmatists pay great attention to the context of the given inquiry.

c. The Second Step to Interdisciplinarity: the Importance of Context to Inquiry

'[…] neglect of context is the greatest single disaster which philosophic thinking can incur.'[396]

This is a statement made by pragmatist John Dewey in his piece on *Context and Thought*. That context is important to any inquiry may seem trivial. However, underestimating the level of its importance can be detrimental to any analysis. Dewey even went as far as stating that the neglect of context constitutes a fallacy in philosophical thought.[397] What exactly, then, does context mean (here)?

David Kennedy stated in his Julius Stone Memorial Address on 'Challenging Expert Rule: The Politics of Global Governance' that '[w]e have context in mind whenever we extract an ought from an is'.[398] What does he mean by this? He distinguishes between foreground, context, and background. According to him, context is made up of impersonal forces; in the legal realm, the context is factual, the background is legal, and the foreground is political. Kennedy opts for a focus on background rather than on context because focusing on the background allows us to put a spotlight on the actors and to hold them responsible.

'It is the expert who stands between the foreground *prince* and the lay *context*, advising and informing the prince, implementing and interpreting his decisions for laymen. It is the scientist, the pollster, who interprets *facts* for the *politician*, and it is the lawyer, the administrator, who translates political decisions back into facts on the ground. Both the assertion that something is the context, and the interpretation of its consequences are the acts of experts.'[399]

---

396 Dewey (n 382) 212.
397 ibid 206.
398 David Kennedy, 'Challenging Expert Rule: The Politics of Global Governance' (2005) 27 Sydney Law Review 1, 4.
399 ibid 5.

Dewey's account of context includes 'background' and 'selective interest'. When using the term 'background', he means to include everything (both temporal and spatial) that 'does not come into explicit purview'.[400] Every time we start our thought or reflection process, there are things that come into our minds; things that we have experienced previously (temporal and spatial); we are influenced by tradition and culture. What Dewey means by this is that depending on the time and space we find ourselves in when we start to think about something, we do not start from scratch. There are certain things that are held constant. We are influenced by what great minds have decided and what is generally accepted. Our background knowledge is influenced, for instance, by Darwin and by Newton. Had we been born in medieval times instead, our inherent starting point for any reflection would be different. We cannot escape these underlying 'mental habits' because they are part of who we are.[401]

Dewey's account of 'selective interest' refers to the motivation that influences us when we embark on any thinking process. This specific attitude influences the way we select while thinking. Every thought results in a selection of something and rejection of other things. Even diligent and critical thinkers who take much care not to discard a thought too quickly will have to perform a selection process at some point.[402] Selective interest has a subjective tone to it. Dewey contends that in any thinking process, everyone has 'a unique manner of entering into interaction with other things'.[403] This is not to say that this is a bad thing. It is just a way of expressing that it is not possible to start a reflection with a clean slate. It is more about individuality than about subjectivity. And in Dewey's approach to context, it is important to keep in mind that we all approach, and interact with, other things in our individual manner, with our inherent backgrounds, our prior knowledge, our experiences, etc.

Applying this to the idea of approaching a topic from an interdisciplinary angle, one can hold that any researcher who embarks on a research project selects, consciously and unconsciously, contextual elements they deem relevant and excludes others they deem irrelevant. This selection process is influenced by the researcher's background and disciplinary perspectives.[404] Putting emphasis on the context of any process of inquiry allows

---

400 Dewey (n 382) 212–213.
401 ibid 214.
402 ibid 215.
403 ibid 217.
404 ibid 99–101.

the thinking or research process to duly take into account the disciplinary context that is of interest; and paying attention to the selective interest of the researcher and, thus, the disciplinary background that led the researcher into the direction of choice paves the way for interdisciplinary approaches. Researchers' different disciplinary backgrounds lead them to embark on their inquiry from different perspectives, with a particular focus, and as long as they pay due attention to the context at hand and are aware of their inherent backgrounds and selective interests, there are no real obstacles to taking an interdisciplinary approach from a pragmatist perspective.[405]

The question is, whether principles of scientific method 'fit' into the legal realm. The question comes to the fore because the legal context differs from the scientific context, and the principles of scientific method were developed for the scientific context, not the legal one. In an essay on law and scientific method, Nancy Levit uses principles of scientific method to critique legal decisions and shows that fruitful insights into legal decision-making can be drawn when analysing jurisprudence through the lens of scientific principles.[406] Thus, she paves the way to show that scientific principles do fit into the legal realm. Using the pragmatist terminology from above, the consequence of chosing one possible solution over another must be 'thought through'.[407] This holds true for legal decision-making and scientific decision-making. What principles of scientific method call for is 'careful conceptual refinement'.[408] This holds true for both the scientific and the legal realm. Levit also points out that the values that are promoted in law and in science are similar: 'certainty, predictability, rationality and self-awareness'.[409]

In sum, thus, pragmatism can be seen to be optimistic about interdisciplinary approaches because, firstly, the scientific method of inquiry is considered to be applicable across all disciplines, and secondly, paying attention to context and selective interest allows researchers to be critical of their own background and to pay due attention to the context they are focusing on and at the same time to combine insights from different disciplines in order to arrive at a reliable outcome to their inquiry.

---

405 Klink and Taekema (n 383) 7.
406 Levit (n 358).
407 Taekema (n 368) 5.
408 Levit (n 358) 305.
409 Levit (n 358) 306. See also below, discussion in Part III, pp. 88ss.

3. Positivism's Arguments against Interdisciplinarity

The most powerful arguments against the interdisciplinarity of international law are put forward by authors who assert that 'the law constitutes a self-contained and self-reliant system'.[410] Hans Kelsen's *Pure Theory of Law*, and to a lesser extent Niklas Luhmann's *System Theory*, posit problems for interdisciplinary approaches in law.[411] Kelsen's intention was to construct a foundation for the science of law that would secure its position as a science alongside other sciences, especially the natural sciences. In his opinion, law is unique as a science in that it can be studied from two different perspectives: it can be analysed from either the perspective of the discipline of empirical sociology or that of the normative science of law. From the perspective of explanatory sociology, law can be seen 'as a part of social reality, as a fact or an occurrence that takes place regularly'.[412] Here, the law can be seen as an 'Is' or *Sein* with regard to human behaviour, in the sense that something does or does not occur, or an action is or is not taken.[413] From the perspective of law itself, law can be understood as a norm. According to Kelsen, 'by "norm" we mean that something ought to be or ought to happen, especially that a human being ought to have behaved in a specific way.'[414] The science of law is, thus, a normative science, whereas the sociology of law is a science of reality. Law can be studied from both perspectives, but this cannot be done at the same time because 'an object cannot be construed as something that is done or happens regularly and that ought to be done or happen simultaneously.'[415]

Kelsen held the view that combining perspectives and methodologies from different disciplines is inadmissible. Because an object (e.g., law) and the method of inquiry for that object are correlated, applying different methods will generate different objects. Mixing methods to study law would threaten the unity of knowledge because it would allow contradictory claims about the same object to emerge. If a given norm is studied from a legal perspective, it may be considered valid because of a high-

---

410 Sergio Dellavalle, 'International Law and Interdisciplinarity' [2020] MPIL Research Paper Series 19.
411 Niklas Luhmann, *Systemtheorie der Gesellschaft* (2nd edn, Suhrkamp 2017); Hans Kelsen, *Reine Rechtslehre* (Matthias Jestaedt ed, Studienaus, Mohr Siebeck 2008).
412 Klink and Taekema (n 383) 9.
413 ibid.
414 Hans Kelsen, *Pure Theory of Law (Max Knight Trans.)* (University of California Press 1967) 4.
415 Klink and Taekema (n 383) 9.

er legal norm (basic norm, or *Grundnorm*) having created the norm in question;[416] however, from an empirical viewpoint, a legal norm may be considered invalid because it has no effects on social reality, e.g. because it is not complied with in real life. Mixing the two approaches would lead to contradictory outcomes because from the legal perspective, the legal norm would be valid, whereas from the sociological perspective, it would be invalid. 'Law cannot be valid and not-valid at the same time, so apparently we are dealing with different senses of validity.'[417]

Niklas Luhmann's position in *Ausdifferenzierung des Rechts* (1981) is less radical than Kelsen's. He rejected the dichotomy of Is/Ought Kelsen based his *Pure Theory of Law* on as being impracticable for sociology, which has humans and their actions as its topic.[418] Luhmann saw legal science as having existed in 'disciplinary isolation' since the downfall of natural law. Thus, his system theory aimed at re-connecting law to other disciplines, and he wanted to address the question of the capacity of legal scholarship for interdisciplinary contact ('interdisziplinäre Kontaktfähigkeit der Rechtswissenschaft').[419] Given the extent and complexity of law, Luhmann considered interdisciplinary perspectives pivotal for adding to the understanding of law; to this end, law in his view should develop a steering system that transcends legal dogmatics and allows for interdisciplinary insights to be drawn.[420] Luhmann held that the necessary decisions in law cannot be arrived at by purely logical means of deduction from legal propositions; rather, the case at hand provides assistance in decision-making ('Der Fall leistet Entscheidungshilfe').[421] Luhmann pointed to Josef Esser, who showed how case-orientation guides judicial decisions, makes 'reaching through' ('Durchgriff') to extra-legal evaluations possible by lim-

---

416 On the idea of the basic norm (*Grundnorm*) and Kelsen's hierarchical account of legal systems, see, e.g. Dhananjai Shivakumar, 'The Pure Theory as Ideal Type: Defending Kelsen on the Basis of Weberian Methodology' (1996) 105 Yale Law Journal 1383, 1388. With regard to the question of the validity of (international) legal norms, see Tilmann Altwicker, 'Völkerrecht und Rechtspositivismus - Eine Annäherung mit Kelsen und Hart' (2012) 10 Zeitschrift für Rechtsphilosophie 54.

417 Klink and Taekema (n 383) 10.

418 Niklas Luhmann, *Ausdifferenzierung des Rechts. Beiträge zur Rechtssoziologie und Rechtstheorie* (Suhrkamp 1981) 288–289.

419 Niklas Luhmann, *Kontingenz und Recht. Rechtstheorie im interdisziplinären Zusammenhang* (Johannes FK Schmidt ed, Suhrkamp 2013) 7.

420 ibid 8.

421 ibid 163.

iting its risks, and keeps even strongly dogmatised systems flexible.[422] Law can thus be seen as a 'science of decision' where the legislature decides which legal norms are issued and courts decide how these norms are applied in a given case. Legal theory assists the 'science of decision' in the sense that it functionally analyses, identifies, and helps clarify issues in the different (sub)systems of society and makes suggestions as to how they can be legally solved. As other authors have interpreted Luhmann's position, 'legal theory acts as a kind of portal through which insights from other disciplines are channeled to the science of law; it establishes "meaningful relations" that enable the "transfer of problem awareness, concepts and knowledge achievements"'.[423] According to Luhmann, system theories and decision theories still need to be distinguished. This is where Luhmann's position sets limits to pragmatist optimism about interdisciplinarity. In his opinion, insights from, e.g., sociology can assist the legislature by providing a functional analysis of existing norms or norms that are to be created; however, such methods of clarification do not result in a decision. A sociological analysis mainly focuses on existing legal norms and is, thus, only of limited use for the decision-making task of a court that has to apply a legal norm to a case at hand.[424] However, this position does not amount to asserting that the insights from a sociological analysis cannot have any effect whatsoever on judicial decision-making.

In Luhmann's *System Theory*, communication between systems exists.[425] However, according to Luhmann, systems are autopoietic, meaning that the specifications of a system's structures must be derived from within the system itself, and cannot be imported.[426] This does not entail that systems are entirely self-sufficient. Autopoiesis does not mean that a system exists in isolation with no contribution from the outside. Rather, it refers to the unity of a system and that all of its constitutive elements are produced within the system itself.[427] Thus, this entails a special type of independence which concerns only the mode of operation; systems are operatively closed, but in their existence, they still depend on inputs from the outside. For instance, a system cannot exist in an environment that is physically

---

422 ibid.
423 Klink and Taekema (n 383) 10.
424 ibid 11–12.
425 On the term 'communication', see Niklas Luhmann, *Soziale Systeme* (Suhrkamp 1984) ch 4.
426 Niklas Luhmann, *Die Gesellschaft der Gesellschaft* (Suhrkamp 1997) 86.
427 Niklas Luhmann, *Die Wissenschaft der Gesellschaft* (Suhrkamp 1990) 30.

not functioning.[428] A system that is autopoietic, or organisationally closed, communicates within itself. Thus, there is a back-and-forth within a system between communication and resistance to communication.[429] Whether, or to what extent, the communication between systems, e.g., between society and the environment, is independent can be debated.[430] Luhmann himself acknowledged that the operative independence or closedness of a system is only one aspect of the autopoietic system. He did not deny that social systems depend on inputs from outside, e.g. that the social system is dependent upon inputs from the environment. The question is how this relationship is established if there is no operative contact between the two.[431] This is where the idea of structural coupling comes into play. One system is never determined by another; however, one system can cause irritations in another system.[432] Examples for structural couplings between law and economics are, e.g., property and contracts, whereas universities are structural couplings between education and science. Such structural couplings can illuminate the similarities and the differences between systems. Universities have a different meaning from a scientific perspective than they have from an educational perspective; the same holds true for property or contracts from an economic versus legal perspective. The different systems use universities, or contracts, or property according to their own logic and their own code; this leads to a coupling of the systems where the different understandings of these entities lead to self-irritation within a system.[433] The different meanings thus allow for leeway in the systems' own self-reference.[434]

---

428 Roland Lippuner, 'Die Abhängigkeit unabhängiger Systeme: Zum Begriff der Strukturellen Kopplung in Luhmanns Theorie Sozialer Systeme' [2010] http://www.uni-jena.de/Roland_Lippuner.html 2.

429 Luhmann, *Die Gesellschaft der Gesellschaft* (n 419) 95. In the original: 'Alles, was als Realität erfahren wird, ergibt sich aus dem Widerstand von Kommunikation gegen Kommunikation, und nicht als seinem Sichaufdrängen der irgendwie geordnet vorhandenen Aussenwelt.'

430 See, e.g. Marina Fischer-Kowalski and Karlheinz Erb, 'Epistemologische und konzeptuelle Grundlagen der Sozialen Ökologie' (2006) 148 Mitteilungen der Österreichischen Geographischen Gesellschaft 33, 37.

431 Lippuner (n 428) 3.

432 Niklas Luhmann, *Einführung in die Systemtheorie* (Dirk Baecker ed, Carl-Auer Verlag 2002) 124; Lippuner (n 426) 4.

433 Tania Lieckweg, 'Recht und Wirtschaft: Strukturelle Kopplung', *Das Recht der Weltgesellschaft* (de Gruyter 2003) 33.

434 Luhmann, *Die Gesellschaft der Gesellschaft* (n 426) 782ss.

Information can thus flow between, e.g., sociology and law in the sense that sociological insights can be taken into account in judicial decision-making; however, before the insights from another discipline can have an effect on a judicial decision, these insights must be translated into the logic and code of the legal system and be adapted to its methods and framework of reference.

Luhmann's concept of structural couplings between systems can be taken as meaning that although each system can only communicate on the basis of its own codes (i.e. legal decisions are always self-referential), communication can also occur between systems, i.e. something that happens in one system irritates another system, within which this irritation is then processed according to this system's logic. Interdisciplinarity can expand the structural couplings (e.g. between science and law), but interdisciplinarity will never become the code of the legal system itself, i.e. a legal decision will always have to translate facts into the logic of law.

Thus, Luhmann can be read here as setting limits to pragmatist optimism about interdisciplinary communication between law and science, in the sense that insights from science will not automatically affect or lead to a legal decision. But Luhmann is not entirely opposed to interdisciplinarity. Rather, insights from science can have an effect in the legal realm, but they first have to be translated into the legal code and be adapted to the methods and framework that operate in the legal system.

In a sense, Luhmann occupies a middle ground between Dewey's optimism towards interdisciplinarity and Kelsen's skepticism towards it.[435] The view taken here can also be considered middle-ground, in the sense that it does argue in favour of interdisciplinarity but does not aim at transplanting scientific method to the legal realm in order to arrive at legal decisions. It aims to apply principles of scientific method to assess or critique the fact-assessment in the ECtHR's case-law. The principles of scientific method are not intended to be used as legal principles, nor are they to be used to assess the legal analysis in the cases.

In what follows, it will be shown that the line between facts and law, or factual and legal analysis, is not clear-cut. This will pave the way for the incorporation of scientific principles to the fact-assessment part of the ECtHR's decision-making.

---

435 See also, for a suggestion of a middle-ground solution, the dynamic model suggested by Klink and Taekema (n 380).

4. The Blurred Line between the Factual and the Normative

a. The Chicken or the Egg? – or the Wandering Gaze

There is no 'one-way road' to reaching a legal conclusion. Rather, there is a link between the factual and the normative, which Karl Engisch has famously described as the gaze that wanders back-and-forth between the factual and the legal, *'das Hin- und Herwandern des Blickes zwischen Obersatz und Lebenssachverhalt'*.[436] This back-and-forth between legal and factual allows us to put the legal analysis on par with the facts of a given case; and, thus, to draw a legal conclusion based on the facts.[437] The application of any legal norm presupposes the realisation of its constituent elements by a specific factual situation.[438] In other words, the basis of the application of the law is the determination of those facts that are relevant to the legal assessment of the facts in question.[439] By equalising the facts of the case with the legal norm, Engisch means that the facts 'are equated in their entirety, or at least in their "essential characteristics", with those cases that are undoubtedly meant and affected by the statutory facts'.[440] The equation does not proceed via 'abstract' cases.[441] The fact-norm-synthesis or equation takes place via 'types of cases' ('Falltypen'),[442] i.e. via facts that have already been decided to fulfil the legal bill and with which the facts of a new case also correspond.[443] This can be seen as an equation between statutory facts and the facts of a given case. In Engisch's words: '[e]quality is therefore not logically based on identity, but conversely identity on equality.'[444] Engisch's 'wandering gaze' takes into account the elements that influence legal decision-making and acknowledges that these elements influence each other. However, this insight was rather implied than fully

---

436 Engisch (n 2) 15.

437 Marijan Pavčnik, 'Das „Hin- und Herwandern des Blickes" (Über die Natur der Gesetzesanwendung)' in Shing-I Liu and Ulfrid Neumann (eds), *Gerechtigkeit - Theorie und Praxis. Justice - Theory and Practice* (1st edn, Nomos Verlagsgesellschaft mbH & Co KG 2011) 559.

438 Reinhold Zippelius, *Juristische Methodenlehre* (10th edn, Beck 2006) 91.

439 Aemisegger Heinz and Robert Florence Michèle, 'Sachverhaltsfeststellung und Sachverhaltsüberprüfung', (2015) 9 Aktuelle Juristische Praxis 1223, 1223ss.

440 Engisch (n 2) 26.

441 Pavčnik (n 437) 559.

442 Engisch (n 2) 26.

443 ibid.

444 ibid 36. In the original: 'Gleichheit gründet sich also logisch nicht auf Identität, sondern umgekehrt Identität auf Gleichheit', [translation by the author].

developed by Engisch. He did not explain or analyse how the facts of life and the legal norms lead to the emergence of the concrete facts in a given case and the emergence of the legal norm that is applicable in a given case. The wandering gaze remains an action that is formally and logically required to reach a legal decision, without Engisch problematising or addressing it in terms of content.[445] In other words, it is not clear what came first, the chicken or the egg. Does a norm exist because there are facts that led to the creation or expansion of a norm? Or does the norm always pre-determine which facts can become relevant in a given case?

According to Martin Kriele, the wandering of the gaze takes place in two stages: the first ensures that the decision has a rational framework, and the second stage makes this framework more dynamic and entails looking for the basis on which a legal decision is reached. The rationality of the framework is determined by the legal norms and the facts of a given case. The legal gaze is influenced by the factual gaze, because only those legal norms come into consideration that correspond to the legally relevant facts. The factual gaze is, in turn, influenced by the legal gaze because the determination as to which facts are relevant depends on the deductions made possible by the legal norms.[446] The first stage of the wandering gaze commences with an analysis as to which 'facts of life' or *Lebenswirklichkeiten* are legally relevant and which ones are not.[447] This categorisation of facts into relevant and irrelevant has an influence on what possible legal conclusions can be reached. In the second stage, the lawyer looks at the legal norms and whether the factual circumstances fit a legal bill. Usually, this is not clear-cut because legal norms are necessarily indeterminate in order to fit different but similar factual circumstances. Here, case-law, commentaries, and interpretations are required to determine whether or not a certain factual occurrence fits into an existing legal norm. It may be, then, that a new factual occurrence can influence the scope of a legal norm for future cases.[448]

For instance, the principle of evolution or evolutive interpretation has allowed the European Court of Human Rights to widen and adapt the scope of the Convention gradually.[449] Evolutive interpretation allows the

---

445 Pavčnik (n 437) 559.

446 Martin Kriele, 'Theorie der Rechtsgewinnung' (1976) 41 Schriften zum Öffentlichen Recht 367, 197.

447 Pavčnik (n 437) 559.

448 ibid 560.

449 Janneke Gerards, *General Principles of the European Convention on Human Rights* (Cambridge University Press 2019) 56.

ECHR to be seen as an 'instrument of development and improvement', rather than being frozen to the time when the Convention was called into existence 60 years ago.[450] Over the years, the emergence of new factual circumstances has led the Court to read new rights and obligations into the ECHR. Janneke Gerards mentions the examples of 'public watchdogs', such as journalists and NGOs, who have received the right of access to information,[451] and the duty to legally recognise same-sex partnerships.[452] There are of course limitations to this type of interpretation, and the Court is not always prone to apply an evolutive approach and read new rights into the ECHR.[453] However, the fact that in certain cases new rights are read into the Convention shows that the gaze of the Court itself wanders. New factual situations can impact the scope of a legal norm. The emergence of new technologies or changes in social norms are factual occurrences that, if they result in a case that is brought before the Court, will impact its assessment and may lead to the broadening of the legal scope of a Convention article.[454] These examples all imply that there is no clear answer to the question of whether the chicken or the egg came first. Rather, facts and norms seem to influence each other in complex manners.

However, the categorisation of facts into legally relevant and irrelevant ones, and the claim that there is an inherent indeterminacy of legal norms, are views that are not shared by all legal scholars. The American legal realist and fact-sceptic Jerome Frank, for instance, held the view that there is no such thing as legally relevant or irrelevant facts.[455] His scepticism was rooted in the perception that testimony given by witnesses 'is notoriously fallible', e.g. because witnesses lie or remember something wrongly, and that the trial judges and juries may be wrong in their assessment of the reliability of the presented facts.[456] Frank's analysis of the fallibility of

---

450 Kanstantsin Dzehtsiarou, 'European Consensus and the Evolutive Interpretation of the European Convention on Human Rights' (2011) 12 German Law Journal 1730, 1730.

451 See, e.g., *Animal Defenders International v. the United Kingdom*, App no 48876/08, Judgment of 22 May 2013.

452 Gerards (n 449) 56. See ECtHR, *Schalk and Kopf v. Austria*, App no 30141/04, Judgment of 24 June 2010.

453 ibid.

454 See, e.g., Factsheet on New Technologies, <https://www.echr.coe.int/Document s/FS_New_technologies_ENG.pdf>, last accessed on 12 July 2021.

455 Julius Paul, *The Legal Realism of Jerome N. Frank: A Study of Fact-Skepticism and the Judicial Process* (Martinus Nijhoff 1959) 81–91.

456 Jerome Frank, '"Short of Sickness and Death": A Study of Moral Responsibility in Legal Criticism' (1951) 26 New York University Law Review 545, 547.

trial courts in America raised awareness among lawyers of the potential inadequacies in the process of fact-finding and fact-assessment.[457]

The idea that facts in the legal domain are judicially constructed can also be traced back to Hans Kelsen. Kelsen argued that in the legal realm, facts are not something that is out in the world, waiting to be found; rather, facts in the world of law are created by judicial organs.[458] Thus, in his opinion, the question of whether the chicken or the egg came first can be answered: norms come before facts. Facts only come into existence within the legal sphere if they are assessed within or through a legal procedure. Facts are created through the institution that conducts the fact-assessment procedure.[459] Martti Koskenniemi agrees that facts cannot simply be found. Rather, the context within which they are assessed plays a pivotal role. He holds 'the view of international law as an argumentative practice'.[460] Thus, the distinction between relevant and irrelevant facts is the outcome of an argument within international legal practice, it is the result of a debate within an interpretative community.[461] Facts only count as relevant in the sphere of international adjudication if they are deemed important and their importance is assessed 'within the relevant context of argument'.[462]

These accounts imply some form of fact-scepticism in the sense that facts are not seen as objective entities but as constructions, i.e. facts are not objectively true, they are only perceived as such.[463] However, even extreme fact-sceptics such as Jerome Frank do not hold the view that facts are entirely meaningless. As a generally accepted starting point, it can be said that facts play a role in judicial decision-making in that they

---

457 Roger J Traynor, 'Fact Skepticism and the Judicial Process' (1958) 106 University of Pennsylvania Law Review 635, 635.

458 Hans Kelsen, *General Theory of Law and State* (3rd ed, The Lawbook Exchange Ltd 2009) 136; Hans Kelsen, 'Legal Technique in International Law' (1939) 10 Geneva Studies 12.

459 Kelsen, *General Theory of Law and State* (n 458) 136; Kelsen, 'Legal Technique in International Law' (n 458) 12.

460 Martti Koskenniemi, 'Law, Teleology and International Relations: An Essay in Counterdisciplinarity' (2011) 26 International Relations 3, 3.

461 Ingo Venzke, 'International Law as an Argumentative Practice: On Wohlrapp's The Concept of Argument' (2016) 7 Transnational Legal Theory 9, 9.

462 Koskenniemi, 'Law, Teleology and International Relations: An Essay in Counterdisciplinarity' (n 453) 20.

463 Thomas M Franck and Laurence D Cherkis, 'The Problem of Fact-Finding in International Disputes' (1967) 18 Western Reserve Law Review 1483.

are weighed and interpreted.[464] As Andrea Bianchi holds: '[t]he physical world of reality and data in general does not speak for itself'.[465] Bianchi explains this using John Searle's example of American football where he distinguishes between 'brute facts' and 'institutional facts'.[466] If a group of people were asked to observe a game of American football, they would be able to describe the clustering, the movements, and the outfits of the players (brute facts). However, no matter how long the observers go on describing what they see, or how much data and information is collected, without concepts such as 'touchdown', 'offside', or 'points' (institutional facts), i.e. without concepts surrounding the rules of the game, they would be insufficient to describe American football.[467] Thus the institutional setting, with its concepts and rules, has an influence on our understanding of what is described. Information and data receive importance in the domain of international adjudication because a judicial organ conducts a fact-assessment within the process of legal decision-making.

This section has shown that in the context of law, the gaze does indeed wander between the facts and the law. A clear separation of facts and norms, as Kelsen suggests, is not always possible. As Sanne Taekema rightly notes, 'interpretation of facts in legal cases is always coloured by the legal framework'.[468] As soon as a legal case is analysed, the facts pertaining to that case acquire a 'legal taste'. The factual side of the analysis is influenced by the circumstance that the analysis is taking place 'against a background of legal normativity'.[469] And the legal analysis is influenced by the facts of life that can have an influence on the scope of a legal norm. There is, thus, no clear answer as to what came first – the chicken or the egg.

b. Adjudicative Facts and Legislative Facts

The distinction between adjudicative facts and legislative facts was first made by Kenneth Culp Davis in his 1942 paper 'An Approach to Problems

---

464 Jean D'Aspremont and Makane Moïse Mbengue, 'Strategies of Engagement with Scientific Fact-Finding in International Adjudication' (2013) 05 Amsterdam Center for International Law Research Paper 244.
465 Bianchi (n 354) 8.
466 John Searle, *Speech Acts: An Essay in the Philosophy of Language* (Cambridge University Press 1969) 52.
467 Bianchi (n 354) 8.
468 Taekema (n 368) 12.
469 ibid 4.

of Evidence in the Administrative Process'.[470] He referred to the facts that concern the immediate parties to a case (e.g. what the parties did, the circumstances and the background of the given case) as adjudicative facts, because the agency that finds these facts is performing an adjudicative function. Legislative facts, in contrast, concern questions pertaining to law or policy. Facts of this type inform the legislative judgment. Here, the fact-finders or fact-assessors perform a legislative function.[471] Davis deemed this distinction important because 'the traditional rules of evidence are designed for adjudicative facts, and unnecessary confusion results from attempting to apply the traditional rules to legislative facts'.[472] Thus, adjudicative facts must follow the rules of evidence that provide the framework for the admissibility of evidence and the procedure concerning witness testimony and expert evidence etc., but the framework for legislative facts is much less formal.

Ann Woolhandler defined an adjudicative fact as 'a description of a past, individual physical or mental phenomenon, the proof of which is in the record'.[473] Examples of adjudicative facts are, e.g., that someone failed to stop at a red light or that the defendant shot the victim. The question addressed here is value-neutral, it is about determining events and actions, one wants to find out what happened.[474] Existing laws are then applied to these facts; and, necessarily, these laws are normative, they attach consequences to the facts.[475]

Legislative facts do not presume such pre-existing laws because this type of facts is used to create new law. They show what effect a legal rule may have,[476] they bear on the desirability of law-making and/or legislative change.[477] Legislative facts often take the form of predictions of what consequences a regulatory alternative may entail.[478]

---

470 Kenneth Culp Davis, 'An Approach to Problems of Evidence in the Administrative Process' (1942) 55 Harvard Law Review 364.

471 ibid 402.

472 ibid 402–403.

473 Ann Woolhandler, 'Rethinking the Judicial Reception of Legislative Facts' (1988) 41 Vanderbilt Law Review 111, 113.

474 Mirjan Damaška, 'Truth in Adjudication' (1998) 49 Hastings Law Journal 289, 300.

475 Woolhandler (n 473) 114.

476 ibid.

477 Damaška (n 474) 303.

478 ibid.

A common example used to explain legislative facts, for instance, are the opinions recited by Louis Brandeis in this brief in the 1908 case *Muller v. State of Oregon*, which called for special protection of female workers.[479] Another example is the social science used in *Brown v. Board of Education* on the effects of racial segregation.[480]

The analysis by Davis seems to indicate that it is possible to distinguish between facts that are more easily determinable, value-neutral, and 'out there to be found', and facts that are less easily determinable, where there is a link to policy considerations. However, the distinction between the two is not so easily made. Hans Baade uses Davis' analysis as a basis for his definitions of legislative and adjudicative facts. Baade's analysis pertains to what he calls 'sociological jurisprudence';[481] he distinguishes between adjudicative social facts and legislative social facts. The adjudicative social facts have to be established for the purpose of the case that is being decided, and for no other purpose. Attempting to prove an adjudicative social fact entails, according to Baade, 'the adjustment of the law of evidence to novel scientific methods of fact-finding'.[482] This does not hold true for legislative social facts. These are facts that 'form the basis for the creation of law and the determination of policy'. If a court decides to determine such a legislative social fact, this implies that the court makes a conscious decision e.g. to shape a new rule or to adapt a policy due to changes in the social fact situation.[483] Adjudicative social facts, according to Baade, are not intrinsically different from other facts, other than that adjudicative social facts can be difficult to prove.[484] In his opinion, '[j]ust like the state of a man's mind is a fact, the state of a community's mind is a fact, too. But the latter is far more difficult to determine than the former'.[485] This statement of Baade resembles the fallibility claim that Jerome Frank made with regard to witness testimony and judicial assessment of the reliability of claims.[486]

The distinguishing factor between adjudicative facts and legislative facts is not that the former are particular facts while the latter are general facts, but rather that adjudicative facts are facts that pose as 'evidence whose

---

479 USSC, *Muller v. Oregon*, 208 U.S. 412, 419 (1908).
480 USSC, *Brown v. Board of Education*, 483, 494 n 11 (1954).
481 Baade (n 362) 424.
482 ibid 425.
483 ibid 426.
484 ibid 425.
485 ibid 422.
486 Frank (n 456).

proof has a more established place' and whose effect is more predictable within the existing legal framework whereas legislative facts pose as evidence that is 'more manifestly designed to create the rules'.[487] However, the line between these two types of facts is often not easily drawn.

This is because decision-makers use both particularised and general facts to make legal rules.[488] The starting point of a discussion that will lead to something being perceived as a problem that is relevant to others in society may initially be an individual problem. In other words, adjudicative facts may become legislative facts in the sense that a fact that is initially only relevant to the individual, 'what happened' part of the analysis in a given case may come to be treated as exemplary of determining the effect of a legal rule.[489] Ann Woolhandler uses the case of *Gideon v. Wainwright* as an example: here, it was held that if one indigent defendant is unable to defend himself without the help of a court-appointed lawyer, this means that others face the same plight, and it was concluded that due process requires indigent defendants to be represented by court-appointed lawyers.[490]

Another way in which the gaze wanders between the general and the individual is in cases where, e.g., the statistics of a particular case can be used as a general statement for future cases and, as such, have precedential effect.[491]

Fritz Jost rightly notes that there is a *Deskriptionsproblem*; the important role that the judiciary plays shows that its law-making and decision-making function can often not easily be held apart.[492] Acknowledging the existence of legislative facts implies the recognition that courts have a law-making function.[493] And this function, according to a realist pragmatic stance, should be fulfilled in a manner that has a desirable social end. In other words, a court should make use of its law-making function and create and/or adapt legal rules so as to cause a desirable social result; the

---

487 Woolhandler (n 473) 114.
488 ibid.
489 ibid.
490 USSC, *Gideon v. Wainwright*, 372 U.S. 335, 337 (1963).
491 Woolhandler (n 473) 115.
492 Fritz Jost, 'Soziologische Feststellungen in der Rechtsprechung des Bundesgerichtshofs in Zivilsachen', *Schriften zur Rechtstheorie, Bd. 84* (Duncker & Humboldt 1978) 159.
493 Woolhandler (n 473) 115.

court's balancing act should reflect social needs.[494] Thus, according to Alexander Aleinikoff, pragmatic balancing should result in a change in a legal rule if it can be empirically shown that the rule's initial purpose, i.e. the one it was initially created for, is not advanced, or that another rule, i.e. a change to the existing rule, would better advance the social ends.[495]

Along similar lines, Jost hypothesises that legal judgments make statements that can be proven via social scientific methods. An empirical-analytical approach, as advocated, e.g., in the methodologies of Popper, Albert, Opp, and Stegmüller, is used in the social sciences to analyse factual relationships.[496] Jost mentions the importance of legal norms being open in the sense that a norm will have to be adaptable to a specific context. Any norm that is too 'precise' is too narrow because it is only useful for one specific case. However, social realities change, and thus norms are usually open and adaptable. If the norms themselves are open to interpretation, the focus shifts onto the factual circumstances of a specific case.[497] *The gaze wanders.* When the assessor of the relationship between legal norm and factual circumstances makes a judgment, it is not only the facts of a given case that will influence their decision. Rather, the social background in which the case is embedded will also be taken into account. The social realities play a role in the legal assessment.[498] Any factuality that is relevant and that influences a judgment receives, in a sense, a 'special characterisation'.[499] Thus, the openness of a norm, or the inherent indeterminacy of legal norms, is necessary and useful because a given context will complete the act and allow the norm to fulfil its purpose in that context.[500]

The factual situation provides the background against which a statement can be deemed true or false. As Tilmann Altwicker notes, having a sound factual basis that underlies legal rules is essential from a legitimacy perspective. If a legal decision is not based on a sound factual basis, one can presume that the rule will less likely be followed by its addressees and,

---

494 Alexander Aleinikoff, 'Constitutional Law in the Age of Balancing' (1987) 96 Yale Law Journal 952, 958.
495 ibid 958.
496 Jost (n 492) 14.
497 ibid 18–20.
498 ibid 21.
499 ibid 22.
500 ibid 21.

its general effectiveness may be called into question.[501] If the factual situation is not correctly represented in a judgment, this will be problematic because the 'reality' is not reflected in it. Normativity and factuality are interlinked in highly complex manners. It is a given factual context that provides the starting point for any legal analysis. It is not only the specific facts of a given case that influence the legal assessment; rather, for instance, social realities and scientific standards also play into judgments. However, at the same time, the legal framework is also what pre-determines which facts will be relevant and which ones will not. In legal decision-making the facts have to fit the 'legal bill' in order for the court to be able to decide whether a violation has taken place or not. Necessarily, the focus will be on the facts that fit that bill and the question then becomes whether we are faced with self-fulfilling prophecies if the legal norms pre-determine or at least highly influence the facts that the assessors are interested in.

In what follows, it will be shown that the European Court of Human Rights itself explicitly acknowledges that facts and law are intrinsically linked. This demonstration will complete the argument for the introduction of principles of scientific method to analyse the fact-assessment in cases decided by the ECtHR.

c. The Intrinsic Link between Facts and Law before the ECtHR

The ECtHR itself has acknowledged that facts and law cannot always easily be held apart. For instance, in *Radomilja and Others v. Croatia*, the question that was brought before the Court pertained to the acquisition of ownership of socially owned immovable property by adverse possession.[502] In this case, the Grand Chamber had to decide whether or not a property had been acquired by the applicants in good faith by adverse possession. In order for this to be the case, a certain amount of time needed to have passed. Here, the length of time for which someone had been in possession of a property as factual basis brought with it the legal consequence of ownership. The complication in this case was that the applicants had, in their case before the Chamber, not specified a certain period of time. The Grand Chamber held that because of this omission, that period of

---

501 Tilmann Altwicker, 'Evidenzbasiertes Recht und Verfassungsrecht' [2019] Zeitschrift für Schweizerisches Recht 181, 181.

502 ECtHR, *Radomilja and Others v. Croatia*, App nos 37685/10 and 22768/12, Judgment of 20 March 2018.

time as factual basis had to be excluded from the applicants' complaint. The Chamber had included the period and was considered by the Grand Chamber to have decided beyond the scope of the case. According to the Grand Chamber, 'claim' as written in art. 34 ECHR comprises of, firstly, factual allegations and, secondly, legal arguments underpinning the factual allegations. The example the ECtHR used here was the case of *Eckle v. Germany*,[503] where the factual allegation related to the claimant being the 'victim' of an act or omission and the legal argument comprised of this act or omission amounting to a 'violation' under the Convention. The Grand Chamber held:

> 'These two elements are intertwined because the facts complained of ought to be seen in the light of the legal arguments adduced and vice versa.'[504]

The ECtHR even refers to this link between facts and law as being 'intrinsic'.[505] This link is explicitly referred to in the Rules of Court. Thus, Rule 47(1)(e)–(f) of the Rules of Court requires applications to contain 'a concise and legible statements of the facts'[506] and 'of the alleged violation(s) of the Convention and the relevant arguments'[507]. Failure to comply with these requirements can result in the Court not examining an application, by virtue of Rule 47(5.1).[508]

In the case of *Guerra and Others v. Italy* of 1998, the Court referred to itself as being

> 'master of the characterisation to be given in law to the facts of the case, it does not consider itself bound by the characterisation given by an applicant, a government or the Commission. [...] A complaint is characterised by the facts alleged in it and not merely by the legal grounds or arguments relied on. [...]'[509]

---

503 ECtHR, *Eckle v. Germany*, App no 8130/78, Judgment of 15 July 1982.
504 ECtHR, *Radomilja and Others v. Croatia*, App nos 37685/10 and 22768/12, Judgment of 20 March 2018, para. 110. Reference also to ECtHR, *Eckle v. Germany*, App no 8130/78, Judgment of 15 July 1982, para. 66.
505 ECtHR, *Radomilja and Others v. Croatia*, App nos 37685/10 and 22768/12, Judgment of 20 March 2018, para. 111.
506 Rule 47(1)(e) of the Rules of Court.
507 Rule 47(1)(f) of the Rules of Court.
508 Rule 47(5.1) of the Rules of Court.
509 ECtHR, *Guerra and Others v. Italy*, App no 14967/89, Judgment of 19 February 1998, para. 44.

The majority in the *Radomilja* case held that art. 35(2)(b) ECHR, which refers to the exhaustion of domestic remedies, ties the Court to base its decision on the factual complaint as presented by the applicant.[510] In other words, while the Court may 'view the facts in a different manner',[511] 'it is nevertheless limited by the facts presented by the applicants in the light of national law'.[512] However, this point was taken up by the dissenters in various manners. It was criticised, for instance, that the period of time should have been taken into account because, although a complaint is always characterised by the facts that are alleged, there is no clear case-law that shows which facts are relevant to the determination of the scope of a case.[513] Thus there was discussion as to the 'legal weight' of facts in this case, and the dissenters considered that the facts that were excluded from the decision should have been included.[514]

In the partly dissenting, partly concurring opinion of Judges Yudkivska, Vehebovic and Kūris, the point was made that while the Court can, indeed, be considered 'master of characterisation to be given in law to the facts of the case',

> 'What raises concerns (in particular, but not only, in the instant case) is that this may be seen as a *carte blanche*. It should not be. In order to attain legitimacy, the Court's "mastering" must be consistent in choosing a narrower or broader, a stricter or more lenient approach. In order to come to a correct and just outcome, judges should look at the facts of the case (as well as the applicable law) through a magnifying glass – but it should not be so that each of their eyes uses its own magnifying glass, only for one to be pink and the other grimy.'[515]

Thus, the issue here was that there is no clear rule or case-law with regard to how the Court characterises the facts of a case, and this could lead to the Court using facts in a manner that allows it to reach a certain pre-defined conclusion. If facts are selected in such a manner, they become

---

510 ECtHR, *Radomilja and Others v. Croatia*, App nos 37685/10 and 22768/12, Judgment of 20 March 2018, para. 123.

511 See ECtHR, *Foti and Others v. Italy*, App nos 7604/76, 7719/76, 7781/77, 7913/77, Judgment of 10 December 1982, para. 44.

512 ECtHR, *Radomilja and Others v. Croatia*, App nos 37685/10 and 22768/12, Judgment of 20 March 2018, para. 121.

513 ibid, paras. 20–21.

514 ibid, para. 22.

515 ibid, Partly Dissenting, Partly Concurring Opinion of Judges Yudkivska, Vehebovic and Kūris, para., I. 3.

self-fulfilling prophecies, as the focus can be placed on those facts that allow a pre-defined normative conclusion to be reached.

Two cases that will be discussed in detail in Part III show that the Court, indeed, is not consistent in its approach to being master of characterisation. The case of *Garib v. the Netherlands*[516] concerns social housing legislation in Rotterdam and the case of *S.M. v. Croatia*[517] concerns forced prostitution and human trafficking.

In the case of *Garib,* the applicant was a single mother who had been refused a housing permit due to housing legislation which based minimum income requirements on persons wanting to reside in certain parts of Rotterdam. The applicant who did not meet the minimum income requirement, filed a complaint against the legislation. However, she had not submitted a complaint under art. 14 ECHR (prohibition of discrimination) before the Chamber but had only relied on art. 2 of Protocol No. 4 (right to choose one's residence).[518] The Human Rights Centre of Ghent University and the Equality Law Clinic of the Université libre de Bruxelles acted as a third party intervener and urged the Court to consider the case under art. 14 ECHR taken together with art. 2 of Protocol No. 4 ECHR.[519] It was argued that the Dutch legislation against which the applicant had raised her complaint especially impacted 'persons living in poverty or who [were] socioeconomically disadvantaged, such as people with a non-European background and single parents living on social security, like the applicant'; this led to stigmatisation based on income requirement and resulted in discrimination 'based on poverty or "social position"'; although the interveners did acknowledge that the applicant had not submitted a complaint under art. 14 ECHR before the Chamber, they urged the Grand Chamber to examine the case under art. 14 ECHR, relying on the principle of the Court being 'master of the characterisation to be given in law to the facts of the case' and the principle of *iura novit curia*.[520] The Grand Chamber did agree that it is not bound to 'the characterisation given in law to the facts of the case' by an applicant or a Government, however, in its opinion it does not follow that 'it is free to entertain a complaint

---

516 ECtHR, *Garib v. the Netherlands*, App no 43494/09, Judgment of 6 November 2017.

517 ECtHR, *S.M. v. Croatia*, App no 60561/14, Judgment of 25 June 2020.

518 ECtHR, *Garib v. the Netherlands*, App no 43494/09, Judgment of 23 February 2016.

519 ECtHR, *Garib v. the Netherlands*, App no 43494/09, Judgment of 6 November 2017, para. 96.

520 ibid, para. 96.

regardless of the procedural context in which it is made'.[521] Thus, in the Grand Chamber's opinion, the fact that the applicant had omitted to put forward a claim explicitly referring to art. 14 ECHR in the earlier proceedings, this claim was a new one which the Court did not want to consider.[522] In the domestic proceedings, the applicant had advanced a discrimination-argument based on art. 26 of the International Covenant on Civil and Political Rights (ICCPR), which had been addressed and rejected at both levels of domestic jurisdiction.[523] According to the Court's standing case-law, the Chamber's decision on admissibility determines the scope of a case that is referred to the Grand Chamber under art. 43 ECHR.[524] It then holds the following:

> 'Consequently, while it is true that a complaint is characterised by the facts alleged in it and not merely by the legal grounds or arguments relied on, this does not mean that it is open to an applicant, in particular one who has been represented throughout, to change before the Grand Chamber the characterisation he or she gave to the facts complained of before the Chamber and by reference to which the Chamber declared the complaint admissible and, where applicable, reached its judgment on the merits.'[525]

What is confusing here is that the Court acknowledges that 'a complaint is characterised by the facts alleged in it and not merely by the legal grounds or arguments relied on', yet it restricts its own possibilities with regard to being master of characterisation of the facts by requiring that the applicant should have brought forward a claim under art. 14 ECHR before the Chamber. The Court does acknowledge that the applicant did make a discrimination-argument under the ICCPR, but nevertheless, it required an explicit reference to the Convention article in the instant case. It can also be observed that the material before the Chamber included 'domestic bodies' opinions alerting about discrimination and domestic courts dealing with this issue'.[526] It seems that if the Court is indeed master

---

521 ibid, para. 98.
522 ECtHR, *Garib v. the Netherlands*, App no 43494/09, Judgment of 6 November 2017, para. 102.
523 ibid, para. 99.
524 ibid, para. 100.
525 ibid, para. 101.
526 Valeska David and Sarah Ganty, 'Strasbourg Fails to Protect the Rights of People Living in or at Risk of Poverty: The Disappointing Grand Chamber Judgment in Garib v the Netherlands' (*Strasbourg Observers*) <https://strasbourgo

of characterisation of the facts, the facts in this case should have been characterised as requiring a thorough analysis as to whether or not they fulfil the legal bill under art. 14 ECHR. This is also reflected in the joint dissenting opinion to the Chamber judgment, by Judges Lopez de Guerra and Keller who expressed that in the case of *Garib*, 'the applicable principles concerning discrimination should have been considered relevant'.[527]

There seems to be a tension between the legal and the factual characterisation of a given complaint. On the one hand, the Court considers itself master of characterisation and holds that a complaint 'is not merely determined by the legal grounds', but that rather the legal characterisation much depends on the facts as well,[528] but on the other hand, it restricts itself to the legal labelling of the facts provided by the applicant in this case. Moreover, the legal label seems to be considered particularly relevant here because the applicant was represented by a lawyer throughout the proceedings.[529] In this case, the relationship between legal and factual characterisation and the role of the Court as master of this characterisation seems unclear and warrants further explanation.

In the case of *S.M. v. Croatia*, a young woman filed a complaint against a young man, accusing him of having forced her into prostitution.[530] In this case, the Court did decide to change the legal characterisation of the facts in a case of its own account. The questions that were addressed here related to the scope of art. 4 ECHR (prohibition of slavery and forced labour) and whether and how forced prostitution and human trafficking fit under this article. What is particularly interesting with regard to the Grand Chamber ruling in *S.M. v. Croatia* is that in this case, the applicant made a complaint under art. 3 and 8 ECHR, not under art. 4 ECHR. How-

---

bservers.com/2017/11/16/strasbourg-fails-to-protect-the-rights-of-people-living-in-or-at-risk-of-poverty-the-disappointing-grand-chamber-judgment-in-garib-v-the-netherlands/#more-4046>.

527 ECtHR, *Garib v. the Netherlands*, App no 43494/09, Judgment of 23 February 2016, Joint Dissenting Opinion of Judges Lopez Guerra and Keller, para. 14.

528 ECtHR, *Garib v. the Netherlands*, App no 43494/09, Judgment of 6 November 2017, para. 101.

529 ibid, which reads as follows: 'Consequently, while it is true that a complaint is characterised by the facts alleged in it and not merely by the legal grounds or arguments relied on, this does not mean that it is open to an applicant, in particular one who has been represented throughout, to change before the Grand Chamber the characterisation he or she gave to the facts complained of before the Chamber and by reference to which the Chamber declared the complaint admissible and, where applicable, reached its judgment on the merits.'

530 ECtHR, *S.M. v. Croatia*, App no 60561/14, Judgment of 25 June 2020.

ever, the Grand Chamber decided to rule the case on the basis of art. 4 and to take this chance to clarify the definitional scope of the norm. Here, the Court referred to the principle of *iura novit curia* and being 'master of characterisation to be given in law to the facts' to justify deviating from the applicant's legal complaint.

Judge Koskelo wrote a powerful dissenting opinion in the Chamber ruling, in which she criticised the majority for the confusion caused with regard to the scope of application of art. 4 ECHR and questions surrounding forced prostitution and human trafficking. This criticism of the Chamber judgment may have led the Grand Chamber to clarify the definitional scope of art. 4 ECHR more generally, which would show how important such opinions of judges can be in influencing the future course of case-law.[531] In the case of *S.M.*, the idea that factual occurrences can lead to a reconsideration of the legal scope of a norm becomes apparent. The factual existence of the issue of human trafficking and exploitation of prostitution has an impact on a normative level because only if these circumstances exist in reality, and are presented to the Court as facts of a given case, will the Court have to consider whether these factual circumstances provoke a normative response. As soon as they are considered as falling into the scope of a Convention article that does not expressly include the factual occurrence, the norm's applicability is widened to more cases. This type of norm-creation or norm-development via the Court's case-law is, in the case of *S.M.*, only possible via fact-assessment. Thus, although art. 4 ECHR was not invoked by the applicant, the facts of the case led the Court to decide the case under art. 4 ECHR and take this opportunity to clarify the scope of said article more generally with regard to the concept of human trafficking.

The concept of the Court being 'master of characterisation' seems more and more ominous, and it remains to be seen how and when the Court decides to master the characterisation of the facts in law, and when it does not. This can be seen when comparing the approach in *S.M.* to the approach in *Garib*. In *S.M.*, the Court played its mastering card, in the sense that it re-characterised the facts of the case legally, even though the applicant had not asked for that specific characterisation, whereas in *Garib*, the Court refrained from mastering and did not re-characterise the facts of the case legally, despite the applicant asking the Court to do so.

---

531 ECtHR, *S.M. v. Croatia*, App no 60561/14, Judgment of 19 July 2018, Dissenting Opinion of Judge Koskelo.

In his dissenting opinion in *Hermi v. Italy*, Judge Zupančič underlined the importance of acknowledging the relationship between fact and law and that the two cannot be easily distinguished. In his opinion, an abstract differentiation may be possible, but in any given case, the choice of legal characterisation will influence the facts that come to the fore, or at least the legal characterisation will influence the interpretation of the same facts. He uses an example from Dostoyevsky's novel *Crime and Punishment* to elaborate: 'the killing of the pawnbroker woman [...] can only be called "murder" because there was a pre-existing norm of substantive criminal law that described and punished such conduct as "murder".'[532] He further states that criminal courts in Continental jurisdictions usually are not bound by the prosecutor's legal characterisation of the facts under *iura novit curia*. Here, the prosecutor advances one legal characterisation of a chosen fact-pattern and the defence will attempt to have it rejected. It is, then, up to the court to settle for one of the two sides or to find its own solution.

> 'It is thus fair to say that this dialectic operates through the mutual conversion of the facts into normative choice and normative choice into the selection of the relevant facts. Thus, which norm will initially be selected depends on the primary perception of the facts. Thereafter and conversely, the perception of the relevant facts may in turn determine the choice of (a different) norm. This mental loop will often be repeated several times in order to arrive at the optimal characterisation of the fact pattern. This mental process is silent, that is to say, it is not usually reflected in the final reasoning (grounds) of the judgment. It is nevertheless real and decisive. [...]'[533]

The above has shown that the ECtHR's factual analyses are not always conducted in a consistent manner and that the characterisation of facts is not always transparent and conclusive. Thus, it is important to pay attention to the fact-assessment procedures in the ECtHR's case law and to detect potential flaws in the Court's factual analyses. It is suggested here that a methodology to detect such flaws is to use principles of scientific method as assessment criteria.

---

532 ECtHR, *Hermi v. Italy*, App no 18114/02, Judgment of 18 October 2006, Dissenting Opinion of Judge Zupančič.
533 ibid.

5. Conclusion

It was argued above that facts vs. norms, as well as the judiciary's decision-making vs. law-making function, cannot always be easily held apart. The examples from the ECtHR cases showed how it is a practical reality that facts and law are intertwined. The middle-ground pragmatist position, which is adopted here, acknowledges these specificities of the realm of legal decision-making and allows for interdisciplinary approaches to enter the legal realm. Thus, in what follows in the case analysis in Part III below, principles of scientific method will be introduced as methodological principles to assess and critique the factual assessments conducted by the European Court of Human Rights in its case-law. By incorporating these principles to *assess* the factual analyses conducted within legal decisions, and not to *reach* a decision, this approach occupies a middle ground, similar to Luhmann, between Dewey's optimism towards interdisciplinary approaches in law and Kelsen's scepticism towards them. The idea is to use principles that are well established in scientific disciplines to gain a new perspective on how a judgment can be read, which pays greater attention to the factual side of the case assessment.

The analysis below starts from the premise that the fact-assessment side in judicial decision-making does not receive as much scholarly attention as it should. Arguably, many lawyers quickly skip to 'the law' section in the ECtHR's judgments and only skim 'the facts' section. However, given that the determination as to whether a certain fact was established or not can affect the (entire) conclusion, it seems highly important to pay great attention to the factual arguments that the parties to a case bring to the fore, and to how a court contends with those factual arguments. As will be shown below, there are cases where certain claims with regard to facts are not addressed in a convincing manner, or where a conclusion with regard to the facts is drawn without proper explanation. It is suggested here that using principles of scientific method provides a methodological framework that will detect such flaws in the fact-assessment of the ECtHR. The claim here is not that this is the one and only 'right way' to assess the ECtHR's case-law with regard to its factual analyses; rather, it is presented as one way to shine a new light onto fact-assessments and to pay greater attention to the fact-part of the analysis in a case.

III. Principles of Scientific Method and Case Analysis

The aim in Part III is to assess and critique decisions reached by the European Court of Human Rights with regard to their fact-assessment. As explained in Part I, there are not many clear rules on how the Court ought to contend with the facts of a given case. I propose here to use principles of scientific method to read and critique decisions by the ECtHR because such an approach allows us to critically assess decisions from a new perspective.

Nine cases from the ECtHR's case-law will be analysed in depth. Three cases will be assessed using the principle of simplicity, three cases will be analysed using the principles of explanatory power and external validity and the last three cases will be critiqued based on the principle of falsifiability. The discussion will then turn to the implications of these new categories and how they change the critique of the ECtHR's jurisprudence.

1. Principles of Scientific Method

It is controversial whether or not there exists a general set of principles that guide any inquiry that is claimed to be 'scientific'.[534] In his book *Scientific Method in Brief*, Hugh G. Gauch claims 'that science has general principles that must be mastered to increase productivity and enhance perspective, not that these principles provide a simple and automated sequence of steps to follow'.[535] It can, thus, be said that there is 'no such thing as a distinctly scientific method'.[536] However, scientific inquiries do have a certain common core, and draw on similar modes of inference and inquiry-procedures.[537] Thus, although there is no one single scientific method that can guide procedures of inquiry, there are certain principles that can help us refine our assessment-processes. Susan Haack believes

---

534 Hugh G Gauch Jr, *Scientific Method in Brief* (Cambridge University Press 2012) 6.

535 ibid 5.

536 Dwyer (n 194) 104.

537 See, e.g., Susan Haack, *Defending Science - Within Reason: Between Scientism and Cynicism* (Prometheus Books 2003) ch 4.

that scientific method is merely a refinement of our thinking processes in everyday life.[538] Thus, if such investigative methods can be used to inform our everyday thinking processes, they can also help us read and assess decisions reached by the European Court of Human Rights.

In her paper on 'Law and Scientific Method' from 1989,[539] Nancy Levit defined scientific method in the context of law and analysed the application of scientific method to jurisprudence.[540] She used principles of scientific method to analyse and criticise both theories of jurisprudence and judicial decisions. Levit observed that the use of scientific method in the legal realm had been limited, up to that point, 'by the prevailing assumption that principles of scientific inquiry must be abandoned when law faces value choices'.[541] However, Levit argued that the criteria of validation on which scientific method relies can be applied to decision-making about both facts and values.[542] If one considers the goal of law to be rationality, the analysis of jurisprudence should follow scientific method.[543] The set of principles for scientific theory-building that Levit applies to the legal sphere encompasses, among others, simplicity, explanatory power, depth or constructivity, fertility and extensibility, external validity, internal consistency and logic, and falsifiability.[544] These criteria are not always distinct from each other. In many instances, they are interlinked and complement each other. They all aim at advancing inquiry and knowledge and at promoting the open exchange of thought-processes and ideas.[545] There are many other criteria that go into sound theory-building or decision-making; the list above is not exhaustive. Criteria such as public verifiability, transparency, clarity, originality, and creativity also play into the analysis.[546] Most of these criteria are deeply intertwined, sometimes they conflict, and sometimes they require more or less the same things. There are no clear rules as to what constitutes a 'good theory' or a 'good decision'; rather, the aim of any theory or method of inquiry should always be the improvement of objectivity and rationality.[547] This general aim also implies certain

---

538 ibid 95.
539 Levit (n 358).
540 ibid 265.
541 ibid.
542 ibid.
543 ibid 266.
544 ibid 268–272.
545 ibid 303, fn 248.
546 ibid 271–272.
547 ibid 272.

values that should underlie any factual inquiry. Levit holds that 'openness, humility and non-chauvinism inhere in the criteria of theory validation'.[548]

The following case analysis is divided into three sections. Within each of them, three cases from the ECtHR's case-law will be discussed in light of one particular principle. The first principle that will be applied to three cases adjudicated by the ECtHR is the principle of simplicity, whereas the second section will pertain to the principles of explanatory power and external validity, and the third group of cases will be considered in light of the principle of falsifiability. These three sections aim at exemplifying the use of employing principles of scientific method to assess the fact-assessment conducted in judicial decisions.

2. Analysis of the ECtHR's Case-Law Using Principles of Scientific Method

What I argue in what follows is that the principles of scientific method can be used to analyse and critique judicial fact-assessment in legal decision-making, including but not limited to the decisions of the ECtHR. It must be noted at the outset that there is no 'scientific roadmap' that will guide decision-makers to 'the right' decision. The view is taken here that abstract concepts such as the principles of scientific method cannot guide all decisions, as contexts and factual underpinnings vary from case to case.[549] However, the abstract principles of scientific inquiry can help us tackle and approach the decisions and their underlying arguments from a different perspective; they will allow us to analyse how arguments are used and whether statements stand when they are tested against the criteria of confirmation. Applying these principles can thus serve as a method of testing the reliability of a given factual analysis.

Arguably, lawyers reading a decision by the ECtHR will quickly shift their focus to 'the law' section of a judgment. What is potentially problematic with this approach is that gaps in the handling of the factual claims may thereby be overlooked. As will be shown in what follows, the ECtHR overlooks some claims put forward by applicants. This leads to gaps in the factual basis of the normative assessment, which, in turn, also calls the normative conclusion into question because it is not based on a sufficient or sound factual assessment.

---

548 ibid 265.
549 ibid 297.

Whilst the above-mentioned principles are interrelated – and relying on only one principle can lead to poor results –, they are not fully compatible. For instance, a decision that succeeds in terms of its explanatory power will most likely not fulfil the criterion of simplicity simultaneously.[550] In what follows, the selected principles will be explained in more detail, and it will be demonstrated how the case-law of the ECtHR can be criticised on the basis of these new categories.

The ECtHR's case-law was searched via the HUDOC database[551] using different search terms, including 'scientific principles', 'scientific method', 'scientific facts', 'social science', 'data', and 'sufficient evidence'. All principles Nancy Levit refers to in her paper were applied as individual search terms as well. I decided to focus my analysis on three of the principles listed in Levit's paper. The HUDOC search revealed that the principle of simplicity and the principle of falsifiability had been explicitly invoked by judges of the ECtHR to critique the majority's reasoning. Thus, given that these two principles have already been employed to critique the ECtHR's jurisprudence, I decided to select these two principles for my own analysis as well.

The principles of depth and constructivity and of fertility and extensibility turned out to be more suited for critiquing legal theories and schools of thought rather than judgments.[552] However, the focus of this thesis is on scrutinising judicial decisions rather than legal theories. Thus, these principles were discarded for the case analysis. The principle of internal consistency and logic was omitted as well, as it opens up an entirely new field of criticism and would require a theoretical underpinning of its own. Furthermore, the use and limits of logic in legal reasoning have already been discussed by several legal scholars.[553] Thus, the principles of explanatory power and external validity were chosen as the third starting point of analysis; they were combined because there is considerable overlap between them.

---

550 ibid 267.

551 See Human Rights Documentation database, available at <https://hudoc.echr.co e.int/eng#{"documentcollectionid2":["GRANDCHAMBER","CHAMBER"]}>, last accessed on 12 July 2021.

552 See, e.g., Nancy Levit in her analysis, ibid 275ss.

553 See, e.g. Wilson Ray Huhn, 'The Use and Limits of Deductive Logic in Legal Reasoning' (2002) 42 Santa Clara Law Review 813; Robert H. Schmidt, 'The Influence of the Legal Paradigm on the Development of Logic', (1999) 40 Texas Law Review; Douglas Lind, 'Logic, Intuition, and the Positivist Legacy of H.L.A. Hart 135, 136 (1999)' (1999) 52 SMU Law Review.

In a sense, there was a back-and-forth between the selection of the cases and the selection of the scientific principles that were to be applied as assessment criteria. My gaze wandered between looking for cases where facts played an important role (which were detected via the search terms in HU-DOC) and choosing the principles that would be most useful for analysing cases. Thus, the choice of principles influenced which cases were chosen, and the cases had an impact on the selection of the principles.

a. Simplicity

i. The Principle

The principle of simplicity, also known as the principle of parsimony or efficiency or as Ockham's razor,[554] recommends that if there are multiple theories that fit the data equally well, the simplest theory should be chosen.[555] For a theory to fulfil the principle of simplicity implies that it has the 'ability to explain all of the relevant phenomena in a single set of ideas'.[556] In short, this principle prefers the least complicated explanation.[557]

Ironically, the principle of simplicity is not so simple itself as it encompasses numerous sub-principles, 'including syntactical simplicity (economy of the structure of the theory), semantic simplicity (limitation on the number of presuppositions), epistemological simplicity (economy of concepts with transcendent or generalized components) and pragmatic simplicity (ease of testability).'[558] Simplicity aims at the integration and unification of knowledge, and it warns against the protection of favoured theories by resorting to *ad hoc* explanations.[559] Any explanation for a phenomenon that does not provide a coherent answer to all aspects of that phenomenon will run counter to the principle of simplicity because this principle requires

---

554 Named after William of Ockham, see 'William of Ockham' (*Stanford Encyclopedia of Philosophy*, 2019) <https://plato.stanford.edu/entries/ockham/>. Last accessed on 12 July 2021.
555 Gauch Jr (n 534) 174.
556 Levit (n 358) 268.
557 ibid.
558 ibid.
559 ibid.

the explanation to be neat. Any requirement for exceptions or adaptations of the main theory will be a red flag.[560]

Gauch explains this principle as demanding that everyone must provide sufficient reason for a statement's truth.[561] What can be deemed a sufficient reason is 'either the observation of a fact, or an immediate logical insight, or divine revelation, or a deduction from these'.[562]

Apart from being an epistemological principle that calls for the preference of the simplest theory that fits the facts, simplicity is also an ontological principle that expects nature to be simple.[563]

Interestingly, in his partly dissenting opinion in *Muršić v. Croatia*, Judge Pinto de Albuquerque criticises the majority's decision using Ockham's razor.[564] The question, which will be discussed in greater detail below, related to the issue of prison overcrowding and the normal conditions that can be expected of prison cells. In Judge Pinto de Albuquerque's opinion, the majority's criteria for assessing the conditions of the prison facilities did not withstand Ockham's razor.[565] It is, thus, not entirely uncommon to criticise the Strasbourg Court on the basis of this principle.

---

560 ibid.
561 Gauch Jr (n 534) 176. See also chapter 10 on parsimony.
562 ibid 176; Gauch quotes (Boehner 1957:xxi).
563 ibid 193.
564 ECtHR, *Muršić v. Croatia*, App no 7334/13, Judgment of 20 October 2016, Partly Dissenting Opinion of Judge Pinto de Albuquerque, para. 53.
565 ibid: 'Furthermore, the offsetting factors referred to by the majority should already be part of the normal conditions within a prison, such as "sufficient freedom of movement outside the cell and adequate out-of-cell activities", and even very broadly speaking the existence of "an appropriate detention facility". There is a serious logical flaw in this reasoning. Here the majority's criteria can hardly withstand Ockham's razor. *Pluralitas non est ponenda sine necessitate.* In an absolutely redundant way, the majority make use of what should be ordinary features of a prison facility in order to justify an extraordinarily low level of personal space for individuals in detention. For the majority, normal living conditions justify abnormal space conditions. Logic would require that extraordinary negative circumstances be offset only by extraordinary positive counter-circumstances. This is not the case in the majority's logic. No extraordinary positive features of prison life are required by the majority to compensate for the deprivation of each prisoner's right to adequate accommodation in detention.'

ii. Case Analysis

Jalloh v. Germany. The case of *Jalloh v. Germany* of 11 July 2006 concerns the use of emetics on a person who was suspected of dealing with drugs.[566]

On 29 October 1993, policemen observed the applicant, on more than one occasion, taking a plastic bag out of his mouth and handing it over to another person in exchange for money. The policemen believed these bags to contain drugs. When they went to arrest the applicant, he swallowed another plastic bag that had still been in his mouth.[567] The applicant was then taken to a hospital where emetics were administered to him forcibly and against his will. This resulted in the applicant regurgitating one plastic bag, containing 0.2182g of cocaine. He was then declared fit for detention by the doctor.[568] The applicant maintained that he suffered from health repercussions of the forced administration of emetics, including stomach troubles and a nose bleed.[569]

The main question in this case was whether forced administration of emetics violated art. 3 of the Convention and therefore evidence obtained in this manner had to be considered illegal and could not be used in court due to being 'fruit of the poisoned tree'. The applicant and the Government disagreed on whether or not the use of emetics amounted to a violation of art. 3 ECHR. The Court assessed approaches of other Member States with regard to emetics and considered the different positions of experts regarding the question of the dangerousness of the use of emetics.[570] After taking into account the different arguments, the Court decided that the forced use of emetics in this case did amount to inhumane and degrading treatment under art. 3 ECHR.[571] There is one paragraph in the judgment that reflects a problematic line of reasoning by the Court. In that paragraph, the Court notes that drug trafficking is a serious offence and that it is aware of the Member States' efforts in addressing this issue, which causes harm to societies. The problematic part of the paragraph reads as follows:

---

566 ECtHR, *Jalloh v. Germany*, App no 54810/00, Judgment of 11 July 2006.
567 ibid, para. 11.
568 ibid, para. 13.
569 ibid, paras. 16–18.
570 ECtHR, *Jalloh v. Germany*, App no 54810/00, Judgment of 11 July 2006, paras. 41–44.
571 ibid, para. 83.

> 'However, in the present case it was clear before the impugned measure was ordered and implemented that the street dealer on whom it was imposed had been storing the drugs in his mouth and could not, therefore, have been offering drugs for sale on a large scale. [...]'[572]

The Court considers this to be reflected in the sentence that the applicant had received, which was at the lower end of the possible range of sentences. It considered it 'vital for the investigators to be able to determine the exact amount and quality of the drugs that were being offered for sale'.[573] The Court was 'not satisfied that the forcible administration of emetics was indispensable' in the present case in order to obtain the evidence, and it pointed out that the authorities could have waited for the drugs to pass through the applicant's system naturally, as was the practice in other States of the Council of Europe in such cases.[574]

Here the majority considers the fact that the applicant had only sold drugs on a small scale as decisive in determining whether or not the forcible administration of emetics was justified. It implies that the lives of small-scale drug dealers have a different weight in the proportionality analysis than those of large-scale drug dealers. In other words, this reasoning implies that had the applicant been a large-scale drug dealer, the forced administration of emetics may have been justified.

This paragraph is also highlighted by Judge Bratza in his concurring opinion. He rightly notes that he cannot accept the implication of this paragraph '[...] that, even where no medical necessity can be shown to exist, the gravity of the suspected offence and the urgent need to obtain evidence of the offence, should be regarded as relevant factors in determining whether a particular form of treatment violates Article 3.'[575]

Similarly, in their dissenting opinion, Judges Wildhaber and Caflisch criticise this paragraph as implying that the majority values 'the health of large dealers less than that of small dealers'.[576]

From the perspective of simplicity, this line of reasoning is untenable. It reduces the arguments regarding the dangerousness of forced administration of emetics to a limited area. The principle of simplicity requires that the conclusions regarding the procedure in question apply to all drug

---

572 ibid, para. 77.
573 ibid.
574 ibid.
575 ECtHR, *Jalloh v. Germany*, App no 54810/00, Judgment of 11 July 2006, Concurring Opinion of Judge Bratza.
576 ibid, Dissenting Opinion of Judges Wildhaber and Caflisch, para. 4.

dealers, no matter if they are selling drugs on a large or a small scale. However, this reasoning implies that the factual conclusions regarding the dangerousness of the forced administration of emetics are not valid for all lives. The principle of simplicity calls for omitting exceptions and *ad hoc* explanations. Here, it seems that the Court built in a caveat for potential future cases where the facts may be interpreted in a different manner because the drug dealer operates on a larger scale.

Muršić v. Croatia. Another case that can be criticised on the basis of principles of scientific method, and the principle of simplicity in particular, is that of *Muršić v. Croatia.*[577] In this case, concerning overcrowding in Bjelovar Prison in Croatia, the question was whether a violation of art. 3 ECHR had taken place due to the amount of personal space available to the applicant. There were different incidents that had to be decided separately. It was concluded unanimously that a violation had occurred in the period the applicant spent in the prison between 18 July and 13 August 2010, during which his personal space had been less than 3 sq. m. By ten votes to seven, it was held that no violation had taken place in the other periods of detention during which the applicant had less than 3 sq. m of personal space, because these periods were non-consecutive. Finally, by thirteen votes to four, non-violation of art. 3 was also found with regard to periods during which the applicant had between 3 and 4 sq. m of personal space.

There is a table enclosed to this case that reflects the cell numbers, the periods of detention, the total number of inmates, the overall surface area in sq. m, the personal space in sq. m, the surface minus sanitary facility in sq. m, and the personal space in sq. m.[578] It was decided that the minimum requirement for personal space in a multi-occupancy cell was 3 sq. m. This was a confirmation of previous cases, where this had been decided to be the applicable standard.[579] If the surface per detainee in such a cell fell below 3 sq. m, there was a strong presumption of art. 3 ECHR being violated. This presumption could be rebutted if mitigating factors could compensate for the lack of personal space.[580] It is clarified that the assessment, i.e. the calculation of the minimum space that should be available to

---

577 ECtHR, *Muršić v. Croatia*, App no 7334/13, Judgment of 20 October 2016.

578 ECtHR, *Muršić v. Croatia*, App no 7334/13, Judgment of 20 October 2016, para. 17.

579 ibid, para. 107.

580 On presumptions in international human rights adjudication, see Tilmann Altwicker and Alexandra E Hansen 'Presumptions in International Human Rights Adjudication' (forthcoming, on file with author).

a prisoner in their cell, is to take into account the in-cell sanitary facilities, the furniture, and the possibility of moving around 'normally' within the cell.[581] However, the (exact) meaning of 'normally' is not clarified in the judgment.

The European Committee for the Prevention of Torture and Inhuman or Degrading Treatment or Punishment (CPT) held in its report that its basic 'rule of thumb' for personal living space in prison establishments is 4 sq. m, this being a minimum standard.[582] The CPT clarified that this standard was not an absolute one, as mitigating factors such as outside-cell activities (workshops, classes, etc.) could influence the assessment. However, even then, the minimum standard was recommended.[583]

The ICRC report on 'Water, Sanitation, Hygiene and Habitat in Prisons' observed that there is no universal standard, but that different countries adopt different standards, ranging from 4 sq. m in Albania to 12 sq. m in Switzerland.[584] The ICRC recommends 3.4 sq. m per person, including beds and facilities in multi-occupancy cells.[585] Because this is a recommendation rather than an absolute standard, the space requirement has to be (factually) assessed on a case by case basis, taking into account, for instance, the individual needs of the person related to their age, gender, and potential disabilities, the physical conditions of the detention facility, outside-of-cell activities, and other factors.[586] The more time a person spent in the cell, the higher the space requirement would be.[587]

In a similar vein to the CPT and to the ICRC, the Court stated that it could not specify 'once and for all' an amount of prison cell space that would in any case comply with the Convention. Rather, relevant factors must be taken into account.[588] In this regard, the Grand Chamber refers to the three-fold test that was established in the case of *Ananyev and Others v. Russia*:[589]

'(1) each detainee must have an individual sleeping place in the cell;

---

581 ibid, para. 114.
582 ibid, para. 51.
583 ibid.
584 ibid, para. 61.
585 ibid, para. 62.
586 ibid, para. 63.
587 ibid, para. 64.
588 ECtHR, *Muršić v. Croatia*, App no 7334/13, Judgment of 20 October 2016, para. 103.
589 ECtHR, *Ananyev and Others v. Russia*, App nos 42525/07 and 60800/08, Judgment of 10 January 2012, para. 148.

(2) each detainee must dispose of at least 3 sq. m of floor space; and (3) the overall surface of the cell must be such as to allow detainees to move freely between furniture. The absence of any of these elements created a strong presumption that the conditions of an applicant's detention were inadequate.'[590]

Although the Grand Chamber refers to cases where the Court had used 3 sq. m as its threshold as well as others where the CPT recommendation of 4 sq. m had been used as a standard,[591] it quickly goes on to state that it sees no reason for departing from its 3 sq. m standard.[592] The Court explains that its reluctance to take the CPT standard as a decisive argument for its finding under art. 3 ECHR 'relates to its duty to take into account all relevant circumstances of a particular case before it when making an assessment under Article 3', whereas the CPT's aim is one of future prevention.[593] However, this does not explain why the Court deems 3 sq. m to be an adequate square footage when it comes to personal space. Without referring to any psychological studies or other empirical evidence that would explain or justify the Court's decision to deviate from the recommendations by the CPT and the ICRC, or to some standard applied by any European country, the Court decides to use a different threshold.[594] In other words, the Court does not choose the simplest solution, but rather decides to create its own threshold without proper explanation as to why. The simplest solution would have been to adopt the qualified recommendations from the CPT and the ICRC as a minimum standard. In any case, deviating from a higher standard recommended by specialised bodies should require more explanation and evidentiary support to justify employing a lower threshold that setting a higher standard would. However, the Court merely states that it will remain 'attentive' to the CPT's recommendations.[595]

---

590 ECtHR, *Muršić v. Croatia*, App no 7334/13, Judgment of 20 October 2016, para. 75.

591 ibid, para. 108, referring to see, inter alia, ECtHR, *Cotleț v. Romania (No. 2)*, App no 49549/11, Judgment of 1 October 2013, paras. 34 and 36; and ECtHR, *Apostu v. Romania*, App no 22765/12, Judgment of 3 February 2013, para. 79.

592 ECtHR, *Muršić v. Croatia*, App no 7334/13, Judgment of 20 October 2016, paras. 109–110.

593 ibid, para. 112.

594 This point can also be criticised from the perspective of the principles of external validity and explanatory power.

595 ECtHR, *Muršić v. Croatia*, App no 7334/13, Judgment of 20 October 2016, para. 141.

Furthermore, the Court states that, although all the facts have to be taken into account with regard to the prison, the cell, and the out-of-cell activities:

> 'Nevertheless, having analysed its case-law and in view of the importance attaching to the space factor in the overall assessment of prison conditions, the Court considers that a strong presumption of a violation of Article 3 arises when the personal space available to a detainee falls below 3 sq. m in multi-occupancy accommodation.'[596]

This 'strong' presumption that the Court employs here can be rebutted by the Government if it can show that the periods of deprivation were short and minor.[597] The problem here is that it is entirely unclear what exactly may be considered 'short and minor'.[598] If the presumption of an art. 3 violation is easily rebutted, the absolute nature of art. 3 ECHR is watered down considerably.[599] The caveat with regard to 'short and minor' periods of deprivation of personal space adds another layer of complexity. The simplest solution here would have been to adhere to the 3 sq. m standard without adding caveats and exceptions.

The next problematic aspect in the reasoning of the Grand Chamber is that even less than 3 sq. m of personal space can be compensated for if mitigating factors are in place to alleviate the lack of cell space. This is where Judge Pinto de Albuquerque himself in his partly dissenting opinion draws upon the principle of simplicity to criticise the majority's reasoning:

> 'Furthermore, the offsetting factors referred to by the majority should already be part of the normal conditions within a prison, such as "sufficient freedom of movement outside the cell and adequate out-of-cell activities", and even very broadly speaking the existence of "an appropriate detention facility". There is a serious logical flaw in this reasoning. Here the majority's criteria can hardly withstand Ockham's razor. *Pluralitas non est ponenda sine necessitate.*'[600]

---

596 ibid, para. 124.
597 ibid, para. 169.
598 Notions such as 'short and minor' can also be criticised under the principle of falsifiability for their vagueness.
599 ECtHR, *Muršić v. Croatia*, App no 7334/13, Judgment of 20 October 2016, Partly Dissenting Opinion of Judge Pinto de Albuquerque, paras. 51–52.
600 ibid, para. 53.

The majority can, thus, be criticised for using ordinary features every prison facility should have to justify extraordinarily little cell space for detainees. This runs counter to the principle of simplicity as stated in the Latin phrase quoted above, which can be translated as meaning 'the essential things should not be multiplied unless necessary'.[601] In the words of Judge Pinto de Albuquerque, 'normal living conditions justify abnormal space conditions' in the reasoning of the majority. However, logic requires matters to be the other way around: if some circumstances are extraordinarily negative, they can only be offset or compensated for by extraordinarily positive circumstances that act as a counter-balance.[602] In the case of *Muršić*, however, this was not fulfilled. There were no extraordinary compensatory features that allowed for the extraordinarily low amount of space to be justified.

The principle of simplicity aims at integrating and unifying knowledge and warns against creating protective caveats to reach a favoured outcome.[603] In this case, the majority did not add to the unification of knowledge, rather, it added more confusion regarding prison cell space. The downward deviation from the CPT minimum standard was not based on any psychological or other empirical evidence, and the mitigating factors that may justify even less cell space should have been interpreted more narrowly, as many of these factors should be considered normal features that ought to be part of any humane living conditions. Furthermore, the possibility for the Government to rebut the presumption of an art. 3 ECHR violation when the prison cell space is less than 3 sq. m is also unclear as the majority failed to provide clear definitions regarding what is meant by short and minor periods of deprivation. These statements provide caveats, exceptions, and the possibility of *ad hoc* explanations that run counter to the principle of simplicity.

Khamtokhu and Aksenchik v. Russia. This delicate Grand Chamber case of 2017 concerns questions surrounding life imprisonment and discrimination on the basis of gender and age. At issue was a Russian law that exempted women in general and males aged under 18 or over 65 from life sentences.[604] The majority of the Grand Chamber ruled by 16 votes to one

---

601 Translation by Benjamin Vargas-Quesada and Félix de Moya-Anegon, *Visualizing the Structure of Science* (Springer 2007) 2.
602 ECtHR, *Muršić v. Croatia*, App no 7334/13, Judgment of 20 October 2016, Partly Dissenting Opinion of Judge Pinto de Albuquerque, para. 53.
603 Levit (n 358) 268.
604 ECtHR, *Khamtokhu and Aksenchik v. Russia*, App nos 60367/08 and 961/11, Judgment of 24 January 2017.

that this constituted no discrimination due to the differential treatment on account of age, and by ten votes to seven that there had been no such violation on account of sex.

The delicateness arose from the potential consequences and repercussions of the decision. The applicants, two men serving life sentences, claimed that men should also be exempted from life sentences, and that the law constituted an unjustified difference in treatment based on gender and age. They pointed out that they were not seeking universal application of life imprisonment to all offenders, i.e. females and males younger than 18 or older than 65 as well. 'Rather, they claimed that, having decided that imprisonment for life was unjust and inhuman with respect to those groups, the Russian authorities should likewise refrain from subjecting men aged 18 to 65 to life imprisonment.'[605] They argued that the difference in treatment between men and women was outdated and stereotypical and was not based on any scientific evidence or statistical data.[606] In the applicants' opinion, women may be treated differently when they are, e.g., pregnant, breastfeeding or child-rearing because in such circumstances there would be justification for difference of treatment.[607] This is, essentially, an argument based on the principle of simplicity: if the argument for exempting specific groups is that life imprisonment is unjust and inhumane, this argument should be applied to people in general, not only to certain groups of people.

What made this case so unique and complex is that the Court was faced with a dilemma: life imprisonment is not as such contrary to the Convention and, thus far, there exists no European consensus for an abolition of life sentences.[608] Russia treats women and males under 18 and over 65 preferentially, in the sense that only men between 18 and 65 can be sentenced to life imprisonment. The consequence of finding a violation on the basis of discrimination would be either A) that everyone, i.e. males under 18 and over 65 and all females as well, would be viable for life sentences, or B) that everyone would be freed from life imprisonment. Russia can either be praised for making a step in the 'right direction', the latter being the abolition of life sentences altogether, or criticised for discriminatory treatment on the base of gender and age.

---

605 ECtHR, *Khamtokhu and Aksenchik v. Russia*, App nos 60367/08 and 961/11, Judgment of 24 January 2017, para. 34.
606 ibid, para. 34.
607 ibid, para. 36.
608 ibid, para. 79.

The Government's position is summarised as follows:

'In sum, the Government believed that, given the biological, psychological, sociological and other particular features of female offenders, young offenders and offenders aged 65 or over, sentencing them to life imprisonment and their incarceration in harsh conditions would undermine the penological objective of their rehabilitation. Besides, the exception concerned in reality a small number of convicted persons. In Russia, as of 1 November 2011, only 1,802 offenders had been sentenced to life imprisonment. Of the total number of 533,024 prisoners, only 42,511 were female.'[609]

Thus, the Government's arguments in favour of the legislation can be considered two-fold. One line of reasoning is that women and the exempted age groups are particularly vulnerable and thus need special protection. The Government argues that the legislation was designed 'to make up, by legal means, for the naturally vulnerable position' of the social groups that were exempted from life sentences.[610] The second line of argument is that there is statistical data that supports the difference in treatment.[611]

The Court, on the one hand, mentions its own progressive stance where it 'has repeatedly held that differences based on sex require particularly serious reasons by way of justification and that references to traditions, general assumptions or prevailing social attitudes in a particular country cannot, by themselves, be considered to amount to sufficient justification for a difference in treatment, any more than similar stereotypes based on race, origin, colour or sexual orientation'.[612] However, it does not condemn the Russian argument for being based on stereotypes and paternalistic reasoning. The majority simply holds that there is a margin of appreciation awarded to Member States to decide on the appropriateness

---

609 ibid, para. 48.
610 ibid, para. 46.
611 A famous case where arguments were put forth on the basis of statistical evidence is ECtHR, *D.H. and Others v. the Czech Republic*, App no 57325/00, Judgment of 13 November 2017.
612 ECtHR, *Khamtokhu and Aksenchik v. Russia*, App nos 60367/08 and 961/11, Judgment of 24 January 2017, para. 78, with reference to ECtHR, *Konstantin Markin v. Switzerland*, App no 30078/06, Judgment of 22 March 2012, para. 127; ECtHR, *X. and Others v. Austria*, App no 19010/07, Judgment of 19 February 2013, para. 99; ECtHR, *Vallianatos and Others v. Greece*, App nos 29381/09 and 32684/09, Judgment of 7 November 2013, para. 77; ECtHR, *Hämäläinen v. Finland*, App no 37359/09, Judgment of 16 July 2014, para. 109.

of detention schemes.[613] Furthermore, this margin is extended in the case at hand by the absence of a European consensus on life imprisonment.[614] The Court then briefly states that the difference in treatment of female offenders seems justified under 'various European and international instruments addressing the needs of women for protection against gender-based violence, abuse and sexual harassment in the prison environment, as well as the needs for protection of pregnancy and motherhood'.[615] It then points to the statistical data that the Government presented, which show the difference between the total numbers of male and female prisoners and the relatively small number of persons who were sentenced to life imprisonment.[616] The data and the circumstances of the case are then considered by the Court's majority as a sufficient basis for the differential treatment of female offenders to be justified by public interest.[617]

The Court enters a slippery slope in that it accepts the Government's two-fold line of reasoning without addressing the stereotypical and paternalistic undertones of the arguments.[618] The Court can be criticised for two reasons: firstly, for not condemning the stereotypical and paternalistic line of reasoning the Government put forward, and secondly, for accepting the statistical data and the circumstances of the case, which were not really addressed in the instant case by the majority, as a sufficient basis for the difference in treatment.

In terms of simplicity, it is unclear why the penological objective of rehabilitation is not undermined by life imprisonment of men between 18 and 65. The harsh conditions that are mentioned by the Government apply to everyone who is imprisoned. This argument is selective and fails to show why the penological objective of rehabilitation is not jeopardised for all people who are imprisoned for life. This flaw should have been pointed out by the majority. The simplest form of proof that should have been required would have been (for the Government) to demonstrate

---

613 ECtHR, *Khamtokhu and Aksenchik v. Russia*, App nos 60367/08 and 961/11, Judgment of 24 January 2017, para. 78.
614 ibid, para. 79.
615 ibid, para. 82, with reference to paras. 27–30.
616 ibid, para. 82, with reference to para. 48.
617 ibid, para. 82.
618 See also Marion Vannier, 'Caught between a Rock and a Hard Place – Human Rights, Life Imprisonment and Gender Stereotyping: A Critical Analysis of Khamtokhu and Aksenchik v. Russia (2017)' in Sandra Walklate and others (eds), *The Emerald Handbook of Feminism, Criminology and Social Change* (Emerald Publishing Limited 2020).

why the negative repercussions of life imprisonment are that much more pronounced for females and for males of a certain age than for people in general. The factual basis used by the Russian Government to justify the difference in treatment merely consists of references to paternalistic and stereotypical ideas. By not addressing these lines of reasoning, the Court is sending a problematic signal, essentially endorsing these ideas.

The question must also be raised as to the relationship between the numbers that the Government provides regarding males and females imprisoned in Russia and the small number of offenders who have been sentenced to life imprisonment; what is the link between the small number of female prisoners (42,511) versus male prisoners (490,513) and the justification of the law exempting females from life imprisonment? These numbers are quoted 'besides' the stereotypical and paternalistic arguments and their relevance is not sufficiently explained. As is rightly pointed out in the joint partly dissenting opinion by various judges, the statistical data provided concern purely quantitative aspects and 'say nothing about women committing particularly serious crimes'.[619] Moreover, it is pointed out that

'the two main trends illustrated by the above-mentioned statistical data – the disproportionate male/female ratio in the prison population and the low number of convicted offenders sentenced to life imprisonment – are not peculiar to Russia. Indeed the Council of Europe's most recent penal statistics show that these two trends can be observed in all the member States.'[620]

There is a complete lack of engagement with the statistical data by the majority and no investigation as to what the situation is in other European countries. It was even pointed out by the dissenters that '[...] the disproportionate ratio referred to by the Government is actually greater at pan-European level than in Russia'.[621] It is this type of inquiry into the factual arguments that is lacking in the majority's reasoning. The assessment of the statistical data in this joint partly dissenting opinion is what would have been required of the majority.

---

619 ECtHR, *Khamtokhu and Aksenchik v. Russia*, App nos 60367/08 and 961/11, Judgment of 24 January 2017, Joint Partly Dissenting Opinion of Judges Sicilianos, Möse, Lubarda, Mourou-Vikström and Kucksko-Stadlmayer, para. 15.

620 ibid, Joint Partly Dissenting Opinion of Judges Sicilianos, Möse, Lubarda, Mourou-Vikström and Kucksko-Stadlmayer, para. 15.

621 ibid, Joint Partly Dissenting Opinion of Judges Sicilianos, Möse, Lubarda, Mourou-Vikström and Kucksko-Stadlmayer, para. 15.

In her concurring opinion, Judge Turković discusses the danger of levelling down, i.e. of life imprisonment being extended to female and male offenders of all ages. In such situations it may 'be preferable to choose a state in which some are better off and none are worse off than under the best feasible equality'.[622] Although this is a valid point, as Judge Turković and other Judges[623] state in their opinions, the majority must still be criticised for their scant analysis with regard to issues of equality and gender and for neglecting to clearly address the stereotypes that underlie the Russian Government's position.[624]

> '[...] the Court should not refrain from naming different forms of stereotyping and should always assess their invidiousness. It is impossible to change reality without naming it. For this reason, in the present case it should be acknowledged that the respondent State's reasoning regarding the legislation exempting women from life imprisonment portrays women as a naturally vulnerable social group [...] and is therefore one that reflects judicial paternalism.'[625]

Although Judge Turković did vote with the majority due to the issue of levelling down, she pointed out the importance of a broader contextual analysis including the discussion of 'criminological and penological literature on gender and sentencing' as well as of potential remedies for addressing the alleged discrimination.[626] As these reflections indicate, the case of *Khamtokhu and Aksenchik v. Russia* can also be criticised from the perspective of other principles of scientific method, including explanatory power and external validity, and for not conforming to core values of scientific inquiry such as avoiding paternalistic and chauvinist stances. Allowing a Government to draw on gender stereotypes in order to limit life imprisonment for women may be well-meant by the majority; however,

---

622 ibid, Concurring Opinion of Judge Turković, para. 10.

623 See, e.g. ibid, Joint Partly Dissenting Opinion of Judges Sicilianos, Möse, Lubarda, Mourou-Vikström and Kucksko-Stadlmayer, para. 8; Dissenting Opinion of Judg Pinto de Albuquerque, paras. 8–11.

624 ibid, Concurring Opinion of Judge Turković, para. 3; refers to paras. 45–48 of the judgment.

625 ibid, Concurring Opinion of Judge Turković, para. 3.

626 ibid, Concurring Opinion of Judge Turković, para. 3. This lack of discussion of evidence and literature from other disciplines links to the principle of external validity, another principle of scientific method that could be used to criticise this case. For interesting analyses, see e.g. Milica Novaković, 'Men in the Age of (Formal) Equality: The Curious Case of Khamtokhu and Aksenchik' (2019) 67 Belgrade Law Review 216.

this well-intended stance may have 'unintended and perverse consequences for the broader landscape of punishment' and by perpetuating the influence of stereotypical lines of argumentation.[627]

Arguably, the majority could have circumvented the issue of levelling down by focusing on the lack of a factual basis and on pointing to the non-conformity with the principle of simplicity at the core of the Russian Government's reasoning, i.e. that the penological objective of rehabilitation is (likely to be) undermined by life imprisonment in general rather than only by life imprisonment of women and of males younger than 18 and older than 65. There is of course a real risk of levelling down in the sense of the scope of life imprisonment being widened to previously protected groups in Russia. However, it is unclear which price is higher: allowing life sentences to be applied to more people than currently lawful or allowing paternalism and stereotypes to enter judicial reasoning.

iii. Summary and Comment

The three cases above were assessed using the principle of simplicity. The above analysis has shown that in cases where the principle of simplicity plays a role, more is needed in terms of a sufficient factual basis to explain why a more complicated solution or line of reasoning is chosen rather than the simplest one available. The principle of simplicity can help detect flaws in the factual basis of an argument by shining a light on complicated explanations or deviations from 'the usual'. It requires more explanation and a more rigid factual analysis if the explanation or justification for a certain approach seems more complicated rather than simple. For instance, in the case of *Jalloh*, the principle of simplicity sounds an alarm bell as soon as the reasoning differentiates between small-scale drug dealers and large-scale ones. In *Muršić*, an alarm bell goes off where less prison cell space than specified in any standard is used as the norm, and another one sounds where ordinary features that should be in place in all prison facilities to guarantee humane living conditions are adduced to justify extraordinary little cell space. In *Khamtokhu and Aksenchik* the difference in treatment between males between 18 and 65 and females with regard to life imprisonment also rings an alarm bell because the simplest approach would be to treat all people equally with regard to life sentences. Once these alarms go off, the Court should engage in a thorough fact-assessment, analysing

---

627 Vannier (n 618) 274.

whether the arguments in the individual case that do not conform with the principle of simplicity have a sound basis. In a sense, the principle of simplicity can help detect the aspects of an argument that require the Court to conduct a particularly thorough fact-assessment for unusual lines of reasoning.

Ockham's razor has played a role in American law.[628] It has even been discussed, albeit hesitantly, whether Ockham's razor may substitute for the burden of proof and instead require the parties to offer the simplest explanation for the events at hand.[629] In this case, the principle of simplicity would operate as a legal principle, which is not the focus of this study. However, in (the context of) assessing the adequacy of a factual statement and the reliability of an analysis, the principle of simplicity can help detect flaws in the factual arguments presented by the parties and by the Court. It can be used to unify and integrate knowledge rather than create protective caveats for favoured outcomes.

It could be argued that one step in the direction of using the principle of simplicity as a legal principle has already been taken: Judge Pinto de Albuquerque, by referring to it in criticising the majority's line of reasoning in one of his opinions, has contributed to translating this scientific principle into the code of the legal realm (using Luhmann's terms).[630] This could be interpreted as a first step in the communication between the different systems; if judges of the European Court of Human Rights use principles of scientific method as criteria to assess the reliability of a decision, then these principles are produced within the system itself and become operatable in the legal realm. If different judges within the same court disagree on a ruling, irritation occurs within the system, amounting to self-irritation within this system. This self-irritation allows for insights from another system to have an effect on a judicial decision, but in order for that effect to occur, an insight from outside the legal system must be translated into the logic and code of the legal realm.[631] It could be, then, that the process of translation is set in motion by judges in their opinions, and if that is the case, using principles of scientific method and translating them into legal principles may not be that far-fetched after all.

---

628 See Richard Helmholz, 'Ockham's Razor in American Law' (2006) 21 Tulane European and Civil Law Forum 109.

629 ibid 122.

630 See above, II.3.

631 See above, II.3.

b. Explanatory Power and External Validity

i. The Principles

A theory must have sufficient explanatory force to pass as sufficiently scientific. This principle requires that the phenomena under study must be accurately explained by the proposed theory. At the least, this principle requires that the explanation or theory advances understanding.[632] Since Hempel and Oppenheim's 1948 'Studies in the Logic of Explanation',[633] much research has been done on the nature of explanation.[634] In the context of this thesis it suffices to note that in order for an argument with regard to the selection of the relevant facts or the interpretation of the facts to pass the threshold of explanatory power, it must promote inquiry rather than bring it to a halt. Any explanation should make for more understanding and less confusion rather than the other way around.

Wild hypotheses should be abandoned as they can 'undo science'.[635] In order to meet the requirement of explanatory power, the factual under-pinnings for any argument or conclusion must avoid being selective or persuasive, because the danger here is that the conclusion is reached due to the existence of a pre-defined goal that can be reached by considering only the selected factual information and data that leads to the desired conclu-sion.[636] Rather, any argument must be fully disclosed; all the different arguments must be weighed against each other and the reasoning behind reaching a certain conclusion must be transparent and clear.[637]

This principle is highly relevant in the legal context considering the discussion above regarding norms being self-fulfilling prophecies.[638] If we consider norms as having a pre-defined goal that is either 'violation' (appli-cant's perspective) or 'non-violation' (Government's perspective), then the facts can be constructed or selected in order to reach that goal. Thus, it is of pivotal importance to analyse the arguments that are presented in terms of the existence or non-existence of sufficient explanatory power.

---

632 Levit (n 358) 269.
633 Carl G Hempel and Paul Oppenheim, 'Studies in the Logic of Explanation' (1948) 15 Philosophy of Science 135.
634 Jonah N Schupbach and Jan Sprenger, 'The Logic of Explanatory Power' (2011) 78 Philosophy of Science 105.
635 Gauch Jr (n 534) ch 81.
636 Levit (n 358) ch 299.
637 Gauch Jr (n 534) ch 83.
638 II.4.c.

Merely providing selected information that will allow for the preferred legal conclusion will not constitute a reliable solution to a case.

The principle of external validity requires a theory to 'be consistent with the generally accepted body of knowledge, both within its own discipline and in other areas'.[639] Whilst the above-mentioned principles often push for 'more', this principle puts some restraint on new ideas in the sense of a 'healthy scepticism'.[640] The idea behind this scepticism is that positions and arguments must be tested and validated. They must be compatible with conclusions that are reached by other means and in other areas of inquiry. Any idea or theory that is based on (factual) evidence from other disciplines as well will seem more reliable and will more likely be valid.[641] Thus, ideas and arguments must be externally valid, in the sense that they must be tested and validated against existing knowledge, both within the legal discipline and beyond. This principle calls for the promotion of validation, e.g., of facts that are presented by the parties or by third parties, the validation of expert opinions, and validation of reports that are discussed within a case. The question must be asked as to whether the information that is presented provides a sound and reliable basis for the normative conclusion that is drawn.

ii. Case Analysis

Fernandes de Oliveira v. Portugal. The case of *Fernandes de Oliveira v. Portugal* of 31 January 2019 concerns the question of medical negligence with regard to a patient's suicide during voluntary hospitalisation in a Portuguese State psychiatric institution. The question referred to the potential violation of positive obligations under art. 2 of the Convention (right to life) due to the State's duty to protect the lives of voluntary psychiatric patients.[642] What is of interest in the context of this thesis is the scope of facts that can call for positive obligations under art. 2 ECHR.

The applicant in this case was the mother of the patient A.J. who committed suicide on 27 April 2000 during his voluntary hospitalisation in the Sobra Cid Psychiatric Hospital (HSC) in Coimbra, Portugal. A.J.

---

639 Levit (n 358) 270.
640 ibid.
641 ibid.
642 ECtHR, *Fernandes de Oliveira v. Portugal*, App no 78103/14, Judgment of 31 January 2019.

had been hospitalised in the HSC on eight occasions between 1984 and 2000.[643] A.J. was diagnosed with alcohol dependence and several other diagnoses were considered, including 'dependent personality [...]; delirious outbreaks [...]; schizophrenia; manic-depressive psychosis'.[644] All of these symptomologies that were mentioned in A.J.'s medical records were considered by a psychiatrist appointed by the Medical Association in a report as predictive of future suicidal behaviour, thus what happened in this case was not deemed unusual by the appointed psychiatrist.[645]

In the domestic proceedings, the facts were established by the Coimbra Administrative Court as follows:

> 'On 7 January 2010 the court held a hearing at which it adopted a decision concerning the facts. The court considered, inter alia, that it should not explicitly define A.J.'s pathology. Regarding the episode on 25 April 2000, the court decided to view it simply as an abuse of alcohol, taking into account his underlying chronic alcoholism and the fact that the drinking had taken place in the afternoon and mainly at a café.'[646]

The incident on 25 April 2000 that is referred to here took place two days prior to A.J.'s suicide. On this occasion, A.J. had been committed to the emergency services due to an alcohol intoxication episode.[647] Thus, according to the domestic authorities, it was not necessary to explicitly define A.J.'s pathology, and the incident just two days prior to his suicide was not considered a factor that warranted special attention in the assessment of the present case.

The applicant argued that the factual and legal analysis of the court had been wrong, and appealed against the findings.

The Deputy Attorney-General provided an opinion which, inter alia, discussed A.J.'s medical report and the risk of him committing suicide. He recommended that the first-instance judgment should be reversed because it had failed to conduct a proper assessment of the level of monitoring that should have been required in A.J.'s particular case.[648] However, the

---

643 ibid, para. 12.
644 ibid, para. 33.
645 ibid.
646 ibid, para. 37.
647 ibid, para. 33.
648 ibid, para. 42.

Administrative Supreme Court upheld the factual findings of the Coimbra Administrative Court and dismissed the applicant's appeal.[649]

This factual assessment in the domestic proceedings should have been criticised by the ECtHR with regard to its explanatory power and external validity. A.J.'s pathology was a crucial factor regarding the risk of him committing suicide. From the perspective of external validity, the lack of a proper diagnosis of A.J.'s pathology prevented a clear assessment of the level of monitoring that was required from a medical perspective. Furthermore, the reason for not diagnosing A.J. properly was never provided by the domestic authorities, which points to a lack of explanatory power for the fact-assessment conducted in the national proceedings. If this pathology is not defined explicitly, then the factual ground for reaching the normative conclusion is nonexistent. In order for the fact-assessment to be externally valid, there should have been a proper diagnosis in the domestic proceedings. Furthermore, the episode on 25 April, two days prior to the suicide, seems to be of pivotal importance with regard to assessing the stability of A.J.'s condition. If this episode were to be interpreted as reflective of his unstable condition, or even as an attempt to commit suicide, this would have to be taken into account in assessing the risk that A.J. was posing to himself.

The question that is most relevant here is whether there existed a real and imminent risk of A.J. committing suicide, and whether that should have led the hospital staff to monitor A.J. more closely and to follow the 'emergency plan'. Under normal circumstances, the patients were free to move around, and their presence was controlled only during the meal-times.[650] The applicant, A.J.'s mother, argued that this level of monitoring was not sufficient. However, closer monitoring of the patients was only provided for in certain circumstances, and the Government argued that A.J.'s condition had been stable and that he did not fall under the emergency standard.[651] Thus, there was disagreement on whether the authorities ought to have known that A.J. was at risk of committing suicide.

The Court provided a list of relevant factors that are to be taken into account 'to establish whether the authorities knew or ought to have known' there was a real or imminent risk of suicide, triggering a 'duty to take appropriate preventive measures', which include:[652]

---

649 ibid, para. 45.
650 ibid, para. 50.
651 ibid, paras. 40 and 128.
652 ibid, para. 115.

'i) a history of mental health problems [...]
ii) the gravity of the mental condition [...]
iii) previous attempts to commit suicide or self-harm [...]
iv) suicidal thoughts or threats [...]
v) signs of physical or mental distress.'

The disagreement in this case arose with regard to this list: the applicant's argument essentially is that the criteria listed are fulfilled, meaning that the facts match the factors in the list and that thus, the normative conclusion is that the authorities should have taken measures to prevent A.J.'s death. The Government's argument is that the facts of the case do not fulfill the requirements in the list and that, thus, it had no duty to protect A.J. in any special manner. Thus, whether or not the facts are interpreted as fulfilling the requirements in the list will have normative implications.

The majority discusses the points in its list and states that there was agreement among the parties that A.J. had suffered from mental health problems.[653] However, regarding the principles of explanatory power and external validity, the majority too quickly accepts the domestic courts' reasoning with regard to A.J.'s pathology and his behaviour prior to his suicide. The majority accepts the Government's assessment that A.J.'s excessive alcohol consumption just two days before he ended his own life had been due to his addiction to alcohol. There is no sufficient engagement with the applicant's argument and with the statements made by A.J.'s sister . Here, the majority simply follows the Government's line of reasoning without properly engaging with the counterarguments, i.e., that the drinking episode should have been interpreted as indicating that A.J. required a higher level of monitoring, and that a correct assessment of his pathology would have been necessary. There is a lack of explanation as to why the Court did not call into question the domestic authorities' decision not clearly define A.J.'s pathology.[654] This can also be criticised from the perspective of external validity, in the sense that A.J.'s pathology was not validated using the body of medical or psychological knowledge.

One point that should be emphasised is point iii) concerning previous attempts to commit suicide. Here, the majority pointed to the case *Renolde v. France.*[655] What the majority fails to point out is that in *Renolde*, the

---

653 ibid, para. 127.

654 ibid, para. 128 and para. 50 of Judge Pinto de Albuquerque joined by Judge Harutyunyan's Opinion.

655 ECtHR, *Renolde v. France*, App no 5608/05, Judgment of 16 October 2008, para. 85.

person had already attempted suicide 18 days prior to the suicide attempt in question. In the case of A.J., the time lapse had been 26 days.[656] The majority does not address the question as to how many days need to have passed since a previous suicide attempt, for special protective measures to be allowed to cease, and why the case of *Fernandes de Oliveira* is treated differently from the case of *Renolde*, where a duty to take measures had been accepted.[657] In terms of external validity and explanatory power, for this case as well as for the purpose of clarification for potential future cases, it should have been explained why these two cases were treated differently, and evidence from psychology or medical science should have been discussed with regard to this time lapse, providing external validity for using a certain amount of days as a threshold requirement.[658]

The domestic proceedings were not conducted thoroughly, yet the ECtHR accepted most of the factual assessments from the domestic proceedings without validating them properly or engaging with the factual accounts made by the applicant. There is a complete lack of explanatory power, and it seems that the majority simply followed the domestic court's assessment. Of course, sometimes domestic authorities are better placed than the ECtHR to assess the facts of a case; however, if the facts of a case are disputed, the ECtHR cannot simply state that it finds no reason for deviating from the fact-assessment conducted in the national proceedings. The ECtHR ought to validate the statements and conduct its own inquiry, by weighing the different arguments against each other, not by easily dismissing one side of the argument. This is also pointed out by Judge Pinto de Albuquerque as a Catch-22 issue: the lack of adequate assessment of the facts, and the lack of a correct diagnosis of A.J. by the State in particular, cannot be used as an excuse for the State to not foresee the risk of suicide. In other words, the State cannot use 'its own faulty omission to excuse itself for the resulting harm'.[659]

---

656 This can also be criticised from the perspective of falsifiability with regard to vague concepts and definitions.

657 ECtHR, *Renolde v. France*, App no 5608/05, Judgment of 16 October 2008, para. 86; see also ECtHR, *Fernandes de Oliveira v. Portugal*, App no 78103/14, Judgment of 31 January 2019, Partly Concurring, Partly Dissenting Opinion of Judge Pinto de Albuquerque joined by Judge Harutyunyan, para. 22.

658 This also links closely to the *Muršić* case with regard to using certain figures as the basis for a normative conclusion.

659 ECtHR, *Fernandes de Oliveira v. Portugal*, App no 78103/14, Judgment of 31 January 2019, Partly Concurring, Partly Dissenting Opinion of Judge Pinto de Albuquerque joined by Judge Harutyunyan, para. 24.

In this case, the Court missed the mark with regard to the external validity of its fact-assessment because it failed to validate the factual arguments provided by the Government. It did not engage with the applicant's point of view but rather accepted the facts as provided by the domestic courts. As a result, there is a lack of explanatory power in the reasoning that led to the conclusion, which seems to have been a pre-defined goal.

N. v. the United Kingdom. The case of *N. v. the UK* of 27 May 2008 concerns the forced return of a Ugandan woman who was HIV positive to her country of origin.[660] The Court has been criticised, by academic commentators and by members of the Court in their opinions, for this decision, and has been seen as being complicit in sending severely ill people 'toward their (near) certain death in unacceptable circumstances'.[661]

The applicant, N., arrived in the UK in 1998. She was seriously ill and was admitted to hospital where she received the diagnosis of being HIV positive with 'considerable immunosuppression and [...] disseminated mycobacterium TB'.[662] A few days later, solicitors submitted an asylum application on N.'s behalf, claiming that she had faced ill-treatment and that on returning to Uganda her life would be in danger.[663] While her application was pending, N. developed a second Aids-related illness, Kaposi's sarcoma. This resulted in her CD4 count being extremely low (hers was down to 10, that of healthy people is above 500). Under treatment with antiretroviral drugs and frequent monitoring, her condition stabilised. By the time the House of Lords began to examine her case, her CD4 count was at 414.[664] The applicant's solicitor requested an expert report by a consultant physician, which stated that without regular antiretroviral treatment and frequent monitoring for the correct use and combination of drugs, the CD4 count could again drop rapidly and N.'s life expectancy would be less than a year. The medications that N. needed would be available in her hometown, Masaka, but only at considerable cost and in limited supply. It

---

660 ECtHR, *N. v. the United Kingdom*, App no 26565/05, Judgment of 27 May 2008.

661 Eva Brems, 'Moving Away from N v UK – Interesting Tracks in a Dissenting Opinion (Tatar v Switzerland)' (*Strasbourg Observers*) <https://strasbourgobserver s.com/2015/05/04/moving-away-from-n-v-uk-interesting-tracks-in-a-dissenting-o pinion-tatar-v-switzerland/>. See also Serge Slama and Karine Parrot, 'Étrangers Malades: L'Attitude de Ponce Pilate de La Cour Européenne Des Droits de L'Homme' (2014) 101 Plein Droit I.

662 ECtHR, *N. v. the United Kingdom*, App no 26565/05, Judgment of 27 May 2008, para. 9.

663 ibid, para. 10.

664 ibid, para. 11.

was also pointed out in the report that 'in Uganda there was no provision for publicly funded blood monitoring, basic nursing care, social security, food or housing'.[665]

The domestic proceedings ended in 2005, with the House of Lords unanimously dismissing N.'s complaint.[666] N. appealed to the ECtHR and claimed that if she were forced to return to Uganda, she would not have sufficient access to the medical treatment she needed for her illness, and that this would result in her rights under art. 3 and art. 8 of the Convention being violated.[667]

The case of *N. v. the UK* is interesting from the perspective of external validity because it can be debated whether the factual conclusion reached by the ECtHR conforms with the body of knowledge available regarding the medical treatment that N. would require and the actual situation in Uganda. It is a case where a factual situation regarding the medical condition of an applicant and the availability of health care may lead to an inclusion under the scope of art. 3 ECHR.

The factual analysis in *N. v. the UK* that was conducted by the ECtHR includes certain positive aspects, but it is also flawed. In terms of the principles of explanatory power and external validity, it is commendable that the ECtHR, in this case, gathered information on the situation with regard to the medical treatment of HIV/Aids patients in the UK and in Uganda *proprio motu*. This was also something that one Lord had asked for in the domestic proceedings in the UK. He argued that more information should have been sought in the domestic proceedings because in his opinion it was not possible to clearly state that art. 3 ECHR was not applicable, given that N. would face a completely different situation with regard to a health support system in Uganda as opposed to the treatment she was receiving in the UK.[668] Furthermore, the information that was presented in the domestic proceedings in the expert report by N.'s doctor showed that N.'s medical condition was stable only as long as N. received the

---

665 ibid, para. 12.
666 ibid, para. 16.
667 ibid, para. 20.
668 Lord Justice Carnwath had dissented because he 'was unable to say that the facts of the case were so clear that the only reasonable conclusion was that Article 3 did not apply. Given the stark contrast between the applicant's position in the United Kingdom and the practical certainty of a dramatically reduced life expectancy if returned to Uganda with no effective family support, he would have remitted the case to the fact-finding body in the case, the Immigration Appeal Tribunal.' ibid, para. 16.

necessary drugs and monitoring via the so called HAART (highly active antiretroviral medication treatment). Without this treatment, the doctor held that N.'s prognosis would be 'appalling'. The doctor's report was summarised by one Lord as follows:

> 'she will suffer ill health, discomfort, pain and death within a year or two. [...] The cruel reality is that if the [applicant] returns to Uganda her ability to obtain the necessary medication is problematic. So if she returns to Uganda and cannot obtain the medical assistance she needs to keep her illness under control, her position will be similar to having a life-support machine turned off.'[669]

Thus, without the treatment and necessary monitoring (i.e. availability of regular blood monitoring and of doctors who can closely and regularly monitor N.'s health), N. would not survive her illness. Deciding whether or not sending N. back to her hometown would amount to inhumane or degrading treatment under art. 3 ECHR involves determining the medical situation (i.e. the external validity with regard to medical knowledge) that she would find upon her arrival and whether the required treatment and monitoring were available.

The ECtHR did gather more information on the HAART treatment and referred to reports and research which had been conducted by the World Health Organization (WHO) and the Joint United Nations Programme on HIV/Aids (UNAIDS) in the judgment.[670] However, what is problematic is that neither the information from the WHO and UNAIDS reports nor the medical information with regard to the HAART treatment are engaged with in a thorough manner. The ECtHR only refers to this information in one paragraph:

> 'According to information collated by WHO [...], antiretroviral medication is available in Uganda, although through lack of resources it is received by only half of those in need. The applicant claims that she would be unable to afford the treatment and that it would not be available to her in the rural area from which she comes. It appears that she has family members in Uganda, although she claims that they would not be willing or able to care for her if she were seriously ill.'[671]

---

669   ibid, para. 17.
670   ibid, paras. 18–19.
671   ibid, para. 48.

The Court continues by stating that N. was, at the time of the decision, not critically ill and that the rapidity in which her condition would deteriorate and the extent to which she would be able to obtain medical treatment and support, including from relatives, 'must involve a certain degree of speculation, particularly in view of the constantly evolving situation as regards the treatment of HIV and Aids worldwide'.[672] There is no further information or explanation as to what is meant by 'a certain degree of speculation'. Thus, although information was gathered, which can be interpreted as an attempt to externally validate the argument with regard to the medical situation in Uganda, there is a lack of engagement with this information. It is not explained why and regarding which particular circumstance a 'degree of speculation' must be involved.[673]

N. in her factual arguments shows that her individual case and the medical context that she would be moved back into in her hometown Masaka would amount to the exceptional circumstances that are required in the Court's case-law for critically ill people to have rights derived from art. 3 ECHR.[674] This shows again how facts and law are intertwined: the scope of art. 3 may be broadened by factual circumstances that arrive. For instance, the question of whether and under what circumstances critically ill people may have rights under art. 3 ECHR is only a question if critical illnesses (factually) exist and if the way people with such illnesses are treated can be seen as inhuman or degrading treatment by a country.

In *D. v. the UK*,[675] which is discussed in the *N. v. the UK* judgment, the applicant, who was at the time of his application suffering from an advanced stage of Aids and appeared the be 'close to death', had been deemed to fall under the 'exceptional circumstances' protection of art. 3 ECHR and could not be expelled from the UK.[676] Since that judgment, the Court has never again found a removal of an alien to amount to a violation of art. 3 ECHR on grounds of a serious illness.[677] The determining factors in *D. v. the UK* that led the Court to find that sending D. to his country

---

672 ibid, para. 50.

673 Vague phrases and notions such as 'degree of speculation' can also be criticised from the perspective of falsifiability, discussed below.

674 As was the case in ECtHR, *D. v. the United Kingdom*, App no 30240/96, Judgment of 2 May 1997.

675 ECtHR, *D. v. the United Kingdom*, App no 30240/96, Judgment of 2 May 1997, paras. 53–54.

676 ECtHR, *N. v. the United Kingdom*, App no 26565/05, Judgment of 27 May 2008, para. 33.

677 ibid, para. 34. See also Brems (n 661).

of origin would amount to inhuman and degrading treatment were that he was 'in the final stages of a terminal illness, Aids, and had no prospect of medical care or family support on expulsion to St Kitts'.[678] Other cases had been dismissed because, e.g., the applicant had family support upon return[679] or the illness was not terminal.[680] However, in the case of N., the particularity of the situation with regard to available medical treatment in her rural hometown of Masaka was not taken into account; N.'s claim of not having any family who would support her was not taken seriously either. All of these points were subsumed by the ECtHR under the necessary 'degree of speculation' without providing an explanation as to why a degree of speculation is warranted given the accounts provided by the WHO, UNAIDS, and the applicant herself. The lack of engagement with this body of knowledge is problematic from the perspective of external validity. In their joint dissenting opinion, Judges Tulkens, Bonello, and Spielmann pointed out that the majority should have found a case of potential violation of art. 3 ECHR 'precisely because there are substantial grounds to believe that the applicant faces a real risk of prohibited treatment in the country of proposed removal'.[681] Furthermore, they pointed to there being 'no doubt that in the event of removal to Uganda the applicant will face an early death after a period of acute physical and mental suffering' and that this certainty was also acknowledged almost unanimously by the judicial authorities in the UK.[682] The opinion thus rightly points to the limited area in which there is any room for any degree of speculation left. The approach by the ECtHR of employing a degree of speculation is misplaced under the principle of external validity.

Thus, the main issue here is that although information was sought, it was not engaged with, and N.'s individual factual context was not taken into account properly. It seems here that the fear that Lord Hope

---

678 ECtHR, *N. v. the United Kingdom*, App no 26565/05, Judgment of 27 May 2008, para. 38; with a reference to ECtHR, *D. v. the United Kingdom*, App no 30240/96, Judgment of 2 May 1997, para. 40.

679 See, e.g. *Arcila Henao v. the Netherlands*, App no 13669/03, Judgment of 24 June 2003.

680 See, e.g. *Bensaid v. the United Kingdom*, App no 44599/98, Judgment of 6 February 2001 and *Amegnigan v. the Netherlands*, App no 25629/04, Judgment of 25 November 2004.

681 ECtHR, *N. v. the United Kingdom*, App no 26565/05, Judgment of 27 May 2008, Joint Dissenting Opinion of Judges Tulkens, Bonello and Speilmann, para. 22.

682 ibid, Joint Dissenting Opinion of Judges Tulkens, Bonello and Speilmann, para. 23.

expressed in the domestic proceedings regarding the UK being 'flooded' with HIV-related asylum applications was weighed more heavily than N.'s dire medical situation. Lord Hope had observed:

> '[Any extension of the principles in D. v. the United Kingdom] would have the effect of affording all those in the [applicant's] condition a right of asylum in this country until such time as the standard of medical facilities available in their home countries for the treatment of HIV/Aids had reached that which is available in Europe. It would risk drawing into the United Kingdom large numbers of people already suffering from HIV in the hope that they too could remain here indefinitely so that they could take the benefit of the medical resources that are available in this country. [...]'[683]

The majority does balance the applicant's suffering against the financial burden that a State would have to carry with regard to health care costs.[684] While it may be considered as commendable that the majority is transparent (i.e. adding to the explanatory power of its own approach) in revealing 'the real reasons behind their finding of non-violation', this line of reasoning runs counter to the absolute nature of art. 3.[685] The dissenters criticise the majority for implicitly accepting the allegation that finding a breach of art. 3 ECHR in the present case 'would open up the floodgates to medical immigration and make Europe vulnerable to becoming the "sickbay" of the world'.[686] They state that a comparison of the total number of requests to the number of HIV cases according to 'the Court's Rule 39 statistics

---

683 ECtHR, *N. v. the United Kingdom*, App no 26565/05, Judgment of 27 May 2008, para. 17.

684 ibid, para. 44: '[...] Advances in medical science, together with social and economic differences between countries, entail that the level of treatment available in the Contracting State and the country of origin may vary considerably. While it is necessary, given the fundamental importance of Article 3 in the Convention system, for the Court to retain a degree of flexibility to prevent expulsion in very exceptional cases, Article 3 does not place an obligation on the Contracting State to alleviate such disparities through the provision of free and unlimited health care to all aliens without a right to stay within its jurisdiction. A finding to the contrary would place too great a burden on the Contracting States.'

685 Eva Brems, 'Thank You, Justice Tulkens: A Comment on the Dissent in N v UK' (*Strasbourg Observers*) <https://strasbourgobservers.com/2012/08/14/thank-you-justice-tulkens-a-comment-on-the-dissent-in-n-v-uk/#more-1685>.

686 ECtHR, *N. v. the United Kingdom*, App no 26565/05, Judgment of 27 May 2008, Joint Dissenting Opinion of Judges Tulkens, Bonello and Speilmann, para. 8.

concerning the United Kingdom' shows this argument to be 'totally mis-conceived'.[687]

Clarity (in the form of explanatory power) as to which factual situation amounts to the standard of 'exceptional circumstances' is required. This was also asked for by the intervening party, the NGO Helsinki Founda-tion. Essentially what they are asking for is a clarification of which factual circumstances will fall under the ambit of art. 3 ECHR. This must be a standard that is externally valid in the sense that it conforms with knowl-edge regarding the medical treatment required for the individual person and the availability of that medical treatment in the country of origin. The argument of speculation that the ECtHR uses is entirely misplaced in this context because the information provided by the WHO and UNAIDS, the information provided by the doctor in the domestic proceedings, and the account provided by N., which was not proven to be wrong, all point to the certainty of the critical situation that N. would face upon return.[688]

What can be drawn from this case is that although it is necessary for concepts to be indeterminate to some extent in order to allow different but similar factual circumstances to be subsumable under a provision, it is all the more necessary for the factual analysis to be conducted thoroughly and for the factual conclusion that is reached to take into account and en-gage with all the relevant information that is available; the fact-assessment procedure must validate the arguments presented and explain why the Court chose to follow one account rather than the other. In this case, it seems that the concept of employing a 'degree of speculation' was used to avoid a proper explanation of the Court's own account of the facts. The argument of speculation is misplaced here because the knowledge and information provided by the WHO and UNAIDS reports and by the appli-cant's account of her rural hometown do not allow for any speculation. It seems to be used solely for the purpose of preventing the opening of the 'floodgates to medical immigration' to Europe. In terms of explanatory power, it seems that a pre-defined goal, i.e. non-violation of art. 3 ECHR, was aimed at, and in order to reach this pre-defined goal, the body of knowledge available from the reports and the applicant's account was subsumed under the idea of there being a necessary 'degree of speculation' for the case at hand. However, this body of knowledge does not allow

---

687 ibid.
688 Vague concepts like these can also be criticised in terms of falsifiability, which will be discussed below.

for much speculation and there is, thus, a lack of external validity for the Court's conclusion.

Garib v. the Netherlands. The case of *Garib v. the Netherlands* of 6 November 2017 concerns the refusal of a housing permit to the applicant, a single mother who was dependent on social-security benefits. Legislation in Rotterdam imposed a minimum income requirement for receiving a permit to live in certain hotspot areas, which the applicant did not fulfil.[689] In the critical words of Judge Pinto de Albuquerque, joined in his dissenting opinion by Judge Vehabović, the refusal was based on legislation which 'introduced a policy of urban gentrification' to promote 'deghettoisation'.[690] The Grand Chamber held by twelve votes to five that the applicant's right to freely choose her residence under art. 2 of Protocol No. 4 ECHR was not violated in this case.[691] A second complaint which the applicant submitted before the Grand Chamber pointed to the discriminatory nature of the legislation under art. 14 ECHR. In the Grand Chamber's opinion, the complaint based on art. 14 ECHR was 'a new one, made for the first time before the Grand Chamber', and therefore, the Court could not 'now consider it'.[692]

The table of contents at the beginning of this judgment reflects a long list of facts, including 'I. The Circumstances of the Case', 'II. Relevant Domestic Law', and 'III. Other Facts' – which include evaluation reports on the designated areas in Rotterdam, legislative developments, and subsequent events concerning the applicant –, 'IV. Drafting History of Article 2 of Protocol No. 4', 'Practice Elsewhere', and 'Relevant International Law'.[693] In cases where so many facts are listed, it is important to reflect on how/where the focus is set and whether the Court aimed at incorporating different perspectives on the issue at hand or whether information was gathered in order to allow a pre-defined conclusion to be reached. The principle of explanatory power requires the Court not to be selective or

---

689 ECtHR, *Garib v. the Netherlands*, App no 43494/09, Judgment of 6 November 2017, paras. 9–12.

690 ECtHR, *Garib v. the Netherlands*, App no 43494/09, Judgment of 6 November 2017, Dissenting Opinion of Judge Pinto de Albuquerque, joined by Judge Vehabović, para. 4.

691 ibid, para. 167.

692 ibid, paras. 95 and 102. This aspect of the case will be further discussed below in the summary and comments. See also the discussion above with the Court being 'master of characterisation to be given in law to the facts of a case', at II.4.c

693 ibid, table of contents.

persuasive in its collection of information because the danger in such an approach is that only that information is gathered and reproduced which allows a pre-defined conclusion to be reached.[694] Rather, the different positions must be weighed against each other and the conclusion for allowing one side of an argument to win over the other must be fully disclosed.[695]

From the perspective of explanatory power, the Grand Chamber judgment can be criticised for different reasons, inter alia, what other authors have criticised as a practice of 'cherry-picking'.[696]

For example, reading the title 'Practice Elsewhere' raises hopes that the Court takes into account various other countries' practices with regard to housing legislation and provides examples that are similar to the policies in Rotterdam as well as examples of different approaches, and then engages with this information, allowing conclusions to be reached with regard to the case at hand. However, the relevant paragraphs only discuss the Social Housing Act in Denmark.[697] This legislation actually is very different from the legislation in Rotterdam, but this fact is not pointed out by the Grand Chamber and there is no explanation of what implications can be drawn from the Danish legislation with regard to the one in Rotterdam. There is no discussion of other countries than Denmark. As Judges Pinto de Albuquerque and Vehabović point out in their dissenting opinion, '[i]n Denmark, the restrictions applicable to "residents out of work" concern only candidates for social housing. That has nothing to do with the applicant's situation in the present case. The specialised literature confirms the uniqueness of the Dutch legislation'.[698] The policy in question in *Garib* is, thus, not reflective of a European consensus or common practice, which is a reason for restricting the margin of appreciation of the Member State in question; however, this point is not touched upon by the Grand Chamber.[699] The lack of a European consensus on the matter can be translated into scientific terminology a implying a lack of external validity for the Dutch position. In such a situation, the margin of appreciation should be narrower and the Court should reflect on whether the Government's position, which is not externally valid, is justified. For instance, the Court

---

694 Levit (n 358) ch 299.
695 Gauch Jr (n 534) ch 83.
696 David and Ganty (n 526). Last accessed on 12 July 2021.
697 ECtHR, *Garib v. the Netherlands*, App no 43494/09, Judgment of 6 November 2017, paras. 87–92.
698 ibid, Dissenting Opinion of Judge Pinto de Albuquerque joined by Judge Vehabović, para. 20, n 43.
699 David and Ganty (n 526).

could have assessed the Government's position in the same manner as the dissenting judges did, by reflecting on the various reports and positions included in the judgment that discuss the legislation, by consulting literature about the Dutch legislation in question, and by contextualising these arguments with other housing legislation.[700] The reports and the literature that are pointed to by dissenting judges show that there is a problem with regard to the external validity of the Government's position, which could have been addressed by the majority using a narrow margin of appreciation based on the non-existence of a European consensus. As Judge Pinto de Albuquerque states, the majority simply ignored the concerns raised by a number of international bodies with regard to the Dutch housing policy.[701]

Another issue in the Grand Chamber's judgment concerning the principle of external validity is the question that was raised by the applicant and by third-party interveners regarding vulnerability. Whether or not an applicant is considered vulnerable (factually) has implications on a normative level in terms of special protection and a narrowing of the margin of appreciation of a Member State.[702] Thus, a correct assessment of the applicant's factual situation would have been necessary in order to assess whether or not she should be deemed 'vulnerable'. The Grand Chamber did not address this question at any point in the judgment. The lack of external validity with regard to the body of knowledge within the ECtHR's own case-law was pointed out by Judges Tsotsoria and de Gaetano. They argue that the applicant's situation should have been discussed with a view of whether or not her situation fell under the ECtHR's case-law regarding 'disproportionate burdens'.[703] This case shows that the Court has the power to form rules; the facts of a case can be interpreted as falling under a normative standard that has been created via case-law, and thus receive a normative colouring, due to the assessment of whether a factual situation matches the normatively coloured idea of, e.g., 'disproportionate burdens'.

The case of *Garib* raises questions regarding the thoroughness of the majority's fact-assessment procedure. It seems here that the majority pursued

---

700 ibid, Dissenting Opinion of Judge Pinto de Albuquerque joined by Judge Vehabović, e.g. n 4 and 5, and paras. 24–30.
701 ibid, Dissenting Opinion of Judge Pinto de Albuquerque joined by Judge Vehabović, para. 28.
702 See, e.g., ECtHR, *Alajos Kiss v. Hungary*, App no 38832/06, Judgment of 20 May 2010, para. 42.
703 ECtHR, *Garib v. the Netherlands*, App no 43494/09, Judgment of 6 November 2017, joint Dissenting Opinion of Judges Tsotsoria and de Gaetano, para. 3.

a pre-defined goal and cherry-picked the facts that allowed for that conclusion to be reached. Such selectiveness runs counter to the principle of explanatory power. Moreover, the Dutch legislation differed from policies in other European countries and runs counter to recommendations by human-rights bodies. This lack of external validity should have impacted the Court's reflections regarding the margin of appreciation granted to the Government.

iii. Summary and Comment

The three cases discussed in light of the principles of explanatory power and external validity all link to an underlying issue in the domestic fact-assessment procedures that were not addressed by the Court. In *Garib*, the factual situation regarding housing policies in the Netherlands (e.g., as opposed to other European countries) and the applicant's claim regarding her vulnerability were not considered properly. In *Fernandes de Oliveira*, the assessment of the patient's medical condition and a clear diagnosis were missing, and in *N. v. the UK*, the assessment of the applicant's medical condition and the specific possibilities for treatment in the place she was being sent to were not assessed properly. A thorough assessment and external validation of a person's vulnerability, of the existence or non-existence of a European consensus and the broad or narrow margin of appreciation this implies, of the existence and correct determination of pathologies, and of the medical situation in a specific place is pivotal to the outcome of a case: if the facts reflect that there is a vulnerability in a given case, this will influence the normative conclusion that is drawn; similarly, the medical assessment will influence the normative implications with regard to a duty to implement protective measures; and lastly, whether or not the hospital and the staff in the applicant's hometown can provide the necessary treatment is pivotal to answering on a normative level whether the refoulement of a person can be deemed a non-violation of the Convention. The answer as to whether there exists a European consensus on a matter, or whether someone is deemed vulnerable or deemed to fall under a specific diagnosis, is usually not a clear-cut yes or no. Any answer that is provided must have explanatory power and show why the conclusion was reached and what data this conclusion is based on.

The principles of explanatory power and external validity require the ECtHR to be transparent in its factual assessments. The facts of a case can be interpreted differently on a normative level; however, the reasons for choosing one factual conclusion over another must be made clear, the Court ought to properly explain how it interprets the facts and which normative conclusions it derives from the factual basis. Here, Dewey can again be quoted with regard to the use of scientific method: 'the consequences of adopting a particular solution must be thought through':[704] the reasons for not deeming Ms. Garib to be in a vulnerable position must be explained; the reasons for not considering it important for A.J. to be properly diagnosed by the domestic authorities must be explained; and the reasons for considering health care provision in Masaka sufficient despite the reports and information provided by the doctor in the domestic proceedings and by the applicant herself pointing to another conclusion must be explained. Furthermore, because answering any of these questions requires knowledge from other fields, the conclusion reached must also conform with the body of knowledge in the areas that are of concern in a specific case.

The principles of explanatory power and external validity are also relevant to the relationship between the domestic proceedings and the proceedings before the ECtHR. As shown in Part I, although it is the responsibility of the parties to a case to substantiate their claims, it is up to the Court to assess the facts.[705] Art. 38 ECHR provides the Court with the competence of examining the case with the representatives of the parties and with the power to conduct its own investigation if the need arises.[706] Due to the subsidiary nature of the ECtHR's fact-assessment, the Court is usually reluctant to depart from the national authorities' fact-assessment. It was held in *Sadkov v. Ukraine* that the Court would only depart from the domestic authorities' fact-assessment if this were 'unavoidable by the circumstances of the case'.[707] It is unclear what exactly is meant by this formulation; however, Judge Pinto de Albuquerque and Judge Sajó pointed out in their dissenting opinion in the case of *Correia de Matos v. Portugal*[708] that the Court should not employ the concept of considering the national authorities 'better placed' as a 'carte blanche to rubber-stamp any policy adopted or decision taken by national authorities'.[709] In other

---

704 See above, II.2.b.

705 I.6.c.

706 Art. 38 ECHR.

707 ECtHR, *Sadkov v. Ukraine*, App no 21987/05, Judgment of 6 July 2017, para. 90.

708 See also above, I.6.d.

709 ECtHR, *Correia de Matos v. Portugal*, App no 54602/12, Judgment of 4 May 2018, Dissenting Opinion of Judge Pinto de Albuquerque, joined by Judge Sajó, para. 7.

words, although the national authorities will be better placed in some cases to conduct the fact-assessment, this does not alleviate the Court from cohering with the principles of explanatory power and external validity with regard to why it considers the domestic authorities better placed. In all three cases discussed in this section, the fact-assessment in the domestic procedures were flawed in some way or another, and the Court failed to point out and address those flaws. These are cases where the Court can be criticised for using the loophole of subsidiary fact-assessment as a 'carte blanche to rubber-stamp any policy adopted or decision taken by national authorities'.[710] The approach taken by a Portuguese State psychiatric institution, the Dutch housing law, and the UK's asylum policy were all rubber-stamped.

c. Falsifiability

i. The Principle

This Popperian[711] requirement means that 'theories must be testable and refutable'.[712] Non-falsifiable theories and hypotheses are considered unscientific and of no value.[713] For instance, a hypothesis regarding supernatural beings that avoids testability is unscientific, as are vague theories, theories that try to explain everything, and theories that are unconditional.[714] Falsifiability is considered a key feature of science because without testing explanations and rejecting those that do not pass the test, there can be no progress in scientific activity.[715]

Levit holds that the criterion of falsifiability entails that definitions must be explicit and unambiguous. Terms that are vague and self-protected do not fulfill the requirement of falsifiability. The example she discussed in

---

710 ECtHR, *Correia de Matos v. Portugal*, App no 54602/12, Judgment of 4 May 2018, Dissenting Opinion of Judge Pinto de Albuquerque, joined by Judge Sajó, para. 7.
711 Karl Popper, *The Logic of Scientific Discovery* (Hutchinson & Co 1959) ch iv.
712 Levit (n 358) 271.
713 Michael BW Sinclair, 'The Use of Evolution Theory in Law' (1987) 64 University of Detroit Law Review 451, 471.
714 Levit (n 358) 271.
715 Jonathan Potter, 'Testability, Flexibility: Kuhnian Values in Scientists' Discourse Concerning Theory Choice' (1984) 14 Philosophy of the Social Sciences 303, 309.

her analysis is the definition of pornography in the Indiana anti-pornography ordinance of 1984, which includes vague terms such as 'who enjoy [...] humiliation; [...] presented in scenarios of degradation; [...] shown [...] as inferior; [...] presented [...] for [...] conquest [...] through postures or positions of servility or submission or display'.[716]

A search of the ECtHR's case-law database HUDOC revealed references to the principle of falsifiability in three judgments. The reference was never made in the majority ruling, it was only used by judges of the ECtHR in their opinions. The earliest reference was made by Judge Zupančič in his concurring opinion in the case of *Kyprianou v. Cyprus*, which concerned impartiality.[717] In his opinion, he points to the differences and similarities between legal and scientific procedure and that a legitimate result can only be reached if the correct procedure is followed. In scientific experiments, falsifiability ensures the correctness of a procedure in the sense that there must exist a possibility to disprove a hypothesis, otherwise the hypothesis cannot be deemed correct.

> 'In legal matters, because it is impossible to ascertain a past historical event, the so-called "truth" can easily, as it did in witch trials, become a self-referential and non-falsifiable myth.'[718]

According to Zupančič, in law, it is a fair trial that ensures the correctness of an outcome of a case, rather than its falsifiability, because in his opinion, law contends with historical events and these 'cannot be experimentally tested as to their objective veracity.[719] However, in the Chamber judgment of *J.K. and Others v. Sweden* of 4 June 2015,[720] it was again Judge Zupančič who referred to the principle of falsifiability. His partly dissenting opinion links closely to his opinion in the *Kyprianou* case. He again states that legal judgments about historical events are not falsifiable because, 'with rare exceptions', they 'are not adapted to the negative feedback from reality'.[721] However, he develops his position further in this

---

716 Levit (n 358) 302.

717 ECtHR, *Kyprianou v. Cyprus*, App no 73797/01, Judgment of 15 December 2005, Concurring Opinion of Judge Zupančič.

718 ibid.

719 ibid.

720 ECtHR, *J.K. and Others v. Sweden*, App no 59166/23, Judgment of 4 June 2015. (The case was referred to the Grand Chamber which delivered the judgment on 23 August 2016.)

721 ECtHR, *J.K. and Others v. Sweden*, App no 59166/23, Judgment of 4 June 2015, Partly Dissenting Opinion of Judge Zupančič.

opinion, and states that this does not hold true for predictions with regard to what will happen to a person upon refoulement to their country of origin.

> 'Such judgments *are* falsifiable. The person so expelled, extradited or returned in fact will, or will not, suffer the consequences this Court had speculated about. The question remains whether this Court will ever be apprised of them (most likely not). Here, as opposed to most other legal cases, the negative feedback would be made available only if there was a legal instrument in place enabling the Court to verify the consequences of its conjecture concerning the future events.'[722]

The third reference to falsifiability was made in the case of *Nicolae Virgiliu Tănase v. Romania*, by Judge Kūris, who links the Court's departure from its existing case-law to the idea of falsifiability.

> 'Whenever the Grand Chamber endeavours [...] to depart from part of its existing case-law as "incorrect", it should measure twice, thrice, fourfold. [...] There may also be a number of other requirements, but the one mentioned here is a *conditio sine qua non* for not disqualifying the Grand Chamber's own conclusions – not as regards their legally binding character (because whatever the Grand Chamber rules cannot be overruled, except by the Grand Chamber itself), but as regards their falsifiability and reliability.'[723]

Thus, Judge Kūris suggests that the Court should depart from its own case-law only after testing the departure from current practice over and over again; any departure should be tested, so as to allow for falsification, before it is completed. Whether and how this idea is operable seems questionable. Falsifiability means that falsification must be possible. However, if something is actually falsified, it means that this has actually happened, that it has therefore been found to be 'incorrect'. And if that has occurred, one will hardly want to implement the deviation.

---

722 ibid.
723 ECtHR, *Nicolae Virgiliu Tănase v. Romania*, App no 41720/13, Judgment of 25 June 2019, Partly Dissenting Opinion of Judge Kūris, para. 11.

ii. Case Analysis

S.M. v. Croatia. The case of *S.M. v. Croatia* concerns the complaint of a young woman, S.M., against a young man, T.M., regarding human trafficking and forced prostitution. It was the Grand Chamber's first art. 4 ECHR-judgment concerning inter-personal harm and is part of the 'definitional quagmire' with regard to questions surrounding human trafficking and forced prostitution and how these notions relate to the prohibition of slavery and forced labour under art. 4 ECHR.[724]

As mentioned above, Levit criticised a US law that included a vague and self-protected definition of pornography as not fulfilling the principle of falsifiability, which 'requires an explicit, unambiguous definition'.[725] The same criticism can be raised with regard to the unclear scope of art. 4 ECHR (prohibition of slavery and forced labour) regarding questions of human trafficking and forced prostitution, which has led to confusion in various judgments as to which facts actually fit under the scope of this Convention article. The confusion started in the judgment of *Rantsev v. Cyprus and Russia*,[726] where the Court placed 'human trafficking' as defined under art. 3(a) of the Palermo Protocol[727] and art. 4(a) of the Council of Europe's Anti-Trafficking Convention[728] under the scope of art. 4 ECHR but did not clarify why exactly the facts of the specific case were considered 'human trafficking' and how vague terms such as 'sexual exploitation' and 'exploitation of the prostitution of others' should be

---

724 Vladislava Stoyanova, 'The Grand Chamber Judgment in S.M. v Croatia: Human Trafficking, Prostitution and the Definitional Scope of Article 4 ECHR' (*Strasbourg Observers*) <https://strasbourgobservers.com/2020/07/03/the-grand-ch amber-judgment-in-s-m-v-croatia-human-trafficking-prostitution-and-the-definiti onal-scope-of-article-4-echr/>. Last accessed on 12 July 2021.

725 Levit (n 358) 302.

726 ECtHR, *Rantsev v. Cyprus and Russia*, App no 25965/04, Judgment of 7 January 2010.

727 Protocol to Prevent, Suppress and Punish Trafficking in Persons Especially Women and Children, supplementing the United Nations Convention against Transnational Organized Crime, adopted and opened for signature, ratification and accession by General Assembly resolution 55/25 of 15 November 2000.

728 Council of Europe Convention on Action against Trafficking in Human Beings, CETS No. 197, entered into force 1 February 2008.

understood in the context of art. 4 ECHR.[729] This confusion continued[730] to the more recent case of *S.M. v. Croatia* of 25 June 2020, where the Grand Chamber addressed some of the questions surrounding human trafficking, forced prostitution, and the definitional scope of art. 4 ECHR[731] after Judge Koskelo wrote a powerful dissenting opinion on the scope of art. 4 in the Chamber judgment of *S.M. v. Croatia*.[732]

The case concerned a woman, S.M., who filed a criminal complaint against T.M. in September 2012. She alleged that T.M. had physically and psychologically forced her into prostitution in 2011.[733] The police conducted a criminal investigation in which they searched T.M.'s premises and his car. They found condoms, two automatic rifles with ammunition, a hand grenade, and various mobile phones. It was also established that T.M. had a police record with regard to procuring prostitution and rape and had previously been sentenced to six and a half years' imprisonment.[734] T.M. denied S.M.'s allegations. In the course of the investigations, T.M., the applicant, and a friend of the applicant were questioned and T.M. was eventually acquitted by the domestic courts, which concluded that force could not be proven.[735]

Before the Grand Chamber, the applicant complained that the national courts had failed to reclassify her complaint from procurement of forced prostitution, which would not be proven, to procurement of prostitution, which was a lesser charge. The application was based on art. 3 and art. 8 ECHR whereas Art. 4 was not mentioned. The Croatian Government made a preliminary objection against the assessment of the case under

---

729 ECtHR, *Rantsev v. Cyprus and Russia*, App no 25965/04, Judgment of 7 January 2010, para. 282. On the ambiguity of the definition of 'human trafficking', see Vladislava Stoyanova, *Human Trafficking and Slavery Reconsidered* (Cambridge University Press 2017). See also Vladislava Stoyanova, 'Dancing on the Borders of Article 4 Human Trafficking and the European Court of Human Rights in the Rantsev Case' (2012) 30 Netherlands Quarterly of Human Rights 163; Stoyanova, 'The Grand Chamber Judgment in S.M. v Croatia: Human Trafficking, Prostitution and the Definitional Scope of Article 4 ECHR' (n 714).

730 See, e.g., ECtHR, *Chowdury and Others v. Greece*, App no 21884/15, Judgment of 30 March 2017. For a discussion of the Chowdury case see Vladislava Stoyanova, 'Sweet Taste with Bitter Roots: Forced Labour and Chowdury and Others v Greece' (2018) 1 European Human Rights Law Review 67.

731 ECtHR, *S.M. v. Croatia*, App no 60561/14, Judgment of 25 June 2020.

732 ECtHR, *S.M. v. Croatia*, App no 60561/14, Judgment of 19 July 2018, Dissenting Opinion of Judge Koskelo, paras. 15–23.

733 ECtHR, *S.M. v. Croatia*, App no 60561/14, Judgment of 25 June 2020, para. 11.

734 ibid, paras. 18–20.

735 ibid, para. 78.

art. 4 ECHR, but this objection was dismissed by the Grand Chamber, which held that following the principle of *iura novit curia*, and in the view of its case-law, the Court 'could seek to determine whether it fell to be characterised under Article 4 of the Convention'.[736] The Court held that

> 'As to the factual scope of the case, the Court notes that the applicant's complaint raises issues of alleged impunity for human trafficking, forced or alternatively non-forced prostitution relating to a deficient application of the relevant criminal-law mechanisms. It is thus essentially of a procedural nature. This finding, as already stressed above, is without prejudice to the further assessment and conclusion as to the actual applicability and scope of protection guaranteed under the Convention for the acts complained of by the applicant.'[737]

The Court further held that although the nature of the applicant's complaint may also raise issues under art. 3 and art. 8 of the Convention, the Court 'has tended to apply Article 4 to issues related to human trafficking',[738] and addressing the case from the perspective of art. 4 'allows it to put the possible issues of ill-treatment (under Article 3) and abuse of the applicant's physical and psychological integrity (under Article 8) into their general context'.[739] Thus, the Grand Chamber, 'being master of the characterisation to be given in law to the facts of a case', decided to examine the case under art. 4 ECHR.[740]

   In the Grand Chamber judgment, the Court clarified what it means for 'human trafficking' and 'exploitation of prostitution' to be included under Article 4 ECHR. In order for a situation to be considered a case of human trafficking, it had to fulfill 'the criteria for the phenomenon in international law'.[741] In *Rantsev* and in the Chamber Judgment on *S.M.*, the formulations by the Court had been confusing with regard to what 'exploitation' might mean because there was no engagement with the requirements of the international-law definition of human trafficking,

---

736 ibid, para. 224.
737 ibid, para. 229.
738 ibid, para. 241.
739 ibid, para. 242.
740 ibid, para. 243. See also the discussion above with the Court being 'master of characterisation to be given in law to the facts of a case', at II.4.c
741 ibid, para. 290.

where exploitation is linked to certain 'means', 'actions', and 'purpose', and how the facts of the case reflected those requirements.[742]

Although the Court reiterated that these concepts now fall under the ambit of article 4 ECHR, how exactly human trafficking and exploitation of prostitution relate to slavery and forced labour is still not clear, and the level of severity required of an abuse is not clear either.[743] With regard to 'exploitation of prostitution' and 'sexual exploitation', which both fall under the ambit of the definition of human trafficking under the Palermo Protocol and the Anti-Trafficking Convention, the Grand Chamber correctly pointed out that their inclusion opens up 'some very sensitive issues relating to the approach to prostitution in general'.[744] With regard to the Anti-Trafficking Convention, the Explanatory Report to that Convention holds that the terms 'exploitation of the prostitution of others' and 'other forms of sexual exploitation' are not defined by the Convention itself, rather, it is up to the States Parties to deal with prostitution in their domestic laws, allowing different Council of Europe States to address the matter in their own way.[745] With regard to art. 4 ECHR, the Grand Chamber held that

> 'the notion of 'forced or compulsory labour' under Article 4 of the Convention aims to protect against instances of serious exploitation, such as forced prostitution, irrespective of whether, in the particular circumstances of a case, they are related to the specific human trafficking context. Moreover, any such conduct may have elements qualifying it as 'servitude' or 'slavery' under Article 4, or may raise an issue under another provision of the Convention.'[746]

Thus, only forced prostitution falls under the scope of art. 4 ECHR; however, it can fall under the Convention even if it is not linked to human trafficking. What remains unclear is what exactly is meant by 'forced'. The Grand Chamber held that '"force" may encompass the subtle forms of coercive conduct identified in the Court's case-law on Article 4, as well as

---

742 ECtHR, *Rantsev v. Cyprus and Russia*, App no 25965/04, Judgment of 7 January 2010, para. 296.

743 Stoyanova, 'The Grand Chamber Judgment in S.M. v Croatia: Human Trafficking, Prostitution and the Definitional Scope of Article 4 ECHR' (n 714).

744 ECtHR, *S.M. v. Croatia*, App no 60561/14, Judgment of 25 June 2020, para. 298.

745 Explanatory Report to the Council of Europe Convention on Action against Trafficking in Human Beings, CETS No. 197, para. 88.

746 ECtHR, *S.M. v. Croatia*, App no 60561/14, Judgment of 25 June 2020, para. 300.

by the ILO and in other international materials';[747] however, in the case of *S.M. v. Croatia*, there is no assessment as to whether the Court deemed the applicant to have been forced into prostitution or not. The conclusion that the Croatian Government did violate art. 4 ECHR only referred to the lack of investigation as to whether S.M. had been forced into prostitution or not in the domestic proceedings.[748]

In this case, the majority went, on the one hand, beyond S.M.'s complaint in that it examined the case under an article that was not invoked and discusses the concept of human trafficking over more than a hundred paragraphs, referring to international law etc. On the other hand, however, the majority failed to assess the specific circumstances of the case and to provide a clear answer to the question as to whether the authorities should have been investigating human trafficking, forced prostitution, or sexual exploitation.[749] Although some clarifications were provided, the line between forced prostitution and human trafficking is more blurred than ever and this poses a problem under the principle of falsifiability because the definition of these concepts is extremely vague. In the words of Judges O'Leary and Ravarani

> '[...] The solution to the conceptual vagueness thus developed is to refer vaguely to "treatment contrary to Article 4 [...] and to state that irrespective of whether the Court is (or more importantly the domestic authorities were) in the presence of human trafficking or forced prostitution, the core procedural obligation, namely the duty to investigate effectively, is the same.'[750]

They further note that rather than bringing clarity into this case and into the scope of art. 4, the Grand Chamber 'unnecessarily inflated' the case in that it insisted on making it about human trafficking. This was all the more unnecessary since the Grand Chamber was only ever going to decide whether the procedural rather than the substantive limb of art. 4 had been violated.[751]

The majority hides behind allegedly defining and further developing the concept of human trafficking, but what it actually does here is generating more confusion. From the perspective of falsifiability, the claims brought

---

747 ibid, para. 301.
748 ibid, paras. 345–347.
749 ibid, Joint Concurring Opinion of Judges O'Leary and Ravarani.
750 ibid.
751 ibid.

forward by the applicant S.M. were neither tested nor refuted, nor can they really be tested or refuted, because it is unclear what 'forced' entails. This was exactly the question that should have been addressed, but the Grand Chamber decided to duck behind requiring the domestic authorities to (procedurally) conduct a proper investigation, avoiding an answer to the question as to whether the facts of the present case did fall under the newly developed ambit of art. 4 ECHR.

In sum, the Grand Chamber did clarify certain aspects regarding the concepts of human trafficking and forced prostitution; however, from the perspective of scientific inquiry, the definition can still be criticised for being unfalsifiable. The idea of 'forced prostitution' remains extremely vague, and it would have been enlightening if the Grand Chamber had elaborated on the factual scope of 'force'. A clear definition of what is meant by 'force' is required under the principle of falsifiability. Only if there is a definition or notion against which a factual situation can be tested is it possible to prove or disprove that a factual situation falls under the ambit of a norm, which will in turn have normative implications.

Ilnseher v. Germany. The case of *Ilnseher v. Germany* concerns questions surrounding preventive detention and 'dangerousness' of a person. Here, the principle of falsifiability can be used to critique the vagueness of certain terms that played a pivotal role with regard to the justification of preventive detention under art. 5(1)(e) and art. 7(1) of the Convention.

The applicant, Mr. Ilnseher, was born in 1978. At the age of 19, he murdered a woman and was sentenced to ten years' imprisonment by a Regional Court in Germany. The crime was considered to be sexually motivated. Due to his age at the time of his offence, Ilnseher was subject to the German Juvenile Courts Act that exempted juveniles and young offenders from preventive detention. This Act was amended on 8 July 2008 to allow for retrospective preventive detention for juveniles and young adults. Based on this amended Act, the applicant's preventive detention was subsequently extended by domestic court orders, based on psychiatric assessments of the applicant that reported a high risk of him committing similar sexual and violent crimes if he were to be released. Thus, his prison sentence was subsequently extended under various judicial decisions. After a series of appeals, it was ultimately decided by the domestic courts that preventive detention had been necessary due to the high risk of Mr. Ilnseher committing a similar serious crime if he were to be released.[752]

---

752 ECtHR, *Ilnseher v. Germany*, App nos 10211/12 and 27505/14, Judgment of 4 December 2018, paras. 10–47.

The applicant claimed before a Chamber of the ECtHR that with regard to his retrospective preventive detention, his rights under art. 5(1) and under art. 7(1) had been violated because a heavier penalty had been imposed than the one applicable at the time when he had committed the offence in 1997. The Chamber unanimously held that the applicant's retrospectively ordered preventive detention from 20 June 2013 onwards had not violated the Convention because the German authorities' finding that his mental disorder warranted compulsory confinement was justified under art. 5(1)(e) of the Convention, which justifies the detention of 'persons of unsound mind'. Furthermore, because the preventive detention had been ordered due to the applicant's mental condition, the retrospective detention could not be considered a 'penalty' for the purpose of art. 7 ECHR.[753] Mr. Ilnseher requested the case to be referred to the Grand Chamber on 15 March 2017, which was accepted.[754]

The focus of the current analysis will be on two aspects of the Grand Chamber's ruling. Firstly, the Grand Chamber (as opposed to the Chamber) held that art. 7(1) ECHR was not applicable in this case because the applicant's preventive detention could not be considered a 'penalty' but rather constituted a therapeutic measure, to which art. 7 ECHR did not apply, and that it was, thus, lawful for the German courts to impose a heavier penalty onto the applicant than the one that was applicable at the time of the criminal offence. Secondly, the analysis will pertain to the notion of 'persons of unsound mind', which is one exception where the detention of a person can be lawful under art. 5(1)(e) of the Convention.

The first aspect refers to the applicant's claim under art. 7 ECHR of receiving a heavier penalty than the one applicable at the time he committed an offence. The majority of the Grand Chamber argued that the jailing of the applicant was not a 'penalty' as required by art. 7 ECHR because of the therapeutic purposes of the detention. Thus, in the case of Mr. Ilnseher's preventive detention, the protection of art. 7 ECHR did not apply due to the labelling of Mr. Ilnseher as – in the words of Judge Pinto de Albu-

---

753 ECtHR, *Ilnseher v. Germany*, App nos 10211/12 and 27505/14, Judgment of 2 February 2017. For a discussion of the Chamber ruling, see Emilie Rebsomen, Méryl Recotillet and Caroline Teuma, 'Preventive Detention as a "Penalty" in the Case of Ilnseher v. Germany' (*Strasbourg Observers*) <https://strasbourgobserv ers.com/2017/11/10/preventive-detention-as-a-penalty-in-the-case-of-ilnseher-v-ge rmany/#more-4026>. Last acccessed 1 June 2021.

754 ECtHR, *Ilnseher v. Germany*, App nos 10211/12 and 27505/14, Judgment of 4 December 2018, para. 6.

querque – 'mad' rather than 'bad'.[755] Although the preventive detention order was imposed by the criminal justice system,[756] the Grand Chamber used factual arguments with regard to the detention facilities, 'the nature and the purpose of his preventive detention', the cell space, the kitchen unit in the cell, and the separate bathroom as factors indicating that the punitive element of the detention had been erased, and that thus the detention was not a 'penalty' as in the meaning of art. 7 ECHR but rather a 'therapeutic measure'.[757] The arguments for characterising the measure as 'therapeutic' rather than 'punitive' referred to material conditions in the institutions, i.e. to factual considerations. In essence, the Grand Chamber uses factual circumstances of the detention facility to relabel the character of the detention, which then has normative consequences: if the detention is labelled 'punitive', the applicant is protected under art. 7(1) ECHR. If it is labelled 'therapeutic', the applicant is not protected under art. 7(1) ECHR, which means that changing the factual label from someone being 'bad' to someone being 'mad' has legal implications in terms of legal protection. The retrospective change of the label regarding the 'nature' or 'purpose' of the detention is criticised by Judge Pinto de Albuquerque:

> '[...] how many kitchen units, how many separate bathrooms, how many TV sets or body-building machines, how many doctors and nurses, how many visiting hours or phone calls should there be for a preventive detention unit to change nature and for detention therein to change its 'purpose'? [...]'[758]

This, essentially, is a critique based on the principle of falsifiability. The vagueness of what exactly the nature and purpose of the detention must (factually) entail to justify its (legal) relabelling is highly problematic.

The second step, then, is to assess whether the preventive detention, which was considered not to violate art. 7(1) ECHR, was justified under art. 5(1)(e) ECHR. This article justifies the deprivation of liberty in cases of lawful detention of 'persons of unsound mind'. The Grand Chamber

---

755 For a scathing criticism of the 'erasure' of the autonomous meaning of 'penalty', see paras. 95–107 of the Dissenting Opinion of Judge Pinto de Albuquerque joined by Judge Dedov, ECtHR, *Ilnseher v. Germany*, App nos 10211/12 and 27505/14, Judgment of 4 December 2018.

756 ECtHR, *Ilnseher v. Germany*, App nos 10211/12 and 27505/14, Judgment of 4 December 2018, para. 229.

757 ibid, para. 236.

758 ibid, Dissenting Opinion of Judge Pinto de Albuquerque joined by Judge Dedov, paras. 108–110.

held that in order for the applicant's preventive detention to be justified under art. 5(1)(e) of the Convention, three minimum conditions had to be satisfied:

> 'firstly, he must reliably be shown to be of unsound mind, that is, a true mental disorder must be established before a competent authority on the basis of objective medical expertise; secondly, the mental disorder must be of a kind or degree warranting compulsory confinement; thirdly, the validity of continued confinement depends upon the persistence of such a disorder.'[759]

The questions that are of interest from the perspective of scientific inquiry, and especially from the perspective of falsifiability, are: how do the notions of 'true mental disorder', 'mental disorder', and being of 'unsound mind' relate to each other? And what can be deemed 'objective medical expertise'?

Two of the applicant's lines of argument pointed to these issues. Firstly, he argued that his preventive detention was not justified under art. 5(1)(e) of the Convention as it had not been shown in a reliable manner that he was of unsound mind. More than half of the experts who had examined the applicant since 1999, including expert F., who had been consulted as one of the experts in the proceedings at issue, had not found the applicant to suffer from a true mental disorder, and none of the experts who had examined him had the specific qualifications to examine young people.[760] Secondly, the notion of 'mental disorder' under the German Therapy Detention Act might be less restrictive than the notion of 'unsound mind' under art. 5 of the Convention, and might therefore not warrant compulsory confinement.[761]

The Government argued that the conditions established in the Court's case-law for detaining a person of unsound mind had been satisfied and that the applicant had been found by the Regional Court relying on 'two renowned external psychiatric experts to suffer from a true mental disorder, namely from a serious form of sexual sadism, at the relevant time'.[762] The domestic authorities referred to the case of *Glien v. Germany*,[763] where

---

759 ECtHR, *Ilnseher v. Germany*, App nos 10211/12 and 27505/14, Judgment of 4 December 2018, para. 127.
760 ibid, para. 111.
761 ibid, para. 112.
762 ibid, para. 118.
763 ECtHR, *Glien v. Germany*, App no 7345/12, Judgment of 28 November 2013, paras. 84 and 87.

a person was considered as a person of unsound mind under art. 5(1) (e) of the Convention despite not having suffered from a condition that ruled out or diminished their criminal responsibility at the time of the offence.[764]

The European Prison Litigation Network (EPLN) acted as a third party and submitted that the Chamber's interpretation of 'persons of unsound mind' was 'too broad and imprecise'.[765] In terms of the principle of falsifiability, what the intervening party argued is that the terminology used is vague and non-refutable. The EPLN noted that the Federal Constitutional Court of Germany used a broad understanding of 'mental disorder', which under German law covered non-pathological disorders as well.[766] However, the notion should only apply to persons with severe pathological disorders whose capacity to understand the wrongfulness of their acts at the time when they did commit them was 'non-existent or at least diminished'.[767] The notion of 'persons of unsound mind' should not be assimilated to or confused with a person being considered dangerous.[768] In other words, the 'bad' should not be labelled 'mad' simply for the purpose of keeping them incarcerated.

Thus, the Grand Chamber's assessment of the facts of the case must be assessed keeping in mind the question of how the concept of 'mental disorder' under the German procedure relates to the notion of 'unsound mind' under art. 5 ECHR. Judge Pinto de Albuquerque in his dissenting opinion, joined by Judge Dedov, criticises the notion of 'person of unsound mind' as a 'catch-all construction'.[769]

> 'The majority in the present judgment are undecided: on the one hand, they say that the notion of 'unsound mind' 'might be more restrictive' than that of 'mental disorder', but on the other hand they say that the notion of 'unsound mind' does not warrant a mental condition that excludes or even diminishes criminal responsibility. With this convenient ambiguity, the door is wide open to establish 'a disorder which can be said to amount to a true mental disorder' and

---

764 ECtHR, *Ilnseher v. Germany*, App nos 10211/12 and 27505/14, Judgment of 4 December 2018, para. 119.
765 ibid. 124.
766 ibid.
767 ibid.
768 ibid, para. 125.
769 ibid, Dissenting Opinion of Judge Pinto de Albuquerque joined by Judge Dedov, paras. 108–110.

'treat' dangerous offenders as 'mentally ill' or 'mentally disordered' persons and keep them detained for the rest of their lives, even on the basis of a detention regime that did not exist at the time of the commission of the offence.'[770]

The Grand Chamber interprets the notion of 'unsound mind' expansively and thereby opens up the possibility of more easily categorising someone as being of 'unsound mind', allowing the preventive detention of that person to be lawful under art. 5(1)(e) of the Convention. The applicant argued that he was neither suffering from a true mental disorder nor that he was a 'person of unsound mind'. He claimed that the requirement of 'objective medical expertise' was not fulfilled. The two experts the Government relied on were K. and F. However, throughout the time that the applicant had been examined, more than half of the experts, including F., had not found the applicant to suffer from a mental disorder, and sexual sadism in particular; a true mental disorder could, thus, not be proven.[771]

The Grand Chamber argued that domestic courts have 'certain discretion' with regard to the clinical diagnoses;[772] however, as Judge Pinto de Albuquerque points out, 'there are limits to this hands-off approach'.[773] In May 2017, the contact between the applicant and his psychologist at the time, M.K., were discontinued because there were no signs of any 'hidden sadistic undercurrent'.[774] Judge Pinto de Albuquerque criticises the 'scientific quality' of the diagnosis and points to the fact that the alleged mental illness of sexual sadism had been diagnosed fifteen years after the criminal act had taken place. The majority had also wrongly held that the applicant had 'a history of offences',[775] even though the offence in 1997 had been his first one.[776]

---

770 ibid, Dissenting Opinion of Judge Pinto de Albuquerque joined by Judge Dedov, para. 109. References to paragraphs omitted.
771 ECtHR, *Ilnseher v. Germany*, App nos 10211/12 and 27505/14, Judgment of 4 December 2018, para. 111.
772 ibid, para. 155.
773 ibid, Dissenting Opinion of Judge Pinto de Albuquerque joined by Judge Dedov, para. 112.
774 ibid, Dissenting Opinion of Judge Pinto de Albuquerque joined by Judge Dedov, para. 112. The Opinion refers to 'Enclosures 10 and 11 joined to the applicant's observations of 10 August 2017' in n 295.
775 ECtHR, *Ilnseher v. Germany*, App nos 10211/12 and 27505/14, Judgment of 4 December 2018, para. 157.
776 ibid, Dissenting Opinion of Judge Pinto de Albuquerque joined by Judge Dedov, para. 113.

These points show that there are serious flaws in the majority's fact-assessment in the present case. As the factual labels have a normative effect, their use should be clear and transparent. However, in this case, the labels did not conform with the requirements of falsifiability because they were vague and self-protective. The first element of vagueness can be seen in the weakening of (the protective effect of) art. 7(1) of the Convention because this article can be circumvented by labelling detention 'therapeutic' rather than 'punitive'. The second vagueness is that the notion of 'person of unsound mind' is interpreted so broadly, and the fact-assessment as to whether a person really suffers from a 'true mental disorder' was conducted so poorly, that the possibility of labelling someone who is considered 'dangerous' by the domestic authorities as 'mad' is opened up, allowing for that person to be held in detention for the rest of their life.

S.H. and Others v. Austria. In ethically and morally sensitive cases, the principles of scientific method can be used to analyse arguments and decisions in a manner that increases analytic utility and helps avoid emotional responses to the sensitiveness of a case. If we consider, for instance, the question of artificial procreation, the reading of a case with the help of scientific principles will help focus on the question that is at stake in the individual case rather than getting lost in the sensitive and often emotional debates over questions of life and death and family relations. The case of *S.H. and Others v. Austria*[777] that came before the Grand Chamber is replete with highly 'emotional sentences'. For instance, the Italian Government as a third-party intervener stated that 'to call maternal filiation into question by splitting motherhood would lead to a weakening of the entire structure of society'.[778]

The case concerns the legality of artificial procreation. Two infertile couples brought claims before the European Court of Human Rights against prohibitions they were facing by Austrian legislation of 1992 that banned sperm donation for the purpose of IVF (in vitro fertilisation) and all forms of egg donation. The first couple could only conceive with the help of donor spermatozoa and IVF, whereas the second couple required egg donation. They claimed violations of their rights under art. 8 ECHR and under art. 14 ECHR. The claim that is of interest here is their complaint of unjustified discrimination due to the incoherence in which techniques were allowed versus prohibited. Ovum donation was generally prohibited

---

777 ECtHR, *S.H. and Others v. Austria*, App no 57813/00, Judgment of 3 November 2011.
778 ibid, para. 73.

whereas sperm donation was permitted only if the semen is placed directly into the womb of a woman. The First Section held in 2010, with a 6–1 vote for the first couple and a 5–2 vote for the second, that art. 14 in conjunction with art. 8 of the Convention had been violated by the Austrian Government.[779] The case was then referred to the Grand Chamber, which reversed the decision in 2011 with a 13–4 vote, concluding that the Austrian laws on assisted reproduction did not violate Convention rights. The majority reached this decision because they deemed the Austrian Government to have a wide margin of appreciation on this ethically and morally sensitive topic.[780]

One issue that arises with the discussion of 'ethically and morally sensitive questions' is that it is not entirely clear what this moral sensitivity is based on and who is to decide what is considered 'ethically and morally sensitive' and how. What is of interest here is the use of social and moral sensitivity as an argument in a case. It is an 'easy' argument to make; however, as Alexandra Timmer rightly notes, such arguments are 'hardly ever concretely substantiated with statistics or other evidence'.[781] Thus arguments based on social and moral sensitivity are easy in the sense that they are not falsifiable because it is unclear what can be tested in order to refute an argument that is based on a vague concept such as 'moral sensitivity'.

Austria appealed to the notion of public interest to justify the ban on sperm donation for in vitro fertilisation and the general ban on egg donation.[782] However, the arguments are not persuasive and the vague concepts invoked by the Government are unfalsifiable.

Firstly, the Government argued that the difference in treatment between sperm and ovum donation was justified in order to protect women. It observed that economically disadvantaged women in particular may be exploited and humiliated.[783] This is a paternalistic line of argument that should have been criticised by the majority. It was not clarified what exactly was meant by the danger of women being exploited and humiliated, nor

---

779 ibid.

780 ibid, paras. 94 and 97.

781 Alexandra Timmer, 'S.H. and Others v Austria: Margin of Appreciation and IVF' (*Strasbourg Observers*) <https://strasbourgobservers.com/2011/11/09/s-h-and-others-v-austria-margin-of-appreciation-and-ivf/#more-1268>.

782 ECtHR, *S.H. and Others v. Austria*, App no 57813/00, Judgment of 3 November 2011, see especially paras. 64–67.

783 ibid, para. 66.

why such dangers do not affect men as well.[784] In order to be falsifiable, the statements would have to be refutable. Here, however, the paternalistic stance remains vague and self-protected.

Secondly, the Government argued that fears regarding split motherhood justified the legislation. The Government argued that IVF 'raised the question of unusual family relationships in which the social circumstances deviated from the biological ones, namely, the division of motherhood into a biological aspect and an aspect of "carrying the child", and perhaps also a social aspect.'[785] The terminology in this line of reasoning is problematic as it reflects the idea that there exist 'usual' and 'unusual' families. The majority acknowledged that the Austrian Government was guided by 'the basic principle of law – *mater semper certa est*' and that

> '[i]n doing so, the legislature tried to reconcile the wish to make medically assisted procreation available and the existing unease among large sections of society as to the role and possibilities of modern reproductive medicine, which raises issues of a morally and ethically sensitive nature.'[786]

This observation by the majority, which implies that preventing 'unusual family relations' from developing is a legitimate goal, is a step backwards from the Court's case-law where it acknowledged the diversity of familial and other human relationships.[787] The issue here, again, is that gender roles are being enforced where the biological mother ought to raise the child and biological and social motherhood must not be separated. This line of reasoning should have been unpacked and condemned by the majority.[788] From the perspective of falsifiability, it is unclear what is meant by 'usual' and 'unusual' family relations and what the 'social aspect' is that the Government refers to.

Thirdly, it was argued that there was a need to protect the child's welfare. It was also argued that split motherhood might jeopardise the child's wellbeing and 'the child's legitimate interest' to know their actual descent, which was considered impossible in most cases where a child

---

784 This can also be criticised under the principle of simplicity.
785 ECtHR, *S.H. and Others v. Austria*, App no 57813/00, Judgment of 3 November 2011, para. 67.
786 ibid, para. 104.
787 See, e.g. ECtHR, *Marckx v. Belgium*, App no 6833/74, Judgment of 13 June 1979; ECtHR, *Schalk and Kopf v. Austria*, App no 30141/04, Judgment of 24 June 2010.
788 See also Timmer (n 781); Michele Bratcher Goodwin (ed), *Baby Markets - Money and the New Politics of Creating Families* (Cambridge University Press 2010).

was conceived using donated sperm or ova.[789] Again, there is no evidence provided for these claims, which seem to solely reflect the Government's own convictions regarding what 'normal' family relationships should look like. The only basis for this argument seems to be 'the unease existing among large sections of society as to the role and possibilities of modern reproductive medicine'.[790] However, no evidence is provided to substantiate this statement. It is unclear what a 'large section of society' means and how many people have to feel uneasy – and indeed how such uneasiness should be expressed – for a law prohibiting certain forms of artificial procreation to be justified on these grounds. Such statements are scientifically unfounded and fail under the principle of falsifiability because there is no possibility of testing or refuting this claim as there is no factual basis to support it. Thus the argument provided by the Austrian Government is vague, and this vagueness is not adequately addressed by the Grand Chamber.

The last aspect of the argument is the fear of selective reproduction, of 'Zuchtauswahl'. Although this fear can be considered legitimate, the Government did not specify why addressing it requires an absolute ban on ova donation and on sperm donation for IVF.[791]

The Grand Chamber decided to award the Austrian Government a margin of appreciation due to the moral and ethical sensitivity on the issue. It can be criticised on the basis of the principle of falsifiability for allowing vague notions to be used as the basis of the Government's argument and for not rejecting the paternalistic and stereotypical lines of reasoning the Austrian Government employs with regard to notions of family relations and women's need for protection. It can also be criticised for accepting unfounded lines of reasoning by the Austrian Government. No empirical evidence is provided by the Austrian Government for its arguments. Concrete, falsifiable arguments are lacking as to why exactly 'split motherhood' should endanger the best interest of the child.

Moreover, there is a back-and-forth in the Grand Chamber's position with regard to the existence or non-existence of a European consensus with regard to artificial procreation. Three documents, dating from 1998

---

789   ECtHR, *S.H. and Others v. Austria*, App no 57813/00, Judgment of 3 November 2011, para. 67.
790   ECtHR, *S.H. and Others v. Austria*, App no 57813/00, Judgment of 3 November 2011, para. 99.
791   Timmer (n 781).

to 2007,[792] are compared and deemed by the Court to show that the legal provisions in the field of medically assisted procreation were developing quickly.[793] The Court also states that 'there is now a clear trend' in the laws in the Member States towards allowing gamete donation for IVF.[794] This is seen as reflecting an emerging European consensus. However, the Court then takes a step back and holds that this consensus is not 'based on settled and long-standing principles established in the law of the member States'[795] but is only one stage in the development of this highly dynamic and fast-evolving field that does not lead to a narrowing of the margin of appreciation.[796] This is highly contradictory: the Court first holds that 'a clear trend' exists, but then deems this trend not established enough, or not sufficiently reflected in the field of law, to narrow the margin of appreciation of the Austrian Government (or any other member State). The idea here seems to be that this field of law is, at the moment, still too dynamic for there to be a clear position that can be used as a 'European stance' and enforced as a standard for all States. Here, it seems quite confusing what, then, a trend entails. In its conclusion, the Court does warn the Austrian Government to pay attention to the future developments in this field, reiterating

'that the Convention has always been interpreted and applied in the light of current circumstances [...]. Even if it finds no breach of Article 8 in the present case, the Court considers that this area, in which the law appears to be continuously evolving and which is subject to a particularly dynamic development in science and law, needs to be kept under review by the Contracting States [...]'.[797]

---

792 ECtHR, *S.H. and Others v. Austria*, App no 57813/00, Judgment of 3 November 2011, para. 35: 'Medically Assisted Procreation and the Protection of the Human Embryo: Comparative Study on the Situation in 39 States" (Council of Europe, 1998); the replies by the member States of the Council of Europe to the Steering Committee on Bioethics' "Questionnaire on access to medically assisted procreation (MAP) and on right to know about their origin for children born after MAP" (Council of Europe, 2005); and a survey carried out in 2007 by the International Federation of Fertility Societies'.

793 ECtHR, *S.H. and Others v.* Austria, App no 57813/00, Judgment of 3 November 2011, para. 40.

794 ibid, para. 96.

795 ibid, para. 96.

796 ibid para. 96.

797 ibid, para. 118.

This shows that the factual situation with regard to artificial reproduction can influence the scope of art. 8 ECHR. The gaze of the Court will continue to wander between the facts of the cases that are presented before it and the Convention articles.

In conclusion to this analysis, even if we agree that there is no European consensus yet that would be strong enough to call for the narrowing of the Austrian Government's margin of appreciation and, thus, a change in the Austrian laws, this still should not prevent the Court from condemning highly paternalistic lines of argumentation and requiring a sound factual basis for the vague and self-protective arguments presented by the Government, which run counter to the principle of falsifiability. Especially in cases that concern ethically and morally sensitive issues, it is important for the arguments that are presented by the parties to be based on factual evidence. One's own moral approach to a sensitive question may all too easily influence the selection of information that is chosen to build an argument. However, the assessment of the arguments must be rigorous and must not allow the data and information to be cherry-picked in order to lead to a pre-defined conclusion.

iii. Summary and Comment

The three cases discussed above all fell short when analysed against the background of the principle of falsifiability. The principle of falsifiability shines a critical light on vague terms and over-inclusive definitions. In all three cases, vague terms or labels were used as the basis for key normative conclusions. It was not clarified what is required on a factual level for specific normative consequence to come into play. In *S.M.*, it was never clarified what is required for a factual circumstance to amount to 'force'; in *Ilnseher*, there was confusion regarding the assessment of Mr. Ilnseher as 'bad', as 'mad', or as 'dangerous', where these labels have different consequences on a normative level; and in *S.H.*, the Austrian Government used stereotypical lines of arguments and the vague concept of 'moral sensitivity' with regard to artificial procreation.

In cases where terms have to be interpreted in order to determine their effect, the underlying factual situation warrants special attention. If the factual basis on which the normative conclusion rests is vague, and this vague situation is considered to fall under the ambit of the vague term that is employed, the reliability of the solution is diminished. In the cases analysed above, vague and self-protective terms were used as criteria without proper analysis or explanation as to what the criteria require or entail (factually) in a specific case in order to reach a (normative) conclusion. If vague notions are used, of which it is unclear what they require from the facts, it is all the easier to cherry-pick those facts that do fit under the vague concept in order to fill the legal bill.

Harking back to the opinions by Judges Zupančič and Kūris, who invoked the principle of falsifiability with regard to shifts in case-law,[798] Judge Zupančič expresses the opinion that usually, decisions reached by the Court 'are not adapted to the negative feedback they receive from reality'.[799] This holds true for the specific case that was decided: because the ECtHR's decision is final, the decision will not be adapted if, e.g., the principle of falsifiability calls for its refutation. However, with regard to future decisions, this does not hold true. Looking at the 'bigger picture' of adjudication, negative feedback from reality – e.g., in the form of judges' dissenting opinions, disagreement voiced in academic commentaries, criticism in newspaper articles, or reactions from NGOs – may have an influence with regard to factually similar cases. In that sense, there is a back-and-forth – a wandering gaze – between case-law and feedback from reality. Although the principle of falsifiability does not require the actual physical testing of theories, of arguments, or of conclusions to a case, this principle does require their 'conceptual refinement'.[800] There must be a back-and-forth, a testing process, and this testing process might influence the Court towards changing its case-law.

A back-and-forth – a wandering gaze – also occurs between factual occurrences and labels they can receive. These labels can have normative implications, and they change as changes happen in society. However, if the labels are too vague and self-protective, the danger is that the facts can easily be interpreted in order to fit a vague label, thus the facts may be 'constructed'[801] in a manner that will allow a pre-defined goal, with or without normative implications, to be reached. For instance, as shown in the cases discussed above, the labels 'morally sensitive', 'dangerous', or 'forced' have normative implications. However, the existence or non-existence of moral sensitivity, of danger, and of force must be interpreted on

---

798 III.2.c.i.

799 ECtHR, *J.K. and Others v. Sweden*, App no 59166/23, Judgment of 4 June 2015, Partly Dissenting Opinion by Judge Zupančič.

800 Levit (n 358) 305.

801 See, e.g., Ana Luisa Bernardino, 'The Discursive Construction of Facts in International Adjudication' [2020] Journal of International Dispute Settlement 175.

a case-by-case basis and depending on the facts of a given case. Whether or not artificial procreation is 'morally sensitive' and how society 'feels' about IVF treatment becomes a relevant question only if this form of procreation exists (factually). Again, this is linked to the idea of the wandering gaze discussed in Part II. This does not imply that there is a requirement for courts to rapidly adapt to changes in society. Such changes take time, and adaptations to conventions must be thought through, refined, and be based on and supported by a wealth of evidence. In this sense, principles of scientific inquiry suggest a cautious attitude towards novel ideas.[802] However, courts must remain attentive to changes in society. In this sense, the ECtHR pointing a warning finger at the Austrian Government to keep under review the fast-evolving situation with regard to artificial procreation can be interpreted as meaning that in the present case, the Austrian Government was deemed not to have violated the Convention, however, in future cases, this may be different. Thus the Austrian Government must remain attentive to the changes that are taking place in society and in the science of reproduction, and might have to adapt its legal rules to the needs of society, and to reality.

3. Implications of these New Categories

Above, the question was addressed as to how the case-law of the ECtHR can be criticised on the basis of principles of scientific inquiry. The question that is of interest now is what implications these new categories have, and how they change the critique of jurisprudence.

a. Focusing on the Quality of the Fact-Assessment Procedure

A first implication can be seen in the way using these new categories to critique jurisprudence puts a spotlight on the quality of the process of inquiry, i.e., the process of fact-assessment, rather than on the labels that are applied to statements. For instance, it is easy to label something (explicitly or implicitly) a 'fact' or 'proven'; however, the difficulty lies in assessing whether the label is actually warranted. For instance, whether prostitution was 'forced' in a given case must be assessed by looking at the facts in the particular case. The facts and the underlying assumptions, generalisations,

---

802   Levit (n 358) 305.

and inferences they are based on, and the quality of the process of inquiry with regard to this assessment procedure will show whether the label 'forced' is warranted or not. The correctness of this label is essential to the normative conclusion that will be drawn. The same holds true for the question of whether some practice or policy of a Government relates to a 'morally sensitive issue'. If the answer is in the affirmative, this will have an implication on a normative level with regard to how broad or narrow the country's margin of appreciation will be. Thus, it is necessary for the Court to show why in the case at hand, the facts can be subsumed under a particular normative concept. This requires a thorough and transparent assessment of the facts.

At the beginning of this thesis, it was stated that labelling something a 'fact' usually implies that this product receives special importance within a debate, and that this label gives a statement a certain authority.[803] The label implies that the person who is making the utterance can provide proof for the statement in some way or another. One can try to distinguish between facts and opinions by testing a statement's reliability, although the line between facts and opinion is often not clear-cut. In cases where there are different interpretations and points of view with regard to an observation or a subject matter, HLA Hart requires that the utterer must be of 'superior knowledge, intelligence, or wisdom which makes it reasonable to believe' what that person utters and that this perspective is 'more likely to be true than the results reached by others through their independent investigations'.[804] Norwood Russell Hanson's example of two people who observe the same thing but may interpret the same visual data in different ways, and thus construe the evidence differently, comes to mind again here. It must be shown, then, 'how these data are moulded by different theories or interpretations or intellectual constructions'.[805]

Applying these ideas to the case analysis above, the parties to a case usually have different accounts of the events, and the Court is then required to decide how the facts should be assessed. The Court has to assess the reliability of the factual accounts provided in a given case, it has to assess the parties' submissions, the expert reports, and all other relevant information submitted in a case. The Court itself must conduct its fact-assessment in a reliable manner. Applying the Norwood Russell Hanson's statement with regard to observations by different people to the sphere of

---

803 See above, I.1.
804 Hart (n 11) 261–262.
805 Hanson (n 12) 5.

legal decision-making, in a first step, the different parties are required to show how the facts, i.e. the data, statistical data, and other information, fits their theory of how the case should be decided. In a second step, the Court is required to do the same thing: the presented data, the different accounts of the facts, i.e. the different observations must be discussed and weighed against each other, and it must be shown how the evidence can be construed differently. The Court's account and interpretation of the facts of the case at hand must then be shown in a clear and transparent manner, and it must be explained why the outcome of the case was based on observation A rather than observation B (or C, or D, …).

In the case-law of the ECtHR, facts and opinions cannot always easily be held apart, and it is not always clear who carries the burden of proof for what. Usually, there are only very few clear labels, or none at all, regarding what is deemed a 'fact' and what is deemed an 'opinion'. In other words, it is rarely entirely clear who bears the burden of proving (or disproving) that something is to be considered a 'fact'. Arguably, it is not the labels that are most important in the process of fact-assessment. Dwyer even states that it is not really useful to approach the analysis of 'evidence of facts' versus 'evidence of opinions' differently.[806] If we consider facts here to include basic sense data and inferences we draw from them, then all of these, including the social and legal significance of those facts, can carry the label of 'fact'.[807] Any statement or observation or perception that is made within judicial decisions can be labelled a 'fact'; categorising these into different entities does not bear on the present discussion. The present discussion aims at showing that all of these 'facts', or factual statements, must be assessed by the Court in order to determine their reliability. The manner in which their reliability can be tested is using the principles of scientific method as guiding principles or framework. When we want to assess and scrutinise how the ECtHR contends with facts, the distinction between facts, opinions, etc. does not assist us in answering this question. In Dwyer's words:

> 'This is because the underlying question, of how inferences have been drawn from basic experiences and generalizations, is structurally the same for questions of both fact and opinion. Therefore when we say 'facts' we are usually referring to a set of propositions which have been inferred through the application of generalizations to other inferences.

---

806   Dwyer (n 194) 75.
807   ibid 93–94.

We may choose to draw the line somewhere and say that some of these inferences should be classified as 'brute facts', but the inferential chain properly goes back to basic experiences.'[808]

The manner in which inferences should be drawn, it is argued here, is by following the principles of scientific inquiry. For instance, the Court may listen to an expert's opinion during a process. Here, the specialist advice refers to how appropriate generalisations should be applied to the set of facts in the given case. However, whether and how this advice is applied and integrated into the final conclusion of a case is still in the Court's power. The Court is not obliged to follow a particular assessment of the facts. What it should be required to do, however, is to conduct its own fact-assessment in a manner that produces a fair, reliable, coherent, and transparent conclusion. For the purpose of this paper, the label 'fact' is not what is of greatest importance. Rather, it is argued here that the focus should not be on the labels but rather on the importance that is given to different statements, whatever label they may carry, and how and why the labels influenced the statements being or not being a determining feature for the conclusion that was reached. Labels are not central to the present discussion because they can be instrumentalised. This holds particularly true for labels such as 'fact', which entails a certain authority. Thus, it is essential to keep in mind what it means to refer to something as a fact, and to analyse and assess, by (scientifically) inquiring the underlying processes behind the decision on whether the statement is indeed a fact.

b. How Do These Categories Change the Critique of Jurisprudence?

The case analysis above showed that facts and law are intertwined. If the fact-assessment by the Court does not conform with the principles of scientific inquiry, it will provide an unsound basis for the normative conclusions that rest on this factual basis. In Part I of this thesis, it was shown that not many rules exist on how the ECtHR ought to conduct fact-assessment. Moreover, the case analysis showed that certain approaches that have developed via its case-law, such as the Court being the master of characterisation to be given in law to the facts, are not applied consistently. Using the principles of scientific method as a framework for analysing the fact-assessment in jurisprudence enables the reader to bring some order

---

808 ibid 77–78.

into the sometimes chaotic and untransparent lines of factual reasoning by the ECtHR. Using these principles for orientation will allow the reader of a case to detect flaws in the Court's fact-assessment and helps shine a light onto inconsistencies or unclear lines of inference and factual reasoning. Many of the principles of scientific method might seem trivial and appear not to add much to the critique of jurisprudence. For instance, it seems self-explanatory that any decision or conclusion should be properly explained and be based on sufficient evidence (drawing on, and consistent with, (the body of) knowledge within the legal realm as well as from other disciplines). However, as was shown in the case analysis, the principle of explanatory power is not always adhered to in practice and can therefore serve as a tool to detect flaws in the analysis by the Court. Thus, the scientific principles can help structure the way in which lawyers and academics, or any reader of the Court's case-law, can critique the Court's decisions in this regard. They shift the gaze from the legal to the factual, and in doing so, they provide a sound basis for arguments which otherwise may have been overlooked.

The principles provide analytic utility with regard to the decision-making process. They can be used as guiding principles when assessing the way the facts are contended with. They require an assessment procedure and conclusion to be transparent, clear, and – using Dewey's terminology – thought through.[809] They also require the assessors to be self-critical and to examine their own assessment procedure.

The use of statistical evidence, reports, and expert opinions in a decision does not automatically mean that the decision is based on a sound factual basis and that methods of scientific inquiry were adhered to. Reliance on empirical or other forms of evidence does not in itself ensure that the decision is externally valid and has explanatory power. The question to be asked is whether the statistical evidence does provide proof for the statement that is made, whether it is reliable, and even whether it has anything to do with the question at stake. The entire line of argument must be evaluated, and it must be asked what objective the statistical or other form of evidence is being put to and whether that objective has been reached. Using the principles of scientific method 'can offer one means of assessing the rationality of alternative decisional possibilities'.[810]

---

809 II.2.b.
810 For Levit's assessment of 'unscientific use of empirical evidence, see Levit (n 358) 304–305.

The principles of scientific method do not require judicial decisions to incorporate, or rapidly adapt to, (the most) recent empirical studies. Rather, these principles require that before new ideas are adopted and judicial decisions are adapted accordingly, they should be supported by a wealth of evidence. For instance, the principle of external validity requires a new idea to conform with a large body of pre-existing knowledge, and the principle of falsifiability calls for the careful conceptual refinement of theories.[811]

This can be linked to the pragmatist approach where inquiry is, in the words of Peirce, 'not standing upon the bedrock of fact. It is walking upon a bog, and one can only say, this ground seems to hold for the present. Here I will stay till it begins to give way'.[812] In other words, the bedrock of fact that we stand upon now is the current legal practice or the approach to questions that has been developed through long-standing case-law. If changes occur, e.g., due to scientific or technological progress or (factual) changes in society, and sufficient relevant data is collected, then the current approach may give way and a new course of action may be called for. This does not mean that the entire system of adjudication collapses or that it has to adapt rapidly to changes; rather, this shift takes place slowly. What is important is that these changes are acknowledged and taken into account in our processes of inquiry. As the famous philosopher of science Imre Lakatos noted, 'scientific theories are rarely abandoned upon the first observation that purports to refute them'.[813] If one observation was proven right at one point in time, it might be proven wrong at another. If it is proven wrong at a later point, our beliefs and reflections must be adapted to the new situation we find ourselves in.[814] This does not mean that we are in a constant flux and must react quickly to the latest insights from other disciplines. However, insights from other disciplines may be used as guidance for future decisions. This is already done in opinions by judges of the ECtHR.

The principles change the critique of jurisprudence in that certain assumptions that are taken for granted are reconsidered: for instance, it has been shown that why one line of reasoning, or of assessing the facts,

---

811 ibid 305.
812 See above, II.2.a. Peirce (n 377) n 5.589. See also Misak, *Cambridge Pragmatism: From Peirce and James to Ramsey and Wittgenstein* (n 377) 18.
813 Christopher T Wonnell, 'Truth and the Marketplace of Ideas' 19 UC Davis Law Review 712.
814 II.2.a., p. 59.

is chosen over another is not always properly explained. Employing the principles of scientific inquiry when analysing jurisprudence requires the reader to be self-analytical and self-aware and read the case-law with a view to the precision of the factual assessments conducted by the court. It entails for the reader of jurisprudence to pay more attention to the method of inquiry, to the way an assessment or conclusion is reached, and to whether the conclusion conforms to principles of rationality. The aim here is not to transplant science into the legal domain; rather, the idea is to assimilate certain lines of thinking and reasoning by using principles of scientific method, and to invite judges, parties to a case, and academics to employ a different way of thinking and of reading case-law and critically reflecting upon it.

An analogy can even be drawn to proofreading or any form of critical assessment of texts or lines of argument. A proofreader can assess the logic and the underlying arguments made in a thesis without having to be an expert on the subject matter. Neither we nor the judges need to understand the inner workings of the clock – to use James Williams' clock metaphor[815] – in order to assess whether an explanation provided for the inner workings of a clock was done well or not.

As Nancy Levit rightly points out, the principles of scientific method cannot guide all decisions, and there is no universal scientific roadmap that will guide all factual analyses to 'the right' outcome.[816] However, what these principles can do is promote more precise understanding of underlying arguments and greater attention to how lines of reasoning are justified and inferences are drawn (in cases). This can increase rationality, predictability, and certainty in the process of fact-assessment and decision-making. The goal here is to encourage judges, lawyers, parties to a case, and theorists to read jurisprudence more critically and systematically, to reflect on theories, arguments, and conclusions, and to pay attention to areas of ignorance. Using principles of scientific method to assess judgments can pave the way to improving the rationality of fact-assessment procedures.[817]

Judicial fact-assessment must be falsifiable. If the process of fact-assessment is not conducted in a manner that conforms with the principles of scientific inquiry, then the normative conclusions reached can be criticised as having been pre-determined, and the information on which the normative conclusion is based can be criticised as having been cherry-picked.

---

815   II.2.a.
816   Levit (n 358) 297.
817   ibid 266.

Norms can become self-fulfilling prophecies if the process of inquiry is not sound. The quality of the inquiry behind a conclusion is of pivotal importance for the reliability of the conclusion itself. A conclusion is reliable if it is based on a sound factual basis, and a factual basis is sound if it is based on a sound method of inquiry.

It is not entirely uncommon for decisions by the ECtHR to be criticised using principles of scientific method. As shown above, various judges of the European Court of Human Rights have referred to such principles, explicitly or implicitly, in their opinions on majority judgments. In these opinions, language from other disciplines is brought into the legal sphere to criticise the majority's ruling, and this can be interpreted as a first step in the process of translating the principles of scientific method into the legal code.[818] If judges continue to use these principles in their opinions, these references to the criteria of validation may cause so much self-irritation within the system of the ECtHR's decision-making that they will be made operable and even become legal principles.

---

818 See discussion of Luhmann with regard to the principle of simplicity above, III.2.a.iii.

Conclusion

Facts play an important role in the ECtHR's decision-making. The legal analysis in the Court's jurisprudence depends on the facts of a given case. Facts and law are intertwined in complex manners: a given factual occurrence influences what legal norms come into consideration for any legal analysis, whereas the scope of a legal norm brings into focus those facts that may fulfil the legal bill. Furthermore, the scope of a legal norm can be influenced by factual circumstances. For instance, changes in society and technology have an impact on the scope of existing legal rules (besides potentially occasioning new legislation). E.g., the question of whether and how artificial procreation ought to be regulated by law can only arise if artificial procreation factually exists. When the ECtHR decides a case, its gaze wanders between the factual circumstances of the case and the legal framework against which it assesses the facts. Which facts are considered relevant for a given legal analysis is influenced by the normative framework that is in place, while the factual event determines what norms come into consideration. Given that facts play an important role in legal decision-making, it is of pivotal importance for the factual basis on which a legal conclusion is based to be sound.

There are not many (legal) rules on how the ECtHR ought to deal with facts. This leaves the Court with quite wide discretion regarding fact-assessment. The particularities of the sphere of international adjudication and the institutional embeddedness of the European Court of Human Rights must be taken into account when critiquing its fact-assessment procedures. In some cases, the Member State, which is the defendant in a given case, may indeed be considered 'better placed' to assess certain facts than the Court. The principle of subsidiarity, tools such as the margin of appreciation, and the existence or non-existence of a European consensus may influence the way the ECtHR contends with facts. As was shown above, the Court does not always provide sound factual analyses. The Court occasionally employs notions such as being 'master of characterisation to be given in law to the facts of the case' or deeming domestic authorities 'better placed' to make factual assessments in an inconsistent manner. These concepts should not be used by the Court to avoid its own task of conducting a sound assessment of the facts.

From the facts that are presented in a given case, different inferences can be drawn. The Court is usually presented with a vast amount of information, e.g., by the parties to the case, by third party interveners, and by experts. All these participators outline how they would apply generalisations to the set of facts in the case at hand. Whether and how the Court processes these inputs in its own assessment is up to the Court. The ECtHR is not obliged to follow a particular account. At the same time, norms can become self-fulfilling prophecies if the facts are cherry-picked to fit a legal norm and to allow for a pre-defined conclusion. The Court should conduct its own fact-assessment and produce its own account in a manner that is fair, reliable, coherent, and transparent. The Court's reasons for agreeing with one factual account rather than another must be transparent and need to be explained properly. If an applicant and a Government disagree on the factual situation, the Court cannot simply hold that the Government is better placed to assess the facts. In such circumstances, the Court must explain why, in the individual case, it deems one factual account more reliable than another. Different observers can interpret the same visual data differently. It is the Court's task to elaborate on why it chose observation (or argument) A over observation (or argument) B.

Because there are not many (legal) rules on how the ECtHR is to conduct fact-assessment, this thesis introduces a methodology for critiquing the ECtHR's fact-assessment procedures. It introduces principles of scientific inquiry as a framework against which to assess the reliability of fact-analyses conducted by the ECtHR. It was shown that a middle-ground pragmatist approach provides the theoretical basis for allowing (interdisciplinary) principles of scientific method to enter legal thinking. These principles can be used to critique the ECtHR's case-law with regard to how facts are assessed. This allows the reader to detect logical flaws or inconsistencies in the Court's reasoning, and it helps consider the at times chaotic fact-assessment by the Court in a more structured manner. The arguments that are provided by the parties to a case must be dissected, and the Court ought to respond to all relevant factual claims by the parties to the case. This approach provides a new angle for critiquing the ECtHR's jurisprudence. It encourages paying greater attention to 'the facts' of a case rather than focusing only on 'the law'.

The principle of simplicity, the principles of explanatory power and external validity, and the principle of falsifiability were used as examples to show how principles of scientific method can be applied to scrutinise the ECtHR's jurisprudence. The criteria of validation demand that the Court's factual analyses be transparent and consistent. Judicial fact-assessment must be falsifiable; factual analyses should not be pink at one point in time and grimey at another. Applying these principles allows a structured critique to emerge. The criteria of scientific method provide an analytical framework to detect flaws in the largely uncharted terrain of fact-assessment. These new categories do not constitute a one-size-fits-all framework to assess every decision by any court. They can, however, serve as an analytical framework for reading and assessing a decision that requires the reader to analyse the case in its entirety. These principles are not legal principles, nor do they determine which decision a Court ought to reach; they are no scientific roadmap to legal decision-making. The principles are a backdrop against which factual analyses can be tested and validated.

Interestingly, judges of the ECtHR have occasionally referred to principles of scientific method, implicitly or explicitly, in their opinions when pointing out flaws in the majority's line of reasoning. It is, thus, not entirely uncommon to critique the Court using these categories. The argument here does not pertain to using principles of scientific method as legal principles. The principles can be used to analytically assess the Court's manner of contending with facts in its case-law, and they also remind the reader to be self-aware and self-reflective and critical with regard to what background assumptions they bring to any thinking process they embark on. Whether these principles may also be used as legal principles can be debated and should be explored in further research. Applying Luhmann's idea of communication between systems, the criticism voiced by judges of the ECtHR in their dissenting opinions can be seen as self-irritation within the system of the ECtHR's decision-making. If the judges use language from the scientific realm, i.e. refer to principles of scientific method, to critique the majority's reasoning, this can be argued to be the first step in translating these principles into the legal code.

In times where labels such as 'facts', 'alternative facts', and the like are used generously, it is important to focus less on the labels and more on the process of inquiry that led to a label to be issued. Our gaze must continue to wander between what we observe and what inferences we draw from our experiences, but we must also remain critical of our own wandering gaze and how it influences our choices, our thinking processes, and our conclusions. We need to remain self-critical and must always strive to base our ideas on a broad factual and evidentiary basis rather than drawing rash conclusions because we pre-select the facts that fit our pre-defined ideals. Applying principles of scientific method to our thinking processes will help us in doing so.

List of Cases

ECtHR Cases

Ahmet Özkan and Others v. Turkey, App no 21689/93, Judgment of 6 April 2004.

Alajos Kiss v. Hungary, App no 38832/06, Judgment of 20 May 2010.

Amegnigan v. the Netherlands, App no 25629/04, Judgment of 25 November 2004.

Ananyev and Others v. Russia, App nos 42525/07 and 60800/08, Judgment of 10 January 2012.

Animal Defenders International v. the United Kingdom, App no 48876/08, Judgment of 22 May 2013.

Annenkov and Others v. Russia, App no 31475/10, Judgment of 25 July 2017.

Apostu v. Romania, App no 22765/12, Judgment of 3 February 2013.

Arcila Henao v. the Netherlands, App no 13669/03, Judgment of 24 June 2003.

Artico v. Italy, App no 6694/74, Judgment of 13 May 1980.

Aydin v. Turkey, App no 57/1996/676/866, Judgment of 25 September 1997.

Bensaid v. the United Kingdom, App no 44599/98, Judgment of 6 February 2001.

Çakıcı v. Turkey, App no 23657/94, Judgment of 8 July 1999.

Case 'Relating to Certain Aspects of the Laws on the Use of Languages in Education in Belgium' v. Belgium (Belgian Linguistic case), App nos 1474/62, 1677/62, 1691/62, 1769/63, 1994/63, 2126/64, Judgment of 9 February 1967.

Chapman v. the United Kingdom, App no 27238/95, Judgment of 18 January 2001.

Chowdury and Others v. Greece, App no 21884/15, Judgment of 30 March 2017.

Christine Goodwin v. United Kingdom, App no 28957/95, Judgment of 11 July 2002.

Correia de Matos v. Portugal, App no 54602/12, Judgment of 4 May 2018.

Cotleţ v. Romania (No. 2), App no 49549/11, Judgment of 1 October 2013.

D. v. the United Kingdom, App no 30240/96, Judgment of 2 May 1997.

D.H. and Others v. the Czech Republic, App no 57325/00, Judgment of 13 November 2007.

Denmark, Norway, Sweden and the Netherlands v. Greece, ECHR, Commission Report, 1969.

Eckle v. Germany, App no 8130/78, Judgment of 15 July 1982.

Edwards v. the United Kingdom, App no 13071/87, Judgment of 16 December 1992.

Fernandes de Oliveira v. Portugal, App no 78103/14, Judgment of 31 January 2019.

Foti and Others v. Italy, App nos 7604/76, 7719/76, 7781/77, 7913/77, Judgment of 10 December 1982.

Garib v. the Netherlands, App no 43494/09, Judgment of 23 February 2016.

Garib v. the Netherlands, App no 43494/09, Judgment of 6 November 2017.

Glien v. Germany, App no 7345/12, Judgment of 28 November 2013.

Guerra and Others v. Italy, App no 14967/89, Judgment of 19 February 1998.

Gultyayeva v. Russia, App no 67413/01, Judgment of 1 April 2010.

Hämäläinen v. Finland, App no 37359/09, 16 July 2014.

Handyside v. the United Kingdom, App no 5493/72, Judgment of 7 December 1976.

Hermi v. Italy, App no 18114/02, Judgment of 18 October 2006.

Ilascu and Others v. Moldova and Russia, App no 48787/99.

Ilnseher v. Germany, App nos 10211/12 and 27505/14, Judgment of 2 February 2017.

Ilnseher v. Germany, App nos 10211/12 and 27505/14, Judgment of 4 December 2018.

Ireland v. the United Kingdom, App no 5310/71, Judgment of 13 December 1978.

Ireland v. the United Kingdom, App no 5310/71, Judgment of 18 January 1978.

J.K. and Others v. Sweden, App no 59166/23, Judgment of 4 June 2015.

Jalloh v. Germany, App no 54810/00, Judgment of 11 July 2006.

Kaya v. Turkey, App no 158/1996/777/978, Judgment of 19 February 1998.

Khamtokhu and Aksenchik v. Russia, App nos 60367/08 and 961/11, Judgment of 24 January 2017.

Khlaifia and Othes v. Italy, App no 16483/12, Judgment of 15 December 2016.

Kılıç v. Turkey, App no 22492/93, Judgment of 28 March 2000.

Klaas v. Germany, App no 15473/89, Judgment of 22 September 1993.

Kokoshkina v. Russia, App no 2052/08, Judgment of 28 May 2009.

Konstantin Markin, App no 30078/06, Judgment of 22 March 2012.

Kudeshkina v. Russia (No. 2), App no 28727/11, Judgment of 17 Feburary 2015.

Kudła v. Poland, App no 30210/96, Judgment of 26 October 2000.

Kyprianou v. Cyprus, App no 73797/01, Judgment of 15 December 2005.

Lautsi and Others v. Italy, App no 30814/06, Judgment of 18 March 2011.

Loizidou v. Turkey, App no 15218/89, Preliminary Objections of 23 March 1995.

Mamatkulov and Askarov v. Turkey, App nos 46827/99 and 46951/99, Judgment of 4 February 2005.

Mantovanelli v. France, App no 21497/93, Judgment of 18 March 1997.

Marckx v. Belgium, App no 6833/74, Judgment of 13 June 1979.

Mentes and Others v. Turkey, App no 58/1996/677/867, Judgment of 28 November 1997.

Muršić v. Croatia, App no 7334/13, Judgment of 20 October 2016.

N. v. the United Kingdom, App no 26565/05, Judgment of 27 May 2008.

Nachova and Others v. Bulgaria, App no 43577/98, Judgment of 6 July 2005.

Nicolae Virgiliu Tănase v. Romania, App no 41720/13, Judgment of 25 June 2019.

Pelladoh v. The Netherlands, App no 16737/90, Judgment of 22 September 1994.

Placì v. Italy, App no 48754/11, Judgment of 21 January 2014.

R.D. v. France, App no 34648/14, Judgment of 16 June 2016.

Radomilja and Others v. Croatia, App nos 37685/10 and 22768/12, Judgment of 20 March 2018.

Rantsev v. Cyprus and Russia, App no 25965/04, Judgment of 7 January 2010.

Renolde v. France, App no 5608/05, Judgment of 16 October 2008.

S. and Marper v. United Kingdom, App nos 30562/04 and 30566/04, Judgment of 4 December 2008.

S.A.S. v. France, App no 43835/11, Judgment of 1 July 2014.

S.H. and Others v. Austria, App no 57813/00, Judgment of 3 November 2011.

S.M. v. Croatia, App no 60561/14, Judgment of 19 July 2018.

S.M. v. Croatia, App no 60561/14, Judgment of 25 June 2020.

Sadkov v. Ukraine, App no 21987/05, Judgment of 6 July 2017.

Saïdi v. France, App no 14647/89, Judgment of 20 September 1993.

Sara Lind Eggertsdóttir v. Iceland, App no 31930/04, Judgment of 5 July 2007.

Schalk and Kopf v. Austria, App no 30141/04, Judgment of 24 June 2010.

Scozzari and Giunta v. Italy, App nos 39221/98 and 41963/98, Judgment of 13 July 2000.

Shamayev and Others v. Georgia and Russia, App no 36378/02, Judgment of 12 April 2005.

Storck v. Germany, App no 61603/00, Judgment of 16 June 2005.

Tanli v. Turkey, App no 26129/95, Judgment of 10 April 2001.

Tanrikulu v. Turkey, App no 23763/94, Judgment of 8 July 1999.

Tepe v. Turkey, App no 27244/95, Judgment of 9 May 2003.

Trepashkin v. Russia (No. 2), App no 14248/05, Judgment of 16 December 2010.

Tyrer v. the United Kingdom, App no 5856/72, Judgment of 25 April 1978.

Vallianatos and Others v. Greece, App nos 29381/09 and 32684/09, Judgment of 7 November 2013.

Veznedaroğlu v. Turkey, App no 32357/96, Judgment of 11 April 2000.

Vidal v. Belgium, App no 12351/86, Judgment of 22 April 1992.

X. and Others v. Austria, App no 19010/07, Judgment of 19 February 2013.

ICJ Cases

Appeal Relating to the Jurisdiction of the ICAO Council—Aerial Incident of 10 August 1999 (Pakistan v. India) (Merits) [1972] ICJ Rep 1972, 46.

Case Concerning Delimitation of the Maritime Boundary in the Gulf of Maine Area (Canada v. US) (Special Agreement of 25 November 1981).

Case Concerning Kasikili/Sedudu Island (Botswana v. Namibia) (Merits) [1999] ICJ Rep 1999, 1045.

Case concerning Pulp Mills on the River Uruguay (Argentina v. Uruguay) (Merits), [2010] ICJ Rep 2010, 14.

Corfu Channel (United Kingdom v. Albania) (Assessment of Compensation) [1949] ICJ Rep 1949, 244.

Corfu Channel (United Kingdom v. Albania) (Special Agreement concluded on 25 March 1948).

Corfu Channel Case (United Kingdom v. Albania) (Merits) [1949] ICJ Rep 1949, 4.

Gabčikovo-Nagymaros Project, (Hungary v. Slovakia) (Order, Site Visit) [1997] ICJ Rep 1997, 3.

Military and Paramilitary Activities in and against Nicaragua (Nicaragua v. United States of America) (Merits) [1986] ICJ Rep 1986, 14.

Military and Paramilitary Activities in and against Nicaragua (Nicaragua v. United States of America) (Judgment on Jurisdiction and Admissibility) [1984] ICJ Rep 1984, 392.

Oil Platforms (Islamic Republic of Iran v. US) (Merits) [2003] ICJ Rep 2003, 161.

Request for Interpretation of the Judgment of 31 March 2004 in the Case concerning Avena and Other Mexican Nationals (Mexico v. United States of America) (Merits) [2009] ICJ Rep 2009, 3.

South West Africa (Ethiopia v. South Africa) (Order of 29 November 1965) [1965] ICJ Rep 1965, 9.

Temple of Preah Vihear (Cambodia v. Thailand) (Merits) [1962] ICJ Rep 1962, 6.

WTO Cases

Argentina: Measures Affecting Imports of Footwear, Textiles, Apparel and Other Items–Report of the Panel (25 November 1997) WT/DS56/R.

Australia: Measures Affecting the Importation of Salmon–Recourse to Art. 21.5 by Canada–Report of the Panel (18 February 2000) WT/DS18/RW.

Canada: Measures Affecting the Export of Civilian Aircraft–Report of the Appellate Body (2 August 1999) WT/DS70.

Canada: Measures Affecting the Importation of Milk and the Exportation of Dairy Products– Report of the Panel Second Recourse to Article 21.5 of the DSU by New Zealand and the United States (26 July 2002) WT/DS103/RW2, WT/DS113/RW2.

European Communities: Measures Concerning Meat and Meat Products (Hormones)–Report of the Complaint by Canada (13 February 1998) WT/DS48/R/CAN.

European Communities: Tariff Preferences–Report of the Appellate Body (20 April 2004) WT/DS246/AB/R.

Japan: Measures Affecting Consumer Photographic Film and Paper–Report of the Panel (23 April 1998).

Japan: Measures Affecting the Importation of Apples–Report of the Panel (10 December 2003) WT/DS245/R.

United States: *Import Prohibition of Certain Shrimp and Shrimp Products–Report of the Panel* (6 November 1998) WT/DS58/23.

United States: *Measures Affecting Imports of Woven Wool Shirts and Blouses from India–Report of the Appellate Body* (23 May 1997) WT/DS33/AB/R and Corr. 1.

Cases from Other Jurisdictions

HRC, *Bordes and Temeharo* (1996) HRC Decision No. 645/1995.

IACtHR, *Velásquez Rodríguez* (Merits) [1988] 95 ILR 259.

IACtHR, *Velásquez Rodriguez* (Reparations and Costs) [1989] 28 ILM 291.

ICSID, *Biwater Gauff (Tanzania) Ltd v. Tanzania*, (Procedural Order No. 2 of 24 May 2006) ICSID Case No. ARB/05/22.

ICSID, *Plama Consortium Ltd v. Bulgaria* (Decision on Jurisdiction of 8 February 2005) ICSID Case No. ARB/03/24.

ICSID, *Suez, Sociedad General de Aguas de Barcelona S.A. and Interagua Servicios Integrales de Agua S.A. v. Argentina* (Order in Response to a Petition for Participation as Amicus Curiae, 2006) ICSID Case No. ARB/03/17.

PCA, Reports of International Arbitral Awards, *Island of Palmas* 2 RIAA 829, 840–841 (US-Netherlands, PCA, 1928).

PCIJ, *Legal Status of Eastern Greenland*, PCIJ Series A/B No. 53, 1933.

PCIJ, *Mavrommatis Jerusalem Concessions*, PCIJ Series A No. 5, 1925.

PCIJ, *SS Lotus*, PCIJ Series A No. 9, 1927.

Reports of International Arbitral Awards, General Claims Commission, *Lillie S. Kling (USA) v. United Mexican States*, 4 RIAA 581–584 (US—Mexico CC, 1930).

Reports of International Arbitral Awards, General Claims Commission, *Parker v. Mexico*, 4 RIAA 35, 39, para. 6 (US—Mexico GCC, 1926).

Reports of International Arbitral Awards, General Claims Commission, *Pinson v. Mexico*, 5 RIAA 411–414.

UNCITRAL, *Canfor Corporation v. US* (Order of the Consolidation Tribunal of September 7 2005.

USSC, *Brown v. Board of Education*, 483, 494 n 11 (1954).

USSC, *Gideon v. Wainwright*, 372 U.S. 335, 337 (1963).

USSC, *Muller v. Oregon*, 208 U.S. 412, 419 (1908).

List of Legislation

ACHR: American Convention on Human Rights, Pact of San José, Costa Rica, adopted on 22 November 1969, available at <https://www.oas.org/dil/treaties_b-32_american_convention_on_human_rights.pdf>, last accessed on 12 July 2021.

Annex 2 of the Agreement on Implementation of Article VII of GATT 1994, adopted on 2 March 1955, available at <https://www.wto.org/english/docs_e/legal_e/20-val.pdf>, last accessed on 12 July 2021.

Council of Europe Convention on Action against Trafficking in Human Beings, CETS No. 197, entered into force 1 February 2008, available at <https://www.coe.int/en/web/conventions/full-list/-/conventions/treaty/197>, last accessed on 12 July 2021.

DSU: Understanding on rules and procedures governing the settlement of disputes, Annex 2 of the WTO Agreement, available at <https://www.wto.org/english/tratop_e/dispu_e/dsu_e.htm>, last accessed on 12 July 2021.

ECHR Protocol No. 11: Protocol No. 11 to the Convention for the Protection of Human Rights and Fundamental Freedoms, Restructuring the Control Machinery established thereby, 11.V.1994, ETS 155, available at <https://www.echr.coe.int/Documents/Library_Collection_P11_ETS155E_ENG.pdf>, last accessed on 12 July 2021.

ECHR Protocol No. 14: Protocol No. 14 to the Convention for the Protection of Human Rights and Fundamental Freedoms, amending the Control System of the Convention, 13.V.2004, CETS 194, available at <https://www.echr.coe.int/Documents/Library_Collection_P14_ETS194E_ENG.pdf>, last accessed on 12 July 2021.

ECHR: Convention for the Protection of Human Rights and Fundamental Freedoms (European Convention on Human Rights), as amended, available at <https://www.echr.coe.int/documents/convention_eng.pdf>, last accessed on 12 July 2021.

ECJ Statute: Statute of the Court of Justice of the European Union, available at <https://curia.europa.eu/jcms/upload/docs/application/pdf/2016-08/tra-doc-en-div-c-0000-2016-201606984-05_00.pdf>, last accessed on 12 July 2021.

ECSC Treaty: Treaty establishing the European Coal and Steel Community, available at <https://eur-lex.europa.eu/legal-content/EN/TXT/?uri=LEGISSUM%3Axy0022>, last accessed on 12 July 2021.

ECtHR Rules of Court: Rules of Court, European Court of Human Rights, amended on 2 June 2021, available at <https://www.echr.coe.int/documents/rules_court_eng.pdf>, last accessed on 12 July 2021.

EFTA Statute: Statute of the European Free Trade Agreement Court (amended 2010), available at <https://eftacourt.int/the-court/statute/>, last accessed on 12 July 2021.

Euratom Statute: Treaty establishing the European Atomic Energy Community, OJ C 327 (26 October 2012), available at <https://eur-lex.europa.eu/legal-content/EN/TXT/?uri=CELEX%3A12012A%2FTXT>, last accessed on 12 July 2021.

IACtHR Rules of Procedure: Rules of Procedure of the Inter-American Court of Human Rights, approved on 16–25 November 2000, available at <https://www.oas.org/36ag/english/doc_referencia/Reglamento_CorteIDH.pdf>, last accessed on 12 July 2021.

ICJ Rules of Court: Rules of Court (1978), entry into force on 1 July 1978, available at <https://www.icj-cij.org/en/rules>, last accessed on 12 July ne 2021.

ICJ Statute: Statute of the International Court of Justice, available at <https://www.icj-cij.org/en/statute>, last accessed on 12 July 2021.

ICSID Convention: International Centre for Settlement of Investment Disputes Convention Arbitration Rules, entry into force on 14 October 1966, available at <https://icsid.worldbank.org/sites/default/files/ICSID%20Convention%20English.pdf>, last accessed on 12 July 2021.

Iran-US Claims Tribunal Rules of Procedure: Tribunal Rules of Procedure, 3 May 1983, available at <http://www.iusct.net/General%20Documents/5-TRIBUNAL%20RULES%20OF%20PROCEDURE.pdf>, last accessed on 12 July 2021.

ITLOS Rules of the Tribunal: International Tribunal for the Law of the Sea Rules, adopted on 28 October 1997, available at <https://www.itlos.org/fileadmin/itlos/documents/basic_texts/Itlos_8_E_17_03_09.pdf>, last accessed on 12 July 2021.

ITLOS Statute: Statute of the International Tribunal for the Law of the Sea, available at <https://www.un.org/ruleoflaw/files/statute_en.pdf>, last accessed on 12 July 2021.

PCA Arbitration Rules: Permanent Court of Arbitration Rules 2012, available at <https://pca-cpa.org/en/services/arbitration-services/pca-arbitration-rules-2012/>, last accessed on 12 July 2021.

Protocol to Prevent, Suppress and Punish Trafficking in Persons Especially Women and Children, supplementing the United Nations Convention against Transnational Organized Crime, adopted and opened for signature, ratification and accession by General Assembly resolution 55/25 of 15 November 2000, available at <https://www.ohchr.org/en/professionalinterest/pages/protocoltraffickinginpersons.aspx>, last accessed on 12 July 2021.

Rome Statute: Rome Statute of the International Criminal Court, in force on 1 July 2002, UNTS vol. 2187 No. 38544, available at <https://www.icc-cpi.int/resource-library/documents/rs-eng.pdf>, last accessed on 12 July 2021.

SCM Agreement: Agreement on Subsidies and Countervailing Measures, available at <https://www.wto.org/english/docs_e/legal_e/24-scm_01_e.htm>, last accessed on 12 July 2021.

UNGA Declaration on Fact-finding by the United Nations in the Field of the Maintenance of International Peace and Security: UN GA Res. A/RES/46/59, 9 December 1991, available at <https://legal.un.org/avl/ha/ga_46-59/ga_46-59.html>, last accessed on 12 July 2021.

Bibliography

Aleinikoff A, 'Constitutional Law in the Age of Balancing' (1987) 96 Yale Law Journal 943

Alston P and Knuckey S, 'The Transformation of Human Rights Fact-Finding: Challenges and Oppotunities' in Philip Alston and Sarah Knuckey (eds), *The Transformation of Human Rights Fact-Finding* (Oxford University Press 2016)

Altwicker T, 'Evidenzbasiertes Recht und Verfassungsrecht' (2019) 138(2) Zeitschrift für Schweizerisches Recht 181

——, 'Völkerrecht und Rechtspositivismus - Eine Annäherung mit Kelsen und Hart' (2012) 10 Zeitschrift für Rechtsphilosophie 46

Altwicker T and Diggelmann O, 'How Is Progress Constructed in International Legal Scholarship?' (2014) 25 European Journal of International Law 425

Altwicker T and Hansen AE, 'Presumptions in International Human Rights Adjudication' (forthcoming, on file with author)

Alvarez JE, 'Are International Judges Afraid of Science?: A Comment on Mbengue' (2011) 34 Loyola of Los Angeles International and Comparative Law Review 81

Amerasinghe CF, *Evidence in International Litigation* (Martinus Nijhoff 2005)

Arnardóttir OM, 'Res Interpretata, Erga Omnes Effect and the Role of the Margin of Appreciation in Giving Domestic Effect to the Judgments of the European Court of Human Rights' (2017) 28 European Journal of International Law 819

Baade HW, 'Social Science Evidence and the Federal Constitutional Court of West Germany' (1961) 23 The Journal of Politics 421

Barceló III JJ, 'Burden of Proof, Prima Facie Case and Presumption in WTO Dispute Settlement' (2009) Paper 119 Cornell Law Faculty Publications 23

Behboodi R, '"Should" Means "Shall": A Critical Analysis of the Obligation to Submit Information Under Article 13.1 of the DSU in the Canada - Aircraft Case' (2000) 3 Journal of International Economic Law 563

Benvenisti E, 'Margin of Appreciation, Consensus and Universal Standards' 31 New York Journal of International Law and Policy 843

Bernardino AL, 'The Discursive Construction of Facts in International Adjudication' [2020] Journal of International Dispute Settlement 175

Besson S, 'Subsidiarity in International Human Rights Law-What Is Subsidiary About Human Rights?' (2016) 61 American Journal of Jurisprudence 69

Besson S and Martí JL, 'Legitimate Actors of International Law-Making: Towards a Theory of International Democratic Representation' (2018) 9 Jurisprudence 504

Bianchi A, *International Law Theories* (Oxford University Press 2016)

Bowett DW and others, 'Efficiency of Procedures and Working Methods: Report of the Study Group Established by the British Institute of International and Comparative Law as a Contribution to the UN Decade of International Law' (1996) 45 International and Comparative Law Quarterly 1

Bratcher Goodwin M (ed), *Baby Markets - Money and the New Politics of Creating Families* (Cambridge University Press 2010)

Brems E, 'Moving Away from N v UK – Interesting Tracks in a Dissenting Opinion (Tatar v Switzerland)' (*Strasbourg Observers*) <https://strasbourgobservers.com/20 15/05/04/moving-away-from-n-v-uk-interesting-tracks-in-a-dissenting-opinion-tat ar-v-switzerland/>, last accessed on 12 July 2021

——, 'Thank You, Justice Tulkens: A Comment on the Dissent in N v UK' (*Strasbourg Observers*) <https://strasbourgobservers.com/2012/08/14/thank-you-justice-t ulkens-a-comment-on-the-dissent-in-n-v-uk/#more-1685>, last accessed on 12 July 2021

Breuer M, '"Principled Resistance" to ECtHR Judgments: An Appraisal' in Marten Breuer (ed), *Principled Resistance to ECtHR Judgments - A New Paradigm?* (Springer 2019)

Brown C, *A Common Law of International Adjudication* (Oxford University Press 2009)

Brunner A, 'Subsidiaritätsgrundsatz und Tatsachenfeststellung unter der Europäischen Menschenrechtskonvention', *Max-Planck-Institut für ausländisches öffentliches Recht und Völkerrecht, Beiträge zum ausländischen öffentlichen Recht und Völkerrecht 283* (Springer 2019)

Bürli N, *Third-Party Interventions before the European Court of Human Rights: Amicus Curiae, Member-State and Third-Party Interventions* (Intersentia 2017)

Cassese S, 'Ruling Indirectly Judicial Subsidiarity in the ECtHR' Paper for the Seminar on "Subsidiarity: a double sided coin?" held to coincide with the ceremony marking the official opening of the judicial year of the European Court of Human Rights, 30 January 2015 1

Chang YC, 'How Does the Amicus Curiae Submission Affect a Tribunal Decision?' (2017) 30 Leiden Journal of International Law 647

Charney JI and others, 'The "Horizontal"Growth of International Courts and Tribunals: Challenges Or Opportunities?' (2002) 96 Proceedings of the Annual Meeting (American Society of International Law)

Christoffersen J, *Fair Balance: Proportionality, Subsidiarity and Primarity in the European Convention on Human Rights* (Nijhoff 2009)

Clermont KM and Sherwin E, 'A Comparative View of Standards of Proof' (2002) 50 American Journal of Comparative Law 243

Crawford J, *Brownlie's Principles of Public International Law* (9th edn, Oxford University Press 2019)

D'Aspremont J, *Participants in the International Legal System - Multiple Perspectives on Non-State Actors in International Law* (Jean D'Aspremont ed, 2011)

D'Aspremont J and Mbengue MM, 'Strategies of Engagement with Scientific Fact-Finding in International Adjudication' (2013) 05 Amsterdam Center for International Law Research Paper

Damaška M, 'Truth in Adjudication' (1998) 49 Hastings Law Journal 289

Danisch R, *Pragmatism, Democracy, and the Necessity of Rhetoric* (University of South Carolina Press 2007)

David V and Ganty S, 'Strasbourg Fails to Protect the Rights of People Living in or at Risk of Poverty: The Disappointing Grand Chamber Judgment in Garib v the Netherlands' (*Strasbourg Observers*) <https://strasbourgobservers.com/2017/11/16/strasbourg-fails-to-protect-the-rights-of-people-living-in-or-at-risk-of-poverty-the-d isappointing-grand-chamber-judgment-in-garib-v-the-netherlands/#more-4046>, last accessed on 12 July 2021

Davis KC, 'An Approach to Problems of Evidence in the Administrative Process' (1942) 55 Harvard Law Review 364

de Been W, Taekema S and van Klink B, 'Introduction: Facts, Norms and Interdisciplinary Research' in Wouter de Been, Sanne Taekema and Bart van Klink (eds), *Facts and Norms in Law - Interdisciplinary Reflections on Legal Method* (Edward Elgar 2016)

Dellavalle S, 'International Law and Interdisciplinarity' (2020) MPIL Research Paper Series

Descartes, R, *Discourse on the Method of Rightly Conducting the Reason, and Seeking Truth in the Science* (John Veitch trans., Cosimo Books 1st ed. 2008) (1924)

Devaney JG, *Fact-Finding before the International Court of Justice* (Cambridge University Press 2016)

Dewey J, 'Context and Thought' (1931) 12 University of California Publications in Philosophy 203

——, 'The Quest for Certainty' in Jo Ann Boydston (ed), *The Later Works, 1925-1953, Volume 4* (Southern Illinois University Press 1984)

Dodge WS, 'Res Judicata' (Jaunary 2006), in Peters A and Wolfrum R (eds), *Max Planck Encyclopedia of Public International Law* (online edn)

Dworkin R, 'Pragmatism, Right Answers and True Banality' in Michael Brint and William Weaver (eds), *Pragmatism in Law and Society* (Westview Press 1991)

Dwyer D, *The Judicial Assessment of Expert Evidence* (Cambridge University Press 2008)

Dzehtsiarou K, 'European Consensus and the Evolutive Interpretation of the European Convention on Human Rights' (2011) 12 German Law Journal 1730

ECtHR, 'Practical Guide on Admissibility Criteria' (2019)

Engisch K, *Logische Studien zur Gesetzesanwendung* (3rd edn., Winter 1963)

Fischer-Kowalski M and Erb K, 'Epistemologische Und Konzeptuelle Grundlagen Der Sozialen Ökologie' (2006) 148 Mitteilungen der Österreichischen Geographischen Gesellschaft 33

Føllesdal A, 'Subsidiarity and International Human-Rights Courts: Respecting Self-Governance and Protecting Human Rights - Or Neither?' (2016) 79 Law and Contemporary Problems 147

——, 'Exporting the Margin of Appreciation: Lessons for the Inter-American Court of Human Rights' (2017) 15 International Journal of Constitutional Law 359

Føllesdal A and Tsereteli N, 'The Margin of Appreciation in Europe and Beyond' (2016) 20 International Journal of Human Rights 1055

Foster CE, 'Court-Appointed Experts' (February 2019) in Ruiz-Fabri H (ed), *Max Planck Encyclopaedia of Public International Law* (online edn)

Franck TM and Cherkis LD, 'The Problem of Fact-Finding in International Disputes' (1967) 18 Western Reserve Law Review 1483

Frank J, '"Short of Sickness and Death": A Study of Moral Responsibility in Legal Criticism' (1951) 26 New York University Law Review 545

Gauch Jr HG, *Scientific Method in Brief* (Cambridge University Press 2012)

Gerards J, 'Margin of Appreciation and Incrementalism in the Case Law of the European Court of Human Rights' (2018) 18 Human Rights Law Review 495

——, *General Principles of the European Convention on Human Rights* (Cambridge University Press 2019)

Glanzberg M, 'Truth' (*Stanford Encyclopedia of Philosophy*, 2018) <https://plato.stanford.edu/entries/truth/>, last accessed on 12 July 2021

Grando MT, *Evidence, Proof, and Fact-Finding in WTO Dispute Settlement* (Oxford University Press 2009)

Haack S, *Defending Science - Within Reason: Between Scientism and Cynicism* (Prometheus Books 2003)

Habermas J, *Faktizität und Geltung* (Suhrkamp 1998)

Hage J, 'Facts, Values and Norms' in Sanne Taekema, Bart van Klink and Wouter de Been (eds), *Facts and Norms in Law: Interdisciplinary Reflections on Legal Method* (2016)

Hamann H, *Evidenzbasierte Jurisprudenz* (Horst Dreier, Ulrike Müssig and Michael Stolleis eds, Mohr Siebeck 2014)

Hanson NR, *Patterns of Discovery* (Cambridge University Press 1958)

Hart HLA, 'Essays on Bentham' [1982] Studies in Jurisprudence and Political Theory

Heinz A and Robert Florence Michèle, 'Sachverhaltsfeststellung Und Sachverhaltsüberprüfung', (2015) 9 Aktuelle Juristische Praxis (AJP) 1223

Helmholz R, 'Ockham's Razor in American Law' (2006) 21 Tulane European and Civil Law Forum 109

Hempel CG and Oppenheim P, 'Studies in the Logic of Explanation' (1948) 15 Philosophy of Science 135

Holmes OW, 'The Path of the Law' (1897) 10 Harvard Law Review 457

Huhn WR, 'The Use and Limits of Deductive Logic in Legal Reasoning' (2002) 42 Santa Clara Law Review 813

Hume D, *An Enquiry Concerning Human Understanding*, (L A Selby-Bigge ed, Oxford University Press 1902)

Jachec-Neale A, 'Fact-Finding' (March 2011) in Peters A and Wolfrum R (eds), *Max Planck Encyclopaedia of Public International Law* (online edn)

Jachtenfuchs M and Krisch N, 'Subsidiarity in Global Governance' (2016) 79 Law and Contemporary Problems 1

James W, 'Pragmatism's Conception of Truth' in Simon Blackburn and Keith Simmons (eds), *Truth* (Oxford Readings in Philosophy 2010)

Jones KA, 'The WTO and National Sovereignty', *Who's Afraid of the WTO?* (Oxford University Press 2004)

Jost F, 'Soziologische Feststellungen in der Rechtsprechung des Bundesgerichtshofs in Zivilsachen', *Schriften zur Rechtstheorie, Bd. 84* (Duncker & Humboldt 1978)

Kazazi M, *Burden of Proof and Related Issues: A Study on Evidence Before International Tribunals* (Kluwer Law International 1996)

Kelsen H, 'Legal Technique in International Law' (1939) 10 Geneva Studies

——, *Pure Theory of Law (Max Knight Trans.)* (University of California Press 1967)

——, *Reine Rechtslehre* (Matthias Jestaedt ed, Studienaus, Mohr Siebeck 2008)

——, *General Theory of Law and State* (3rd ed, The Lawbook Exchange Ltd 2009)

Kennedy D, 'Challenging Expert Rule: The Politics of Global Governance' (2005) 27 Sydney Law Review 1

Klink B Van and Taekema S, 'A Dynamic Model of Interdisciplinarity. Limits and Possibilities of Interdisciplinary Research into Law' (2008) 8 Tilburg Working Paper Series on Jurisprudence and Legal History 1

Koskenniemi M, *From Apology to Utopia* (Cambridge University Press 2009)

——, 'Law, Teleology and International Relations: An Essay in Counterdisciplinarity' (2011) 26 International Relations 3

——, 'International Law as "Global Governance"' 199

Krebs S and others, 'The Legalization of Truth in International Fact-Finding' (2017) 211 Chicago Journal of Internadional Law 83

Kriele M, 'Theorie der Rechtsgewinnung' (1976) 41 Schriften zum Öffentlichen Recht 367

Letsas G, 'Two Concepts of the Margin of Appreciation', *A Theory of Interpretation of the European Convention on Human Rights* (Oxford University Press 2007)

Leurdijk JH, 'Fact-Finding: Its Place in International Law and International Politics' (1967) 14 Netherlands International Law Review 141

Levit N, 'Listening To Tribal Legends: An Essay on Law and the Scientific Method' (1989) 58 Fordham Law Review 263

Lieckweg T, 'Recht und Wirtschaft: Strukturelle Kopplung', *Das Recht der Weltgesellschaft* (de Gruyter 2003)

Lind D, 'Logic, Intuition, and the Positivist Legacy of H.L.A. Hart 135, 136 (1999)' (1999) 52 SMU Law Review 135

Lippuner R, 'Die Abhängigkeit unabhängiger Systeme: Zum Begriff der Strukturellen Kopplung in Luhmanns Theorie Sozialer Systeme' [2010] <http://www.uni-jena.de/Roland_Lippuner.html>, last accessed on 12 July 2021.

Livingston SG, 'The Politics of International Agenda-Setting: Reagan and North-South Relations' (1992) 36 International Studies Quarterly 313

Luhmann N, *Ausdifferenzierung des Rechts. Beiträge zur Rechtssoziologie und Rechtstheorie* (Suhrkamp 1981)

——, *Soziale Systeme* (Suhrkamp 1984)

——, *Die Wissenschaft der Gesellschaft* (Suhrkamp 1990)

——, *Die Gesellschaft der Gesellschaft* (Suhrkamp 1997)

——, *Einführung in die Systemtheorie* (Dirk Baecker ed, Carl-Auer Verlag 2002)

——, *Kontingenz und Recht. Rechtstheorie im interdisziplinären Zusammenhang* (Johannes FK Schmidt ed, Suhrkamp 2013)

——, *Systemtheorie der Gesellschaft* (2nd edn, Suhrkamp 2017)

Mbengue MM, 'International Courts and Tribunals as Fact-Finders: The Case of Scientific Fact-Finding in International Adjudication' (2011) 34 Loyola of Los Angeles International and Comparative Law Review 53

McCormick MS, *Believing Against the Evidence: Agency and the Ethics of Belief* (Routledge 2015)

Mégret F, 'Do Facts Exist, Can They Be "Found," and Does It Matter?' in Philip Alston and Sarah Knuckey (eds), *The Transformation of Human Rights Fact-Finding* (Oxford University Press 2016)

Meyer-Ladewig J, 'Art. 25', *Europäische Menschenrechtskonvention Handkommentar* (4th edn, Nomos 2017)

Misak C, *Truth and the End of Inquiry* (Oxford University Press 2004)

——, *Cambridge Pragmatism: From Peirce and James to Ramsey and Wittgenstein* (Oxford University Press 2016)

——, 'The Pragmatist Theory of Truth' in Michael Glanzberg (ed), *The Oxford Handbook of Truth* (Oxford University Press 2018)

Nissani M, 'Fruits , Salads , and Smoothies: A Working Definition of Interdisciplinarity' (1995) 29 The Journal of Educational Thought 121

Novaković M, 'Men in the Age of (Formal) Equality: The Curious Case of Khamtokhu and Aksenchik' (2019) 67 Belgrade Law Review 216

Oellers-Frahm K, 'Article 92 UN Charter' in Andreas Zimmermann and others (eds), *The Statute of the International Court of Justice: A Commentary* (2nd edn, Oxford University Press 2012)

Palchetti P, 'Opening the International Court of Justice to Third States: Intervention and Beyond' (2002) 6 Max Planck Yearbook of United Nations Law 139

Paul J, *The Legal Realism of Jerome N. Frank: A Study of Fact-Skepticism and the Judicial Process* (Martinus Nijhoff 1959)

Pauwelyn J, 'Defenses and the Burden of Proof in International Law' in Lorand Bartels and Federica Paddeu (eds), *Exceptions and Defences in International Law* (Oxford University Press)

——, 'The Use of Experts in WTO Dispute Settlement' (2002) 51 International & Comparative Law Quarterly 325

Pavčnik M, 'Das „Hin- und Herwandern des Blickes" (Über die Natur der Gesetzesanwendung)' in Shing-I Liu and Ulfrid Neumann (eds), *Gerechtigkeit - Theorie und Praxis. Justice - Theory and Practice* (1st edn, Nomos Verlagsgesellschaft mbH & Co KG 2011)

Peirce CS, *Collected Papers of Charles Sanders Peirce, Vol. V: Pragmatism and Practicism* (Charles Hartshorne and Paul Weiss eds, Harvard University Press 1934)

Peters A, 'The Refinement of International Law: From Fragmentation to Regime Interaction and Politicization' (2017) 15 International Journal of Constitutional Law 671

Peters A and Altwicker T, *Europäische Menschenrechtskonvention* (2nd edn, Beck 2012)

——, 'Die Verfahren beim EGMR' (2018) MPIL Research Paper Series

Picker C, 'International Law's Mixed Heritage: A Common/Civil Law Jurisdiction' (2008) 41 Vanderbilt Journal of Transnational Law 1083

Plant B, 'Expert Evidence and the Challenge of Procedural Reform in International Dispute Settlement' (2018) 28 Journal of International Dispute Settlement 464

Popper K, *The Logic of Scientific Discovery* (Hutchinson & Co 1959)

Posner R, *Law, Pragmatism, and Democracy* (Harvard University Press 2003)

Potter J, 'Testability, Flexibility: Kuhnian Values in Scientists' Discourse Concerning Theory Choice' (1984) 14 Philosophy of the Social Sciences 303

Putnam H, *Pragmatism: An Open Question* (Blackwell 1995)

——, *The Collapse of the Fact/Value Dichotomy and Other Essays* (2nd edn, Harvard University Press 2003)

Ramcharan BG, *International Law and Fact-Finding in the Field of Human Rights* (Bertrand G Ramcharan ed, 2nd edn, Brill Nijhoff 2014)

Rebsomen E, Recotillet M and Teuma C, 'Preventive Detention as a "Penalty" in the Case of Ilnseher v. Germany' (*Strasbourg Observers*) <https://strasbourgobserv ers.com/2017/11/10/preventive-detention-as-a-penalty-in-the-case-of-ilnseher-v-ge rmany/#more-4026>, last accessed on 12 July 2021

Riddell A, 'Evidence, Fact-Finding, and Experts' in Cesare PR Romano, Karen J Alter and Yuval Shany (eds), *The Oxford Handbook of International Adjudication* (Oxford University Press 2014)

Riddell A and Plant B, *Evidence before the International Court of Justice* (British Institute of International and Comparative Law 2009)

Ridi N, 'Precarious Finality? Reflections on Res Judicata and the Question of the Delimitation of the Continental Shelf Case' (2018) 31 Leiden Journal of International Law 383

Robert H. Schmidt, 'The Influence of the Legal Paradigm on the Development of Logic', (1999) 40 Texas Law Review 367

Romano CPR, 'The Role of Experts in International Adjudication' (2009) Legal Studies Paper No . 2011-04, Société française pour le droit international

Sanders M, 'The Fact / Opinion Distinction: An Analysis of the Subjectivity of Language and Law' (1987) 70 Marquette Law Review 673

Sandifer D V, *Evidence Before International Tribunals* (rev edn, University Press of Virginia 1975)

Sands PJ and Mackenzie R, 'International Courts and Tribunals, Amicus Curiae' (January 2008), in Peters A and Wolfrum R, *Max Planck Encyclopaedia of Public International Law* (online edn)

Schlüter A, 'Beweisfragen in der Rechtsprechung des Europäischen Gerichtshofs für Menschenrechte' in Armin von Bogdandy and Anne Peters (eds), *Beiträge zum ausländischen öffentlichen Recht und Völkerrecht*, vol Band 288 (Springer 2019)

Schürer, S, 'Der Europäische Gerichtshof für Menschenrechte als Tatsacheninstanz – Zur Bedeutung divergierender Sachverhaltsfeststellungen durch den EGMR am Beispiel einiger Schweizer Fälle' (2014) Europäische Grundrechte Zeitschrift 512

Schupbach JN and Sprenger J, 'The Logic of Explanatory Power' (2011) 78 Philosophy of Science 105

Schwebel S, 'A Site Visit of the World Court', *Justice in International Law: Further Selected Writings of Stephen M. Schwebel* (Cambridge University Press 2011)

Searle J, *Speech Acts: An Essay in the Philosophy of Language* (Cambridge University Press 1969)

Shany Y, *Questionsof Jurisdiction and Admissibility before International Courts* (Cambridge University Press 2016)

Shivakumar D, 'The Pure Theory as Ideal Type: Defending Kelsen on the Basis of Weberian Methodology' (1996) 105 Yale Law Journal 1383

Sinclair MBW, 'The Use of Evolution Theory in Law' (1987) 64 University of Detroit Law Review 451

Slama S and Parrot K, 'Étrangers Malades: L'Attitude de Ponce Pilate de La Cour Européenne Des Droits de L'Homme' (2014) 101 Plein Droit I

Stefanelli JN, 'ICJ Arranges for Expert Opinion on Reparations in DRC v. Uganda' (*American Society of International Law, International Law in Brief*)

Stoyanova V, 'The Grand Chamber Judgment in S.M. v Croatia: Human Trafficking, Prostitution and the Definitional Scope of Article 4 ECHR' (*Strasbourg Observers*) <https://strasbourgobservers.com/2020/07/03/the-grand-chamber-judgment-in-s-m-v-croatia-human-trafficking-prostitution-and-the-definitional-scope-of-article-4-echr/>, last accessed on 12 July 2021

——, 'Dancing on the Borders of Article 4 Human Trafficking and the European Court of Human Rights in the Rantsev Case' (2012) 30 Netherlands Quarterly of Human Rights 163

——, *Human Trafficking and Slavery Reconsidered* (Cambridge University Press 2017)

——, 'Sweet Taste with Bitter Roots: Forced Labour and Chowdury and Others v Greece' (2018) 1 European Human Rights Law Review 67

Taekema S, 'Beyond Common Sense: Philosophical Pragmatism's Relevance to Law' (2006) The Tilburg Working Paper Series on Jurisprudence and Legal History. Working Paper 06-02

Tamanaha BZ, *Realistic Socio-Legal Theory: Pragmatisam and a Social Theory of Law* (Claredon Press 1997)

Tams CJ, 'Art. 50' in Andreas Zimmermann and others (eds), *The Statute of the International Court of Justice: A Commentary* (2nd edn, Oxford University Press 2012)

Timmer A, 'S.H. and Others v Austria: Margin of Appreciation and IVF' (*Strasbourg Observers*) <https://strasbourgobservers.com/2011/11/09/s-h-and-others-v-austria-margin-of-appreciation-and-ivf/#more-1268>, last accessed on 12 July 2021

Traynor RJ, 'Fact Skepticism and the Judicial Process' (1958) 106 University of Pennsylvania Law Review 635

Vannier M, 'Caught between a Rock and a Hard Place – Human Rights, Life Imprisonment and Gender Stereotyping: A Critical Analysis of Khamtokhu and Aksenchik v. Russia (2017)' in Sandra Walklate and others (eds), *The Emerald Handbook of Feminism, Criminology and Social Change* (Emerald Publishing Limited 2020)

Vargas-Quesada B and Moya-Anegon F de, *Visualizing the Structure of Science* (Springer 2007)

Venzke I, 'International Law as an Argumentative Practice: On Wohlrapp's The Concept of Argument' (2016) 7 Transnational Legal Theory 9

Vick DW, 'Interdisciplinarity and the Discipline of Law' (2004) 31 Journal of Law and Society 163

Vogiatzis N, 'The Relationship Between European Consensus, the Margin of Appreciation and the Legitimacy of the Strasbourg Court' [2019] European Public Law 445

von Bogdandy A and Venzke I, *In Whose Name? A Public Law Theory of International Adjudication* (Oxford University Press 2014)

Vuille J, Lupària L and Taroni F, 'Scientific Evidence and the Right to a Fair Trial under Article 6 ECHR' (2017) 16 Law, Probability and Risk 55

Walker VR, 'Preponderance, Probability and Warranted Factfinding' (1996) 62 Brooklyn Law Review 1075

White GM, *The Use of Experts by International Tribunals* (Syracuse University Press 1965)

Wieringa S and others, 'Rethinking Bias and Truth in Evidence-Based Health Care' (2018) 24 Journal of Evaluation in Clinical Practice 930

Wiik A, *Amicus Curiae Before International Courts and Tribunals* (Nomos/Hart 2018)

Wildhaber L, Hjartarson A and Donnelly S, 'No Consensus on Consensus?' (2013) 33 Human Rights Law Journal 248

'William of Ockham' (*Stanford Encyclopedia of Philosophy*, 2019) <https://plato.stanford.edu/entries/ockham/>, last accessed on 12 July 2021

Wolfrum R and Möldner M, 'International Courts and Tribunals, Evidence' (August 2013) in Peters A and Wolfrum R (eds), *Max Planck Encyclopedia of Public International Law* (online edn)

Wonnell CT, 'Truth and the Marketplace of Ideas' 19 UC Davis Law Review 669

Woolhandler A, 'Rethinking the Judicial Reception of Legislative Facts' (1988) 41 Vanderbilt Law Review 111

Council of Europe (ed.), *Yearbook of the European Convention on Human Rights* (Brill Nijhoff 1969)

Zippelius R, *Juristische Methodenlehre* (10th edn, Beck 2006)

List of Abbreviations

AB	Appellate Body of the WTO
ACHR	American Convention on Human Rights
App no(s)	Application Number(s)
art(s).	article(s)
Bd.	Band
CD4 count	Cluster of differentiation 4 count
ch	chapter
CoJ	Court of Justice of the European Communities
CPT	The European Committee for the Prevention of Torture and Inhuman or Degrading Treatment or Punishment
DNA	Deoxyribonucleic acid
DRC	Democratic Republic of the Congo
DSU	Understanding on Rules and Procedures Governing the Settlement of Disputes (Dispute Settlement Understanding)
e.g.	for example
ECHR	European Convention on Human Rights
ECJ	European Court of Justice
ECSC	European Coal and Steel Community
ECtHR	European Court of Human Rights
ed(s)	editor(s)
edn	edition
EFTA	European Free Trade Association
EPLN	European Prison Litigation Network
et al.	and others
Euratom	Treaty establishing the European Atomic Energy Community
g	gram(s)
GATT	General Agreement on Tariffs and Trade
GCC	Secretariat General of the Gulf Cooperation Council
HAART treatment	Highly active antiretroviral medication treatment
HIV	Human immunodeficiency virus

HSC	Sobra Cid Psychiatric Hospital in Coimbra, Portugal
HUDOC	Human Rights Documentation, database, available at <https://hudoc.echr.coe.int/eng#{"documentcollectionid 2":["GRANDCHAMBER","CHAMBER"]}>, last accessed on 12 July 2021.
i.e.	that is
IACtHR	Inter-American Court of Human Rights
ibid	in the same place
ICC	International Criminal Court
ICCPR	International Covenant on Civil and Political Rights,
ICJ	International Court of Justice
ICRC	International Committee of the Red Cross
ICSIC	International Centre for Settlement of Investment Disputes
ILC	International Law Commission
ITLOS	International Tribunal for the Law of the Sea
IUSCT	Iran-United States Claims Tribunal
IVF	In vitro fertilisation
Jr.	Junior
MAP	Medically assisted procreation
MPEPIL	Max Planck Encyclopaedia of Public International Law
n	note
NGO	Non-governmental organisation
No.	Number
p(p).	page(s)
para(s).	paragraph(s)
PCA	Permanent Court of Arbitration
PICJ	Permanent International Court of Justice
Res.	Resolution
SCM Agreement	Agreement on Subsidies and Countervailing Measures
SNSF	Swiss National Science Foundation
SPS Agreement	The WTO Agreement on the Application of Sanitary and Phytosanitary Measures
sq. m.	square meters
TB	Tuberculosis
TBT Agreement	Agreement on Technical Barriers to Trade

TV	Television
UK	United Kingdom
UN	United Nations
UN Doc	United Nations Document
UNAIDS	Joint United Nations Programme on HIV/Aids
UNCITRAL	United Nations Commission on International Trade Law
UNCLOS	United Nations Convention on the Law of the Sea
UNGA	United Nations General Assembly
US/USA	United States of America
USSC	United States Supreme Court
v.	versus
vol.	volume
WHO	World Health Organization
WTO	World Trade Organization